THE POLITICS
OF SURVIVAL

BLACK LIVES IN THE DIASPORA:
PAST / PRESENT / FUTURE

THE POLITICS
OF SURVIVAL

BLACK WOMEN SOCIAL WELFARE
BENEFICIARIES IN BRAZIL AND
THE UNITED STATES

GLADYS L.
MITCHELL-WALTHOUR

Columbia University Press   *New York*

Columbia University Press
Publishers Since 1893
New York   Chichester, West Sussex
cup.columbia.edu

Library of Congress Cataloging-in-Publication Data
Names: Mitchell-Walthour, Gladys L., 1978– author.
Title: The politics of survival : Black women social welfare beneficiaries
in Brazil and the United States / Gladys L. Mitchell-Walthour.
Description: New York : Columbia University Press, [2023] |
Series: Black lives in the diaspora: past / present / future |
Includes bibliographical references and index.
Identifiers: LCCN 2022043275 (print) | LCCN 2022043276 (ebook) |
ISBN 9780231207669 (hardback) | ISBN 9780231207676
(trade paperback) | ISBN 9780231557078 (ebook)
Subjects: LCSH: Women, Black—Political activity—Brazil. |
Poor women—Polical activity—Brazil. |
African American women—Political activity. | Poor women—
Political activity—United States.
Classification: LCC HQ1236.5.B6 M583 2023 (print) |
LCC HQ1236.5.B6 (ebook) | DDC 305.48/896081—dc23/eng/20221222
LC record available at https://lccn.loc.gov/2022043275
LC ebook record available at https://lccn.loc.gov/2022043276

Columbia University Press books are printed on permanent
and durable acid-free paper.
Printed in the United States of America

Cover design: Elliott S. Cairns
Cover image: BrazilPhotos / Alamy Stock Photo

Dedicated to all Black women.
May we all become Marielle Franco's seeds.

Dedicado a todas as mulheres negras.
Que todas nos tornemos sementes de Marielle Franco.

CONTENTS

ACKNOWLEDGMENTS

I first thank God that I was healthy during the pandemic and able to write this book. This project began in 2018 and required travel to three Brazilian cities and to North Carolina with my then four-year-old daughter. While I was working, I also homeschooled and traveled monthly, sometimes twice a month, to visit my beautiful grandmother Gladys H. Mitchell, who was sick. She passed away in 2019, but I am forever grateful for her unconditional love, wisdom, and all the care she dedicated to me and our family. When the pandemic began, I was already three years into homeschooling and had learned to balance work, family, and my volunteer service. The homeschooling journey had already taught me to appreciate every day, every moment, and sometimes every second.

This book benefited from the help of many people: research assistants, contacts at field research sites who allowed me to conduct research at their workplaces, and all those who allowed me and my team to interview them. Unfortunately, one respondent in São Paulo passed away due to Covid-19. I am grateful to the following research assistants: Bria Brown, Crystal Ellis, Shavonte Grant, Lester Kern, Mariah Levy, Paulo Victor Pacheco, Dalila Negreiros, Rebecca Sobral, and Nia Wilson. I also thank

Tchernavia Montgomery, Holly Kaster, Damaris Wright, and Lanetta Williams for allowing my research team to conduct interviews with women at their worksites. I thank Fernanda Barros dos Santos, Paulo Victor Pacheco, Dalila Negreiros, and Sales Santos who aided with transcriptions. I am also grateful to Michel Chagas and Ecyla Borges for graciously sharing their beautiful home in Salvador. I am grateful to all the women who participated in this study and gave the interview team time taken from their busy schedules to interview them. I also thank those who funded the project. This research was funded by the University of Wisconsin–Milwaukee's Research Grant Initiative, and I was able to present preliminary research with funding from UWM's Center for Latin American and Caribbean Studies.

My involvement with the U.S. Network for Democracy in Brazil and the Washington Brazil Office has been a wonderful experience and made the time writing this book during a pandemic bearable. I am grateful to all those I have worked with who are committed to democracy and marginalized communities in Brazil: James Green, Dalila Negreiros, Anielle Franco, Marcelle Decothé, Douglas Belchior, Kia Caldwell, Sharelle Barber, Gregory "Duff" Morton, Sidney Chaloub, Juliana Morães, Iman Musa, Natalia Campos, Myriam Marques, and Paulo Abrão. A luta continua!

I am extremely grateful to my daughter Truth Walthour, who accompanied me when I conducted interviews and when I attended my research assistants' interviews. She made the best of each situation. She is an empathetic and nonjudgmental child who was always open to friendship and play with the children she met in Brazil and the United States. I also thank my husband Anthony Walthour, who ensured I had time to write this book. Sunday Daddy-Daughter dates were wonderful opportunities for me to slip away to a local coffee shop to work. I also thank my sisters Cornelia Smith, Davia Lee, and Julia Elam, who have always been supportive. I am also thankful for my prayerful Godmother Elnora Barrier, and I am grateful for my mother, Violet Mitchell who is always helping someone. Like the Black women in this book who serve as caretakers for family members, I thank my cousin Phyllis Lynch for caring for my grandmother so she could remain comfortably in her home as she desired. I thank her sister, Julia Morris, who always provided a positive and loving word to my grandmother. My grandmother passed away during the writing of this book but would be proud to know I completed another book. I also acknowledge the passing of my father-in-law, John E. Walthour, during the writing of this book; he was a kind and humorous person. Finally, I thank my ancestors who poured into me and who taught me humility, commitment to family and the Black community, and social justice: my father David Mitchell Jr. and my grandmother Gladys H. Mitchell.

THE POLITICS
OF SURVIVAL

INTRODUCTION

My everyday experiences as a Black woman in this world provide stark reminders of what diasporic Black women invariably encounter. At a routine doctor's visit in Milwaukee with my four-year-old daughter, the nurse let me know that because I was on Medicaid she would look into a specific flu shot for my daughter (I have never received Medicaid). My husband and I alternated taking my daughter to her Mandarin Chinese class on Sundays, and one day a white mother asked my husband if I was working on completing my college degree because she often saw me working while waiting for my daughter. In Rio de Janeiro in 2012, I frequented a French bakery that sold truffles, macarons, and tea; one day the manager, who was not often in the store, expressed visible shock at seeing me and asked me whether I needed help and if I knew what a truffle was. In Salvador in 2018, the cashier said I needed to provide identification before being permitted to purchase food; I met with the manager, and he reaffirmed that I should carry my passport—to provide proof, he said, that I had not stolen my debit card. Why would people in Brazil see me as a potential thief, and why did people in the United States assume I was low educated?

These examples speak to the experiences of Black women of all socioeconomic classes, and specifically to dark-skinned Black women in the African Diaspora. To clarify that which should not need clarification, I am a university professor with four degrees from elite universities. I have completed postdoctoral fellowships at elite universities and a visiting fellowship at Harvard University. I have never received social welfare. Yet in the eyes of some people in the United States and Brazil, all Black women are social welfare beneficiaries or have low-incomes and are uneducated.

My experiences as a Black mother in Wisconsin have been eye-opening. In coffee shops in Shorewood (a nearby suburb of the university where I teach), people have congratulated me for reading books to my daughter. Once a white man shared how much he wished he could take a picture of my daughter and me—to capture the moment, he explained, as he pretended to take a photo with his hands. Collectively I found these experiences to be unusual, even though I am from the southern United States. What was it about a university professor reading and teaching her daughter that utterly shocked white spectators? Why did people in Milwaukee assume I was on Medicaid or uneducated? The longer I lived in Milwaukee and the surrounding suburbs, the more it began to feel like Brazil—and this was definitely not due to the weather!

The normalization and overrepresentation of Black women as low-income, uneducated, social welfare beneficiaries, regardless of their actual socioeconomic class, brought me to this project. In mainstream discourse, Milwaukee is often cited as the worst place for Black people and Black children to live. As a Black mother, I can attest to that reputation. These racialized and gendered experiences motivated this project, which focuses solely on African-descended women in the United States and Brazil, the two countries in which I have spent time. Conducting and observing interviews with Afro-descendant women social welfare beneficiaries and learning about the similar and unique experiences of these women was eye-opening and humbling.

In some ways I occupied an insider position in interviewing participants because I was seen both as a Black woman and as a mother. My daughter often accompanied me to interviews in Charlotte, Milwaukee, São Paulo, São Luis, and Salvador. When in Brazil, I was introduced as a researcher from the United States, and my daughter's presence at all the interviews made it clear that I was also a mother. In Charlotte one day I forgot to bring my daughter's iPad and had only a pen and paper with me to entertain her. Before beginning the interview, one of my interview participants saw my disgruntled five-year-old and caringly asked me throughout the interview if my daughter was okay. This participant was also a mother. Another mother in Charlotte had two of her children at the interview; my daughter was delighted to have the company and shared her iPad so they could all watch cartoons together. In São Luis, when I accompanied my research assistant, a neighbor invited my daughter to play. My daughter enthusiastically agreed and played at the neighbor's house with their children while my assistant and I conducted the interview. Similar to many of the mothers I interviewed, I also balance work and caring for my daughter.

By focusing on the experiences and voices of Black women beneficiaries of social welfare, I am able to highlight how systemic structures marginalize poor Black women in Brazil and in the United States, and I provide insight into how these women resist these structures and survive in former slaveholding societies. Black motherhood, in particular, was an exceptional experience in slaveholding societies: Black mothers historically occupied the position of caring for white children, caring for their own children and households, and working. During slavery all of this labor was unpaid. Today systemic racism, sexism, and classism make it difficult, challenging, and nearly impossible for Black mothers—especially low- and zero-income Black mothers—to survive. Yet they do; yet we do. Poor Black women have often been erased from public and academic discussions of politics. Even when Black women are lauded for "saving America" through voting or framed as an influential voting bloc in Brazil, the discussion addresses Black women in general and places little focus on *poor* Black women.

In this book, I seek to make visible the historically persistent invisibility of poor Black women social welfare beneficiaries in the United States and Brazil. In the late 1980s and early 1990s, U.S. policy makers deemed these women to be the "undeserving poor." To this day, Black women in the United States and in Brazil are often viewed as undeserving of cash transfers or social welfare. These representations fail to fully capture the lives of these women. To develop a more holistic picture of their experience as political subjects, I ask the following questions of Afro-descendant women social welfare beneficiaries: How do these Black women act as political subjects through the politics of survival in former slaveholding societies that make survival difficult? How do they negotiate societal perceptions of social welfare beneficiaries? Moreover, given their marginalized position as low-income Afro-descendant women, how do they perceive racial, gender, and class discrimination in their lives? How do they engage in formal politics such as voting? Beyond voting, I analyze their opinions of politicians.

I unapologetically claim that poor Black women matter. Their political opinions matter. Their evaluations of political candidates matter, and the way they understand discrimination matters. As Martin Luther King Jr. once noted, many people, in this case women, work full-time jobs for part-time wages. Others have tried to gain employment only to be stymied by discrimination. Still, others have disabilities or have children with disabilities who require their care, making work impossible. I argue that Afro-descendant women engage in a *politics of survival* to provide food for their children and themselves, even in dire circumstances.

Throughout the book I use the term *Afro-descendant* to refer to all the women in the United States and Brazil who participated in the study because all participants were required to be of African ancestry. I interchangeably use the umbrella terms *Black* and *Afro-descendant* in the same sense that Afro-Brazilian activists, academics, and media use the term *Black* (*Negro* in Portuguese), which is an umbrella term for racially mixed Afro-Brazilians and Afro-Brazilians who do not identify as racially mixed.

Participants were asked an open-ended question about their race or color. In the United States we asked about their race, and in Brazil we asked about their color, which is a more common identifier. When specifically referring to how women self-identify, I use the categories participants employed, such as African American, Black, *Negra*, *Parda*, and *Preta*. Parda is a Brazilian census category that allows individuals to acknowledge racially mixed ancestry. Preta is a census category that translates as "Black," but it is less commonly used. Afro-Brazilians more often use the umbrella term Negra, which means Black but is not a census category and includes both Pretas and Pardas. In the United States sample, some women self-identified as multiracial, and I noted their self-identification.

When I include quotations from participants, I note their self-identification. In addition, my questionnaire includes hair texture (see appendix) because Afro-descendants with African features are treated worse than those with European features. Information on skin tone is also included because those with darker skin tend to be treated worse than those with lighter skin.[1] All research assistants used a ten-point color scale that included pictures of people with different skin tones. They memorized the skin tones and recorded the skin tone of respondents. When I describe skin tones, I am referring to skin tones 1–4 as light and 5–10 as dark.

SUPPLEMENTAL NUTRITION ASSISTANCE PROGRAM, WOMEN, INFANTS, AND CHILDREN, AND BOLSA FAMÍLIA

Although mainstream media has paid attention to Black women's electoral power, there has been less focus on poor Black women and a lack of academic research on poor Black women's political opinions, evaluation of politicians, and evaluation of social welfare programs. In the United States, 20.8 percent of people receiving Women, Infants, and Children (WIC) benefits are Black/African American, and Blacks made up 25.6 percent of Supplemental Nutrition Assistance Program (SNAP) beneficiaries in 2016.[2] In 2014, 73 percent of people benefiting from Brazil's social welfare programs were Afro-Brazilians,[3] and 68 percent of Bolsa Família households were women-headed households. Although Black social welfare participation rates are significantly lower in the United States than participation rates of Afro-descendants in Brazil, in both cases Black participation in these programs is overrepresented relative to their population demographics. In Brazil, Afro-descendants are 56 percent of the population, and in the United States they are 13 percent.

Social welfare programs in Brazil and in the United States often provide food assistance. In Brazil, Bolsa Família is a conditional cash program that provides monthly assistance to beneficiaries in the form of a debit card, and these funds are usually used to buy food. The Bolsa Família program is for people with incomes at the poverty line and those who live in extreme poverty. Incomes are reported to the Cadastro Unico, a registration unit where eligibility for Bolsa Família can be determined. In the United States, both SNAP and WIC are social welfare programs that provide food assistance. SNAP assists low-income people and requires that recipients have an income at or 130 percent below the poverty line. The maximum amount of benefits depends on family size. Families are expected to spend 30 percent of their income on food. According to the U.S. Center on Budget and Policy Priorities, families received an average of $246 USD a month in the fiscal year 2020.[4] According to the Food and Nutrition Service of the USDA, 7 percent of SNAP beneficiaries were able-bodied people ages eighteen to forty-nine without children, 44 percent were under the age of eighteen, 14 percent were sixty years or older, and 9 percent were not elderly but had a disability. Thirty percent of beneficiaries earned an income in 2018: 54 percent of the people in households with children worked, and 19 percent had no income.[5] WIC is a program for children and mothers at nutritional risk. It provides food and nutrition education for low-income pregnant, breastfeeding, and nonbreastfeeding postpartum women, and children up to five years of age. The caretakers of these children can be parents, guardians, grandparents, or foster parents. In 2018, the largest share of postrebate costs was 19.59 percent for fruits and vegetables, 18.2 percent for infant formula, and 15.3 percent for cow's milk.[6] The highest postrebate costs were for infants in the amount of $44.97, followed by food package postrebate costs of

$35.79, and $30.72 for postpartum women. WIC served 53 percent of all infants in the United States, and the highest percentage of people benefiting from food programs are children. In addition, many beneficiaries rely on food assistance because they receive low wages. In households with children, more than a majority of beneficiaries work, dispelling the myth that parents or mothers do not work but rely on these programs. In contrast, given child care costs and transportation costs to work, these working families take on an added burden and costs of working.

The Politics of Survival prioritizes previously understudied perspectives of low-income Afro-descendant women in Brazil and the United States who are demographically overrepresented as social welfare beneficiaries. I argue that this overrepresentation is due to structural intersectionality or paradigmatic intersectionality, in which racist, sexist, and classist institutions, policies, and societies shape the experiences and everyday lives of Afro-descendant women.[7] In other words, Afro-descendant women social welfare beneficiaries face racism, sexism, colorism, and classism, all of which collectively threaten their life chances and compel them to rely on food assistance programs. Many women social welfare beneficiaries live in households with children or elderly people, or are unemployed or underemployed. Women with children are often responsible for providing food for those in the household. A lack of employment, child care, or elder care makes it difficult to buy food without government assistance. As Soss, Fording, and Schram state, "By discrediting and deterring welfare usage, . . . desperate workers [are forced] to accept the meanest work at the meanest wages."[8]

The Politics of Survival uses a Black feminist analysis of social welfare to closely examine the impact of institutional racism and sexism. Calls from citizens and politicians that social welfare beneficiaries should work do not consider their locations in structures that overdetermine their placement in society, including employment and caretaking. In 2015, the hourly wages of Black women in the United States were $13 compared to $21 for white men and $17 for white women.[9] Afro-Brazilian women receive 44.4 percent of the salary white men make, and they receive 58.6 percent of the salary of white women.[10] Afro-Brazilian women who graduated from a public university made 159 percent less than white men who graduated from a public university.[11] These glaring disparities, regardless of socioeconomic status, show the impact of what Patricia Hill Collins calls "interlocking systems of domination," in which modes of discrimination such as racism, sexism, classism, and colorism converge and overlap.[12] Social welfare programs, which provide the basic human right of food, allow low-income or zero-income Afro-descendant women to provide food for their families. Learning about these women's political opinions, how they survive, and the ways in which they interpret the political world privileges the voices of Black women, providing a bottom-up approach rather than only paying attention to institutions or those involved in the distribution of social welfare benefits.

LITERATURE REVIEW

By enriching the comparative research between Brazil and the United States and focusing on poor Afro-descendant women in both countries as political subjects, *The Politics of Survival* contributes to existing scholarship across Black studies, Latin American studies, political science, and women and gender studies. Drawing on a Black feminist framework, I analyze poor Black women's opinions about political candidates, how they are empowered, and how they resist systems of domination. Historically, much scholarship has analyzed and compared race relations in Brazil and the United States.[13] In 2020, the increasing attention to global protests focused on anti-Blackness, and the global pandemic provided an opening for comparative work on the experiences of Afro-descendants, especially Afro-descendant women. In *The Politics of Survival*, this comparative work deepens our understanding of the experiences, opinions, and lives of poor Black women in the United States and Brazil.

The Politics of Survival contributes a Black feminist analysis to scholarly debates about (1) whether social welfare empowers women or simply serves as a form of paternalism or state control, (2) perceptions of stereotypes of social welfare beneficiaries and the impact of these stereotypes, and (3) the homogeneity of political preferences among Black Americans and the variation of political preferences among Afro-Brazilians. Much of the literature on social welfare beneficiaries focuses on health and education outcomes of children who benefit from the programs.[14] Few studies on WIC, SNAP, and Bolsa Família consider the role of discrimination.[15] Furthermore, scholarship on social welfare and identity in the United States tends to focus on race and class, and in Brazil it focuses on gender and class. However, some published work on social welfare has used an intersectional lens that considers the simultaneous impact of race, gender, and class. Adding to a growing scholarship that engages such intersectional analyses of social welfare and its beneficiaries, *The Politics of Survival* contributes to African Diaspora research by employing a Black feminist framework in the comparative study of the political attitudes and experiences of Afro-descendant social welfare beneficiaries.

Social Welfare as Empowerment or Paternalism

In the United States and Brazil, scholars debate whether social welfare programs empower beneficiaries or are simply a form of paternalism. In Brazil, there has also been a debate about whether the program is a form of clientelism; that is, a relationship in which a politician delivers goods or services in exchange for votes. Soss, Fording, and Schram found that government policies such as the Temporary Assistance for Needy Families (TANF) for the poor are a form of neoliberal paternalism in which those administering these programs as well as external organizations associated with the programs are incentivized to follow a particular business model.[16] Recipients are also incentivized, but they are often punished if they do not conform to the ways these programs are meant to shape and integrate them into being certain types of citizens.

Scholars who argue that social welfare is a form of empowerment discuss how beneficiaries have learned methods to advocate for themselves, with some even enrolling in training classes to build their social capital. Jamila Michener finds that Medicaid—a program for low-income individuals that aids with health care costs—is unequal throughout the United States because its rules vary from state to state.[17] If beneficiaries move to another state, they have to enroll again and qualify according to that state's rules. Notably, Michener states that beneficiaries become intimately aware of the rules of the program and are able to advocate for themselves. In Silvana Mariano and Cassia Carloto's study of Afro-Brazilian (Black and Brown) women in two Brazilian cities, Uberlandia and Londrina, women believed they gained more respect after receiving Bolsa Família.[18] Natasha Sugiyama and Wendy Hunter stated that Bolsa Família beneficiaries felt empowered by their participation in social welfare: they felt socially included; were able to provide basic needs for their family; did not have to rely on friends, family, or others to provide food; and felt a sense of agency in determining their life course.[19] For Hunter and Sugiyama, the Ministry of Social Development's advertising of the program as a socially inclusive initiative reduced any stigma.[20] They conducted their research in 2009 during the administration of President Luis "Lula" da Silva, who came from a working-class background and emphasized social inclusion throughout his time in office. Moreira et al. found that Bolsa Família beneficiaries felt empowered in their interactions with agents of the Social Assistance Reference Centers (CRAS); they demonstrated interest in attending CRAS workshops and trainings and exhibited increased self-esteem.[21]

In contrast, some scholars believe social welfare programs regulate, control, and disempower women and that programs addressing poverty are designed to punish beneficiaries who deviate from the requirements of these programs. Cecchin and Parente state that women Bolsa Família beneficiaries in the Ilha Verde Camp chose to use any spare money to invest in their families and children.[22] In doing so, these beneficiaries disempowered themselves and felt compelled to fulfill socially accepted gender roles: to stay home and care for their children or, if a family member or friend must work, to care for another person's children. Even working women are pressured to care for the home. It is difficult to participate in politics or other activities when most of their time is spent caring for their families, so these women are inhibited from collective empowerment. Even though Mariano and Carloto found that Bolsa Família beneficiaries in Uberlandia and Londrina felt they gained more respect, Afro-Brazilian women were more likely to feel they had increased obligations and responsibilities. Mariano and Carloto found that Bolsa Família reinforces gender roles in which women have more family responsibilities than do men. As in the general population, Afro-Brazilian women social welfare beneficiaries tend to be more economically marginalized than their white women counterparts. Mariano and Carloto conclude that Bolsa Família does not reduce inequalities between Afro-Brazilian women and non-Afro-Brazilian women.[23] Similarly, David De Micheli found income differences between Brown, Black, and white beneficiaries, with white beneficiaries having the highest incomes among the groups.[24]

My findings do not fit neatly into either side of the debate between empowerment and paternalism. I argue that Afro-descendant women in anti-Black countries resist systems of domination such as racism, colorism, sexism, and classism through survival strategies that sustain their families. Although social welfare programs contribute to their survival, the survival of these women is sustained primarily through informal labor and networks with family and friends. In addition, the social and political institutions that support social welfare programs are responsible for marginalizing the beneficiaries in terms of where they live, work, and go to school. In the United States, local governments legislated segregation. In cities such as Milwaukee and Chicago, racial covenants and redlining produced segregated neighborhoods with underfunded public schools and public services where low-income people live today. In Brazil, customary law allowed for segregation and discrimination without the implementation of Jim Crow laws.[25] Implementation of university affirmative action in Brazil has dramatically increased the number of Afro-descendants attending universities, but public schools still have few resources and most students at these schools are Afro-descendants. Across both the United States and Brazil, I found evidence that Afro-descendant women social welfare beneficiaries survive despite the small amount of social welfare benefits they receive through their individual and collective efforts to sustain their families. The reach of paternalism cannot be defined simply by receiving social welfare benefits. Afro-descendant women's bodies are controlled by institutions that produce Black women's marginalized status through racist and sexist practices. One notable example is that Black women's maternal morbidity is three times that of white women in the United States and is twice as high as that of white women in Brazil.[26] *The Politics of Survival* attempts to represent Black women in the complex positions they inhabit as social welfare beneficiaries: although they suffer from marginalization, they access some modes of empowerment as they survive structural modes of domination that circumscribe their lives and communities.

Impact of Stereotypes on Social Welfare Beneficiaries

Research shows that stereotypes of social welfare beneficiaries have a negative impact on policy support for these programs and that discrimination against Afro-descendant social welfare beneficiaries has a negative impact on the services they receive.[27] The racialized and gendered representations of Black women are a common theme in this research. In Brazil, Layton found that those who hold negative stereotypes of Bolsa Família beneficiaries are less supportive of the program.[28] Beal, Kulthau, and Perrin stated that WIC counselors were more likely to recommend that Black women bottle feed their babies, whereas they encouraged white women to breastfeed.[29] Baran's study on the intersection of race, class, and gender and SNAP beneficiaries in Milwaukee revealed caseworkers' differential treatment of Black American beneficiaries compared to white beneficiaries.[30]

The spatial geography of the city and suburbs, along with the fact that caseworkers do not have to live in the city, contribute to their stereotypes of Black social welfare beneficiaries. Ange-Marie Hancock found a negative relationship between prevalent media stereotypes such as the "welfare queen" and policy support of social welfare.[31] In both countries, negative stereotypes lead to less support for the programs, and discrimination against Afro-descendant beneficiaries leads to lower quality services.

In both the United States and Brazil, the mainstream racialization of poverty programs has given way to reductive stereotypes of beneficiaries as poor, Black, and undeserving.[32] Gilens traces the change from the media's focus on coverage of poor whites to a focus on Blacks in the mid-1960s. He believes the civil rights movement and urban riots contributed to the environment in which media shifted their attention. However, he believes they shifted their attention to Blacks because the "moral tone" of news coverage was less sympathetic to the poor. This led to an increase in stories about poor Black people.[33] As Gilens notes, political, economic, and social conditions combined with stereotypes influenced states to make changes to social welfare programs. In addition, citizens' attitudes toward these programs were influenced by media coverage. Sparks discussed the congressional hearings of the Personal Responsibility and Work Opportunity Act (PRWOA) of 1996 in which critics of welfare often stereotyped beneficiaries, especially Black women.[34] Most of the hearings did not include welfare beneficiaries, and those who were able to express their opinions were unable to influence the final outcome of the act. Sparks focuses on the voices of welfare beneficiaries during congressional hearings on PRWOA and their concerns regarding domestic violence, the need for affordable child care, and enforcement of existing laws such as the requirement to provide child support. Like Sparks, in *The Politics of Survival* I consider the voices of social welfare beneficiaries. Unlike Sparks, I focus on Afro-descendant social welfare beneficiaries in Brazil and the United States. This comparative scholarship allows for an analysis of global stereotypes of social welfare beneficiaries. I analyze how women perceive stereotypes and buy into them or fight against them. Although some believe the stereotype that some beneficiaries are lazy and do not want to work, most acknowledge the need for these programs. They are also acutely aware of larger systems of domination that marginalize them.

Political Preferences of Black Americans and Afro-Brazilians

In general, Black Americans support the Democratic Party and Democratic candidates because that party has a more progressive stance on civil rights and social policies. In the 1930s, the realignment of Black Americans from the Republican Party to the Democratic Party occurred because Republicans were less supportive of policies that would economically and socially benefit Black Americans. In the 1950s and 1960s, Blacks supported federal government intervention in cases of school desegregation and voting rights. For this reason, they have been more supportive of Democratic candidates.[35] In the contemporary context, Black social networks put pressure on Blacks who do not endorse the Democratic Party, which in part explains high levels of support for the party.[36]

Brazil has thirty-three political parties, and Afro-Brazilians have shown more variation in support of political parties. During the height of the Worker's Party (Partido dos Trabalhadores, or PT) in the administrations of Lula da Silva and Dilma Rousseff

(2002–2016), most Afro-Brazilians supported the PT president. In the literature on a "racial vote" or voting as a racial bloc, historically Afro-Brazilians have not voted as a racial bloc;[37] however, in some cases appeals to vote along racial lines may have led to a vote based on color.[38] Although many Afro-Brazilians supported President Lula when he was elected,[39] in 2018 nearly a majority voted for the extreme right president Jair Bolsonaro. Yet the PT candidate Fernando Haddad won in the predominantly Afro-Brazilian Northeast, where a majority of women with less than two salaries voted for Haddad.[40] In Brazil, scholars have found that social welfare beneficiaries are more likely to support leftist presidential candidates. Because of this support, there is a debate about whether Bolsa Famíilia beneficiaries are "clients" in a system of clientelism.

Simone Bohn argues that Lula's voter base of Bolsa Família beneficiaries was not a form of clientelism, a relationship in which politicians provide goods or services including foodstuffs or neighborhood improvements to their voter base (their "clients") in exchange for their support.[41] Historically, clientelism has characterized politics throughout Latin America, including Brazil, but scholars of Brazilian politics have argued that these traditional forms play less of a role in contemporary politics. Other scholars argue, however, that Bolsa Família beneficiaries' support of leftist political candidates is the result of clientelism. Natasha Sugiyama and Wendy Hunter did not find evidence of clientelism, and Brian Fried found evidence that clientelism is in decline.[42] However, Cesar Zucco Jr. and Timothy Power identified a relationship between the program and voter support for Lula.[43] In Lula's 2006 presidential election, Diego Corrêa states that wealthy voters were critical of the use of public resources to support social policies and migrated to the opposition party, which changed the socioeconomic composition of

Lula's voter base.[44] This led to a different voter base than that of his 2002 presidential election, which explains why it appears that more Bolsa Família beneficiaries supported him.

In addition, it is important to consider criticism from Bolsa Família beneficiaries who voted for leftist politicians. A national survey by the Latin American Political Opinion Project (LAPOP) found that self-identified Preta women living in households receiving Bolsa Família had the highest percentage of dissatisfaction with President Dilma Rousseff in 2014.[45] In 2016, however, they had one of the highest percentages of satisfaction with Rousseff. I concluded that they may have had higher expectations of her in 2014 than other beneficiaries due to their experiences as low-income Preta women, but after witnessing the sexism Rousseff faced, they may have been more sympathetic than other groups because of their intersectional identities.

In this book, I am interested in the political opinions of Afro-descendant women social welfare beneficiaries. Because there is less divergence in party affiliation among Black Americans, my expectation is that Black American social welfare beneficiaries are more likely to vote for Democrats. In Brazil, although there is more divergence in political affiliation among Afro-Brazilians generally, I expect social welfare beneficiaries to be more supportive of the PT presidential candidate. There is support for my hypothesis, but an unexpected finding is that Black American women social welfare beneficiaries have less political knowledge than their Brazilian counterparts when measured by their ability to name at least one political party. *The Politics of Survival* contributes to literature on political opinions by focusing on a subset of voters within the larger population of Afro-descendant voters and considering presidential vote choice, opinions of presidents, and political party knowledge.

Black Feminism as a Theoretical Framework

The Politics of Survival focuses on poor Black women, drawing on a theoretical framework of Black feminism inspired by the work of both Black Brazilian and Black American feminists. The main tenets of Black feminism that inform this book include: (1) a focus on the everyday lives and experiences of Black women;[46] (2) an analysis of engagement in the collective and the community and not simply the individual; (3) a study of Black women's voices through narratives;[47] (4) an analysis based on intersectional and interlocking oppressions;[48] and (5) a refusal to analyze Black women's lives through the lens of respectability politics.[49] As Black feminist scholar Brittney Cooper and feminist Mikki Kendall have done, this project challenges respectability politics that promote the idea that societal notions of womanhood will protect women from violence and discrimination. In alignment with the commitments of Black feminism, I argue that a person's human dignity should not be denied based on diction, education, number of children, social welfare status, color, or gender.

Throughout the book I refer to Patricia Hill Collins's notion of the matrix of domination—the interlocking or intersectional oppressions Black women face. One oppression does not have primacy over the others. This matrix of domination acknowledges that racism, sexism, classism, and colorism, along with other forms of domination, intersect in particular ways that have an impact on Black women. Rather than thinking about these forms of oppression in a ranked order in which one has more impact on their lives than another, Collins's theory suggests that they interlock in specific ways that lead to Black women's particular experiences. In other words, race is not their primary identity; rather, it is the intersectional identities of race, color, gender, and class that shape their experiences. Brazilian and American scholars such as Angela Davis, Sueli Carneiro, Leila Gonzalez, Kia Caldwell, Keisha-Khan Perry, Rebecca Sobral, Elizabeth Hordge-Freeman, Tanya Saunders, Djamila Ribeiro, Leila Lemos, Caroline Souza, Flávia Rios, Jasmine Mitchell, Beverly Guy Sheftall, Patricia Hill Collins, Elizabeth Adams, Emanuelle Freitas Goes, and Enilda Rosendo do Nascimento have all discussed various forms of intersectional oppressions as well as empowerment and resistance to these oppressions. This is not a comprehensive list. Many scholars go beyond discussing issues of racism, sexism, classism, transphobia, and colorism.

Black feminism in Brazil is a tool used by Black women even when it is not explicitly named,[50] and it is a framework used in academic writing to offer a more complete analysis of racialized, classed, and gendered structures that shape Black women's daily experiences. It is also a practical tool of self-empowerment that can be used by individuals and activists. Black feminists are aware of and struggle against the multiple oppressions Black women face and acknowledge how these oppressions are symbolized in stereotypes meant to dominate and oppress Black women. Controlling images and stereotypes such as the figure of the "jezebel," which characterizes Black women as sexually available, and the "welfare queen," which characterizes women as lazy and dependent on state resources, are present in both Brazil and the United States. Black feminism fights against these stereotypes through Black women's liberation and empowerment.

Claudia Cardoso discusses an African cosmovision in which Black feminists are guided by non-Western principles and approaches to thinking and structuring life. Cardoso claims that "in the African cosmovision, life is sanctified and ritualized constantly in the daily lives of Black African societies and the universe is interconnected, represented by rites and myths, and understood by analogies and participation, contributing to the common good."[51] This contribution to the common good is not individualistic but considers others. Léila Gonzalez's concept of "Amerfricana" recognizes how African culture shapes life in the African Diaspora and argues that African forms of community and collectivity structure the lives and experiences of Black women.[52] Nikol Alexander-Floyd, Julia Jordan-Zachery, and Evelyn Simien are Black feminist scholars who emphasize the need for narratives that center Black women in Black feminist scholarship.[53] Black feminism is not simply an intellectual framework practiced in academia; its goals are meant to be applied to lead to a more equitable and just society.[54]

Informed by a Black feminist methodology, I push against respectability politics by quoting women as they speak. Throughout my analysis I address the theme of community and family, intersecting oppressions, resistance, and empowerment, and I rely primarily on the narratives of participants. Translating from Portuguese to English is challenging when trying to provide a sense of how women use certain words. Some women express their emotions and thoughts with slang, cursing, or in the U.S. sample, using African American Vernacular English (AAVE). Antonio Bacelar da Silva brilliantly explains how certain language or words are used to express high-level concepts.[55] In Brazil, women sometimes left out the "l" when pronouncing *filha* or *filho* (daughter or son), or *está* (is) was pronounced as tá, and *você* (you) was pronounced as cê. Unfortunately, there are no English equivalents. Language is important in analyzing the political opinions and experiences of discrimination of Afro-descendant women social welfare beneficiaries, but it also reveals the environment from which they come. Some women are articulate, and others use colorful language and AAVE.

"Attempts to tie access to food programs to labor, to respectability, to anything but being a human in need are ultimately less about solving the problem of hunger and more about shame."[56] I push back against the idea that only educated and respectable women should benefit from social programs. Women who suffer from domination are deserving of rights, including the right to food. Shaming women for seeking assistance while ignoring marginalization due to interlocking systems of domination is linked to the American meritocracy idea that hard work automatically leads to success. In Brazil, the idea of being a worker is also tied to the idea of being a respectable person.[57]

Black feminism includes empowerment, and part of empowerment is countering narratives that poor Black women are deserving of living in misery and not deserving of perceived luxuries such as frequenting bars or restaurants outside of their neighborhoods, being able to have their hair styled, or being able to eat certain foods. This book is an intervention to demonstrate that poor Black women are as deserving as their middle-class and high-income counterparts. On a larger scale, I assert that structures of domination should not exist and that poor Black women throughout the Americas should be able to live in a dignified manner. Some Black women politicians in Brazil and the United States—such as Benedita da Silva, Marielle Franco, Cori Bush, and Barbara Lee—have experiences with hardship, and that experience has shaped their lives and the way they see the world. They have advocated for policies that will benefit low-income people, including low-income Black women. Black feminism encompasses acknowledging both the ways that intersectional oppressions shape Black women's lives and their daily resistance to these oppressions. Ways to fight against and abolish these oppressions are examined with the goal of empowering and liberating Black women.

CONCEPTS AND TERMS

The concepts of colorism, classism, racism, and sexism often came up in my interviews. *Colorism* is a practice in which those with lighter skin tones are preferred and valued more than those with darker skin tones. Colorism can occur within Afro-descendant communities, but in the context of this research, I am interested in how societal structures of oppression, along with colorism manifested by these structures, shape the location these women occupy in society and how colorism plays a role in the life experiences of these women.[58] Colorism plays a role in society in Brazil and in the United States. Flaviá Rios discusses colorism in the Brazilian context where color is on a continuum and is not limited to skin color but also includes physical traits. She argues that discussing colorism is not meant to divide Pardos and Pretos, nor is it meant to essentialize racial groups. Lighter-skinned Negros may have a few advantages when compared to darker-skinned Negros, but they are not white. Rios notes that colorism has to be discussed along with other forms of oppression such as classism and racism or other demographic factors that shape the life experiences of Negros.[59] Scholars such as Nascimento and Jasmine Mitchell have discussed the role of colorism in Brazilian media. Jasmine Mitchell finds that race, class, and color determine how mixed-race women are portrayed in media. For example, mixed-race women actresses are sometimes granted the role of the maid, but the storyline may allow for social advancement if she marries a white man.[60] The point is that, similar to Rios's claims, lighter-skinned or mixed-race women are not free from racism, classism, and sexism even though they may suffer these oppressions in slightly different ways. In the United States, skin color also shapes life chances and opportunities, and scholars have shown that darker-skinned women are less preferred as marriage partners in heterosexual relationships, have lower incomes, and have less education than lighter-skinned women.

When I discuss *classism*, I am referring to unequal or disparate treatment of people based on their perceived class. In general, those perceived as having a lower-class status are treated more harshly and with less respect than those with a higher-class status. In the United States and Brazil, it is well documented that Black professionals experience classism.[61] Classism does not exist in a vacuum; those with darker skin may be perceived as having a lower-class status than those with light skin tones. In addition, when people think of poor people, the assumption is that they are Black in the United States and Negro in Brazil. In fact, Brown-Iannuzzi et al. and Lei and Bodenhausen found that when Americans envision a poor person they think of a Black person.[62] Paul, Gaither, and Darity found that study participants most often incorrectly identify the class status of high-income Blacks and high-income Latinx people.[63] In my study, women participants are low income, but some challenge societal expectations that they should not have the freedom to purchase certain types of foods or be able to occupy space in certain leisure areas. Classism also presents as treating people with disrespect because of stereotypes associated with low-income Black women.

Sexism occurs when women are viewed as unequal or less capable than men and are less valued. Sexism manifests in different ways based on color, class, and other intersectional identities. Historically, Black women were not viewed as being equal to European women. In fact, in Brazil and the United States today, Black women receive poorer health treatment. In this book, sexism is demonstrated in employment and personal relationships, but women do not always perceive sexism as such. *Racism*, in this study, indicates a devaluation and the practice of a racialized group or groups being disadvantaged by groups in power based on the belief that the group is inferior to other racialized groups. In this study, women cite examples of not being hired due to their racial background or being called a derogatory name during their childhood.

METHODOLOGY

This book draws on analyses of qualitative interview data to represent the realities of Black women social welfare beneficiaries in Brazil and the United States. I conducted 240 in-depth interviews (forty interviews in each city) in 2018 and 2019 with Afro-descendant women in Salvador, São Paulo, and São Luis in Brazil and Chicago, Charlotte, and Milwaukee in the United States. I organized and coded the interview data, identifying and analyzing common themes mentioned by participants. In addition, I used a qualitative software program to analyze the content of these interviews focusing on commonly used terms. The research assistants for the in-depth interviews were trained in interview methods, and all interviewers were Afro-descendant. In Brazil, two Brazilian graduate students and one recent PhD conducted interviews in São Paulo, São Luis, and Salvador. These three research assistants all have light-skinned complexions and include a cisgender woman who identifies as Negra and has dark wavy hair with highlights, a cisgender man who identifies as Negro and has short dark wavy hair, and a cisgender pansexual woman with short straight dark hair. In the United States, the skin tones varied. Two students from the University of Wisconsin–Milwaukee conducted interviews in Milwaukee. One of the interviewers in Milwaukee is light skinned and sometimes wears braids or flat ironed hair with highlights; she identifies as multiracial. The other Milwaukee interviewer has a medium skin complexion with natural hair. I conducted interviews in Charlotte and am a native of a suburb of Charlotte. The research assistant in Charlotte was dark skinned with natural hair. Three graduate students from the University of Chicago conducted interviews in Chicago. One is a man with dark skin and long locs who identifies as Black. Another is a light-skinned woman with natural hair, and the third is a dark-skinned woman with natural hair. I also conducted a few interviews in Milwaukee. These cities were chosen as a convenience sample. They include cities I have lived in and where I have conducted research. In addition, they differ in overall population size, regional histories, and percentage of Afro-descendant populations. In Brazil, Salvador (located in the northeast of Brazil) is 80 percent Afro-descendant; São Paulo (located in the southeast of Brazil) is 33 percent Afro-descendant; and São Luis (located in the northeast of Brazil) is 71 percent Afro-Brazilian. São Paulo is Brazil's largest city, and Salvador is its third largest city. São Luis's population exceeds one million, making it the seventeenth most populous city in Brazil.

Participants were recruited at nonprofit organizations and through a snowball method, and all participants were paid $20. Most participants in Milwaukee were recruited at the YWCA, which offers a number of services from job training to use of phones. Most participants in Charlotte were recruited at Crisis Assistance Ministry, a nonprofit agency that assists low-income people with emergency assistance such as paying electricity bills and providing food and clothing. Participants in Milwaukee and Charlotte were also recruited via a snowball method through other nonprofit organizations. Participants were recruited at the YWCA in Chicago. Participants in São Paulo were recruited through a snowball method and at a homeless shelter. In Salvador, participants were recruited at a union office. In São Luis, respondents were recruited relying on a snowball method.

Of the cities in the United States, Milwaukee is 39 percent Afro-descendant; Chicago is 30 percent Afro-descendant; and Charlotte is 35 percent Afro-descendant. Chicago, the third largest city in the United States, is known for Black mobilization and Black political power. It is home to Jesse Jackson's Operation Push, a civil rights organization, as well as to former Illinois Senator Barack Obama and Lori Lightfoot, Chicago's first Black lesbian mayor. Chicago was one of the midwestern cities that received southern Blacks during the Great Migration. Blacks were able to find jobs, and a sizable Black middle class developed. However, after deindustrialization, it became difficult for Blacks to maintain jobs. Between 2000 and 2010, 181,000 Blacks who wanted better opportunities left Chicago.[64] This reverse migration to the South was led by educated and middle-class Blacks, and the brain drain and the economic resources they held left the city with their migration. The overall homeownership rate

FIGURE 0.1 Roseland, a predominantly Black neighborhood in Chicago mentioned by a respondent.

Source: Courtesy of Google Maps.

in Chicago is 39 percent, but some suburbs have Black home-ownership rates above 80 percent. Olympia Fields (an affluent predominantly Black suburb) has a Black homeownership rate of 98 percent, and Flossmoor (a nearly 50 percent Black affluent suburb) has a Black homeownership rate of 83 percent.[65]

Charlotte, the fifteenth most populous city in the United States, also has a history of Black activism and Black political power. Vi Lyles, Charlotte's current mayor, is its first Black woman mayor. Harvey Gantt, a Black American man, was Charlotte's first Black mayor in 1983, and he served for two terms. Charlotte, like many American cities, is undergoing gentrification that pushes Black Americans out of majority Black neighborhoods as young whites move into them. North Carolina is home to twelve historically Black colleges and universities (HBCUs), and one of these, Johnson C. Smith University (JCSU), is in Charlotte. In the 1960s, students from JCSU organized sit-ins in restaurants, calling for an end to segregation in public facilities. Famed attorney Julius Chambers filed a lawsuit

FIGURE 0.2 West Charlotte, a predominantly Black neighborhood some respondents mentioned.

Source: Courtesy of Google Maps.

in 1971 on behalf of ten Black families in *Swann v. Charlotte-Mecklenburg Board of Education*, and Chambers's home as well as homes of other Black civil rights activists were bombed as late as 1965. It is in this hostile environment that Blacks fought for their rights in the southern city of Charlotte. The history and legacy of activism and the rise of Black leadership there resulted in political power for Blacks.

The midwestern city of Milwaukee has its own history and legacy of racial strife. Unlike Charlotte, Milwaukee ranks at the bottom of many socioeconomic indicators, including those regarding segregation, Black wealth, and Black social mobility. Milwaukee is the thirty-first most populous city in the country, and it is often considered the worst city for Black people, and especially Black children, to live. High Black infant mortality rates, high incarceration rates, and higher suspension rates of Black children compared to their white peers reveal the nature of the institutionalized bias against Blacks. As an industrial city in the early and mid-twentieth century, Milwaukee provided stable blue-collar employment for its Black residents; however, with the advent of deindustrialization and the destruction of labor unions, jobs for the Black blue-collar middle class virtually disappeared.[66] During much of the twentieth century, redlining and racial prejudice shaped the city's predominantly African American inner core. During the civil rights era, Black activists such as Lloyd Barbee and Vel Phillips fought to desegregate schools and end housing discrimination for Milwaukee's Black residents; Phillips eventually became the first Black woman elected to Milwaukee's Common Council. Today, although Milwaukee's Common Council is 47 percent Black, the city continues to have some of the worst socioeconomic indicators for Black people in the United States. Notably, Milwaukee has the highest Black poverty rate—33.4 percent among the top fifty metropolitan areas—and 44.6 percent of Black children in Milwaukee live below the poverty line.[67] Milwaukee is also home to the well-known 53206 zip code: 62 percent of Black men living in this zip code have been or are incarcerated. The Black homeownership rate in Milwaukee is 27.4 percent[68] compared to 41.6 percent in Charlotte[69] and 39 percent in Chicago. In 2020, Milwaukee was ranked as the most segregated metropolis in the United States, and it has ranked in the topmost segregated cities since the 1970s. These harsh material conditions make Milwaukee a distinctly American city.

The three Brazilian cities include two large cities and one medium-sized city. São Paulo is Brazil's most populous city and is 33 percent Afro-Brazilian. Although it is a major economic hub and a global city, racial disparities persist. The average salary for whites is 2.5 times more than salaries of Afro-Brazilians. São Paulo is known for Black movement activism, including the Frente Negra Brasileira (Brazilian Black Front), which began in the 1930s. Activism continues in the city and includes groups such as

FIGURE 0.3 Homes on the predominantly Black north side of Milwaukee.
Source: Photo by author.

FIGURE 0.4 Neighborhood on the predominantly Black north side of Milwaukee.

Source: Photo by author.

Educafro, which trains Afro-Brazilian and low-income students taking the national college entrance exam. The Mothers of May is a group of mothers—mainly Afro-Brazilian women—who fight against police brutality and seek justice for their murdered loved ones. São Paulo is also home to a number of hip hop groups and activities.[70] In terms of politics, São Paulo elected Erika Hilton its first Black trans woman city council member in 2020, and Erica Malunginho was elected from the state of São Paulo as Brazil's first Black trans woman in 2018. Celso Pitta, who was from a conservative political party, was the city's first Black mayor and served from 1997 to 2000. São Paulo is the site of much Black movement activism, but it is also a deadly city for Afro-Brazilians due to the widespread police executions of Blacks—to borrow the words of Jaime Alves, São Paulo is an anti-Black city.

Salvador is the third largest city in Brazil and is often referred to as the Black Rome, a reference to its large Afro-Brazilian

FIGURE 0.5 Jabaquara, a neighborhood some respondents mentioned in São Paulo.

Source: Photo by author.

population. It is known for the Carnival groups Ile Aiye and Olodum, which embrace Black culture. Salvador is also home to the Steve Biko Cultural Institute, which offers courses to prepare Afro-Brazilian and low-income students for the college entrance exam. The institute also teaches about racism, and students often mention how they began embracing a Black aesthetic while there.[71] Keisha-Khan Perry's work in the Gamboa de Baixo neighborhood in Salvador highlights the importance of local grassroots organizing.[72] Black women leaders, many of them young, organized to stop expulsion from land their families had lived on for generations. The antipolice brutality movement Reaja ou Será Morta (React or Die) was created in Salvador in 2005. Salvador has never elected a Black mayor, and in 2018 the city had the highest level of income inequality between Pretos and whites in Brazil.

FIGURE 0.6 Sussarana, a neighborhood where some respondents reside
in Salvador.

Source: Courtesy of Google Maps.

FIGURE 0.7 Sussarana, a neighborhood where some respondents reside
in Salvador.

Source: Courtesy of Google Maps.

São Luis is located in the state of Maranhão, which ranks third in terms of states in which the number of people receiving Bolsa Família is higher than the number of jobs with a *carteira* (jobs with benefits). São Luis is known as a rich cultural site of African and Indigenous cultures and religions. It is a popular place for theater, music, and dance celebrations of Bumba Meu Boi, which celebrates the death and resurrection of the bull. This event is celebrated all over the country, but it originated in Maranhão. Although 85 percent of the illiterate population in Maranhão is Afro-Brazilian, a higher percentage of Afro-Brazilians than whites in Maranhão have a college education.

PARTICIPANT DEMOGRAPHICS

My study sample includes social welfare beneficiaries from three Brazilian cities (Salvador, São Paulo, and São Luis) and three U.S. cities (Milwaukee, Charlotte, and Chicago). In Brazil, Salvador is in the Northeast and is largely Afro-Brazilian; São Paulo is located in the Southeast and is majority white. São Luis is located in northern Brazil and is predominantly Afro-Brazilian. Milwaukee and Chicago are midwestern cities, and Charlotte is in the South. Most Afro-descendants in the United States live in the South.

I recorded age, racial identification, and skin tone for all participants. Previous research has shown differences in racial attitudes and political opinions based on racial identification in Brazil and in the United States.[73] In the interview, participants were asked their race (race/color in Brazil) in an open-ended question. Along with skin color, I also collected information on skin tone.

Age

The average age of participants in Salvador was 38.5, in São Paulo 33.1, and in São Luis 34.1. In Charlotte, the average age was 34.4, in Milwaukee 28.4, and in Chicago 29.2. In Salvador, the age range was twenty to sixty-three. In São Luis, the age range was eighteen to sixty. In São Paulo, the age range was eighteen to fifty-seven. In Charlotte, the age range was twenty to sixty-six. In Milwaukee, the age range was twenty to forty-six. In Chicago, the age range was eighteen to forty-two.

Racial Identification

In Milwaukee, 34 percent of the sample identified as African American, 37 percent identified as Black, African American, and 5 percent identified as Black. The other 19 percent identified as biracial, multiracial, Cuban, Black-Creole, and other categories. In Charlotte, 25 percent of the sample identified as African American, 28 percent identified as Black, and 13 percent identified as Black, African American. The remaining 34 percent identified as Indigenous Black, African American and Cuban, Afro-American, and other categories. In Chicago, 42 percent of participants identified as African American, 23 percent identified as Black, and 16 percent identified as Black, African American. The remaining 19 percent identified in other categories. In Salvador, 55 percent of the sample identified as Negra (an inclusive category much like African American), 26 percent identified as Parda or Brown (denoting racial mixture), and 10 percent identified as Preta (the census category for Black). In São Luis, 47.5 percent identified as Negra, 42.5 percent as Parda, and 7.5 percent as Morena. In São Paulo, 42.5 percent identified as Negra, 32.5 percent as Parda, and 5 percent each in the categories of Preta, Morena, and branca. The remaining identified in other categories. In Charlotte and Milwaukee, the most popular racial identification among social welfare beneficiaries was Black, African American, indicating that the two are interchangeable. In the United States, Sigelman, Tuch, and Martin found that Afro-descendants were equally likely to choose either term, but the term used depended on the racial composition of the schools attended, the region, their degree of racial consciousness, and city size.[74] The most popular category in Chicago was African American, and in Charlotte the most popular category was Black.

In Salvador the most popular identification was Negra. However, the Brown or racially mixed category was the second most popular. In São Paulo, the two most popular categories were Negra and Parda. Negra was the most popular term in Salvador, São Paulo, and São Luis. In the United States, more than a third of the Charlotte sample identified in other categories, including multiracial categories, and in Milwaukee, nearly one-fifth identified in multiracial and biracial categories. In Chicago, only 7.6 percent of participants identified in categories such as Brown American or Black (multiracial). Table int.1 shows racial self-identification for all study participants by city.

A surprising finding was that more racial identity categories were elicited from Afro-descendant women in the United States than in Brazil. In Milwaukee, Charlotte, and Chicago, identity was related to parentage, heritage, race, religion, nationality, and ethnicity. For example, one respondent identified as Hebrew Israelite, a religious category created by African Americans in the late 1800s. Hebrew Israelites claim blood lineage as Hebrew. In Chicago, a woman identified as a Brown

Racial Identification	Salvador (%)	São Paulo (%)	São Luis (%)	Milwaukee (%)	Charlotte (%)	Chicago (%)
Negra	55	42.5	47.5			
Preta	26	5				
Parda	5	32.5	42.5			
Morena	3	5	7.5			
Branca	11	5				
Sometimes Morena, sometimes Negra		2.5				
Morena clara, Negra clara		2.5				
Negra but certificate says Parda		2.5				
Negra, Preta		2.5	2.5			
Total	**100**	**100**	**100**			
African American				34	25	42
Black				5	30	23
Black, African American				37	6	16
Black (multiracial ancestry)					5	3.8
Black, not African American						3.8
African American (multiracial ancestry)				3	3	

(continued)

TABLE INT.1 (Continued)

Racial Identification	Salvador (%)	São Paulo (%)	São Luis (%)	Milwaukee (%)	Charlotte (%)	Chicago (%)
Biracial (African American & white)				3		
Black, white, German, Puerto Rican				3		
Multiracial					3	
Cuban				3		
Black, Creole				3		
African American & Cuban				3	3	
African American, Native American, Hindu				3		
Indigenous Black					3	
Afro-American, not African					3	
Afro-American					3	
Hebrew Israelite					3	
Human Being					3	
Brown American						3.8
American						3.8
Do not have one						3.8
Other				3		
Total	100%	100%	100%	100%	100%	100%

American. In both Charlotte and Milwaukee, some women claimed identities as African American and Cuban, Cuban, and one mentioned having a Dominican parent. Participants mentioned additional ancestries such as white and Native American, which were categorized as multiracial and biracial. Self-declared racial identification is an understudied area in the United States. Candis Watts Smith's study of college students who were Black immigrants or descendants of enslaved Blacks held differing political opinions on social justice and other issues.[75] Davenport also found that biracial people have different political opinions than monoracial people.[76] Although noteworthy, the study of why low-income Black women in the United States identify in more racial categories is beyond the scope of this project.

Skin Tone

A pobreza tem cor e a cor é pele retinta (poverty has a color and the color is dark skin). Table int.2 shows data in both a two-tone and a three-tone skin tone classification system. In the three-tone classification, skin tones are divided in three groups: light skin (1–3), medium skin (4–5), and dark skin (6–9). In the two-tone classification, 1–4 is considered light skinned, and 5–9 is dark skinned. In Salvador, in the three-tone classification, 21 percent of the sample had light skin, 5 percent had medium skin tone, and 74 percent had dark skin. Under the two-tone classification, 21 percent had light skin, and 79 percent had dark skin. In São Paulo, under the three-tone classification, 43.6 percent had light skin, 38.5 percent had dark skin, and only 17.9 percent had medium skin color.

In the two-tone classification, 51 percent of the sample had dark skin, and 41 percent had light skin. In São Luis, 75 percent of the participants had dark skin, 5 percent had medium skin, and 20 percent had light skin. Under the two-tone category, 25 percent had light skin, and 75 percent had dark skin. In Salvador and São Luís, two cities with majority Afro-Brazilian populations, Afro-Brazilian social welfare beneficiaries overwhelmingly have darker skin complexions on the two-toned and three-toned scales. On the two-toned scale, more than a majority of Brazilian participants are dark skinned in all three cities, indicating that in these samples women tend to have dark skin complexions.

In the cities of Charlotte, Milwaukee, and Chicago, Afro-descendant social welfare beneficiaries in the sample overwhelmingly have dark skin tones using the two-toned categories. In Milwaukee, 91 percent of participants are dark skinned; in Charlotte, 81 percent are dark skinned; and in Chicago, 80 percent of respondents are dark skinned. The remarkably high percentage of dark-skinned social welfare beneficiaries reflects previous research about the economic and societal penalties for people with dark skin, especially Black women.[77] These biases begin early in life, as Blake et al. found in their study of urban Black school girls who were punished more severely than their counterparts.[78] In Brazil and the United States, more than a majority of African-descended social welfare participants are dark skinned, which highlights how societies place these women based on their marginalized intersectional identities. The institutionalization of colorism, sexism, racism, and pigmentocracy in the United States and in Brazil has led to disadvantages for women of darker complexions.

TABLE INT.2 PARTICIPANTS SKIN TONE AND CITY

Skin Tone	Salvador (%)	São Paulo (%)	São Luis (%)	Milwaukee (%)	Charlotte (%)	Chicago (%)
1–3 (light)	21	43.6	20	6	11	15
4–5 (medium)	5	17.9	5	11	14	18
6+ (dark)	74	38.5	75	83	75	67
Total	100%	100%	100%	100%	100%	100%
1–4 (light)	21	49	25	9	19	20
5+ (dark)	79	51	75	91	81	80
Total	100%	100%	100%	100%	100%	100%

CHAPTER OVERVIEW

Chapter 1: The Politics of Survival

Many people cite Audre Lorde's quotation about self-care as a means of resistance, but most social welfare beneficiaries in this sample do not have this luxury. In fact, many are simply trying to survive. In Brazil and the United States, poor Afro-descended women are engaged in resistance through the *politics of survival*. This chapter focuses on the many ways low-income Black women engage in mutual aid efforts, including coming together with friends to help each other, relying on family and friends for aid, and individual efforts that enable them to survive from month to month and day to day. Many supplement their social welfare benefits by, accepting money from family members, and informal work such as painting nails to earn extra income. The Black southern American aphorism "Tryin' to make it" encapsulates the survival efforts of low- and zero-income Black women social welfare beneficiaries. As these women struggle financially, they employ the politics of survival through mutual and cooperative support of friends and family and by participating in the informal economy.

Chapter 2: Support of Social Welfare Programs, Stigma, and Resistance

This chapter focuses on Afro-descendant women's perceptions of discrimination against social welfare beneficiaries. The stereotype of Black women as welfare queens dates to the Reagan era in the United States, but this stereotype became more prevalent in Brazil in the 2014 presidential elections when scholars and media discussed whether leftist politicians received more votes in regions or municipalities with significant populations of Bolsa Família beneficiaries. Memes of Black women Bolsa Família beneficiaries circulated on social media, and academics debated whether Bolsa Família was a form of clientelism. Cesar Zucco Jr. and Timothy Power identified a correlation between Bolsa Família participation and voter support for Lula.[79] However, Diego Corrêa argues that there was a change in composition of Lula's supporters from 2002 to 2006, when he had less support from wealthy voters.[80] Wealthy voters migrated to the opposition party, changing the socioeconomic composition of Lula's voter base. During this time, some people questioned whether Bolsa Família beneficiaries deserved welfare and circulated memes that stereotyped Afro-Brazilian women as lazy and wasteful spenders of government money. Layton found that believing in negative stereotypes of Bolsa Família beneficiaries decreased support for the program.[81] In the U.S. context, Hancock found that media shaped policy outcomes regarding social welfare to the extent that negative media led to less positive support for the programs.[82]

Chapter 3: Perceptions of Class, Skin Color, and Gender Discrimination

This chapter focuses on how Afro-descendant social welfare beneficiaries perceive stereotypes based on class, skin color, and gender. My hypothesis is that Afro-descendant social welfare beneficiaries in the United States are more likely to acknowledge race-based discrimination than class discrimination, and that Afro-Brazilian women social welfare beneficiaries are more likely to perceive class-based discrimination than race-based discrimination. The U.S. sample is less likely to perceive gender-based discrimination even when cases of discrimination based on their gender are discussed. In both countries, Afro-descendant women suffer from discrimination; however, investments in national myths—such as the myth of racial democracy in Brazil and the myths of exceptionalism and meritocracy—inhibit some women from perceiving racial or class discrimination.

Chapter 4: Are Poor Black Women to Blame for Conservative Politicians? Social Welfare Beneficiaries' Political Knowledge, Voting Preferences, and Religion

This chapter examines political knowledge, voter choice, and Black women's opinions of presidents. I assess the political knowledge of Black women social welfare beneficiaries as measured by their ability to cite a political party. Voting is mandatory in Brazil but not in the United States, and Americans in the sample generally have lower levels of political knowledge than Brazilians. In general, political knowledge is positively correlated with political participation. However, like Black women in the general population, Black American social welfare beneficiaries have high levels of voting—an inverse relationship between political knowledge and political participation as measured by voting. I also challenge academic and media conclusions that evangelicals support conservative politicians. Afro-Brazilian evangelical social welfare beneficiaries overwhelmingly support leftist politicians and are harshly critical of conservative politicians. In both countries, Christian social welfare beneficiaries—who are the majority in both samples—overwhelmingly support leftist presidential candidates. I provide an intersectional analysis that considers identities of race, class, gender, and religion. These intersectional identities explain why Afro-descendant social welfare beneficiaries differ from their white counterparts.

I also examine participants' opinions of then President Michel Temer in Brazil and then President Donald Trump in the United States. Participants largely disagreed with the policies and behavior of both presidents, and I focus on their responses as well as how they speak about these former presidents. In both countries, social welfare beneficiaries criticized their respective presidents on class-based claims, such as believing these presidents were only concerned about the rich. Only in the United States was the issue of race brought up.

Chapter 5: Conclusion: Are Poor Black Women the Hope for Progressive Politics?

During the 2020 elections in Brazil and in the United States, much of the media viewed Black women as the hope for leftist politics. However, in the contemporary context, poor Black women are rarely called upon as a potential voting bloc, and their voices are often overshadowed in mainstream discourse. Powerful Black women politicians in the United States and Brazil are often disrespected in the public arena. In Brazil, for example, Black woman politician Marielle Franco was assassinated, and Talíria Petrone Soares has been threatened. The 2020 U.S. congressional and presidential elections and the 2020 municipal elections in Brazil highlighted the energy and commitment of Black women to the political process. Low-income Black women from Brazilian peripheries made their voices heard, and some ran for local office. In 2020 in São Paulo, the activist group Quilombo Periférico (Periphery Quilombo) ran six candidates,

including Elaine Mineiro, an Afro-Brazilian woman, in municipal elections and won a seat on the city council. Benedita da Silva
is a Black Brazilian woman politician who was also from humble
means but has been a politician for more than thirty years and
continues to advocate for low-income Black women. Poor Black
women must be heard and valued rather than stereotyped as lazy
and undeserving. To understand how poor Black women use
political skills and strategies to survive in a system established to
prevent their survival is to understand how they build power and
sustain life democratically. Poor Black women's needs must be
brought to the fore so that they are acknowledged—not only as
the saviors of democracy but as major participants in democracy.
A strong democracy hinges on ensuring that poor Black women
and their children have opportunities not only to survive but also
to flourish. In this chapter, I explore the contemporary political
context, advocate for an increased number of low-income Black
women politicians, and propose that citizens in democracies
view social welfare as a right.

1

THE POLITICS OF SURVIVAL

Some Black Americans and Afro-Brazilians employ these aphorisms to indicate financial hardships:

Robbing Peter to pay Paul.	Vendendo o almoço para comprar o jantar.
	(Selling the lunch to buy dinner.)
Money is acting funny and	O cobertor está curto.
change is looking strange.	(The blanket is short.)
Trying to make a dollar out of	Muito mês para pouco salário.
15 cents.	(A lot of month for little salary.)

These aphorisms demonstrate the common experience of the economic struggle of Black people throughout the Americas. These day-to-day struggles are often shouldered by Afro-descendant women because they are the primary caregivers and caretakers of family members. The survival of Black communities depends on Black women, especially Black mothers. Most of the Afro-descendant social welfare beneficiaries interviewed for this research are mothers, and they use their benefits to purchase food. However, they still face difficulties making ends meet and paying monthly bills for rent, gas, and electricity. In this chapter, I examine the *politics of survival*—how marginalized women engage in survival methods—using a Black feminist framework. Rather than viewing these women as powerless, I argue that their survival is a form of resistance.

What is the politics of survival? Throughout this book, the politics of survival focuses on five key elements of Black feminism: (1) narrative and the original voice of Black women, (2) empowerment, (3) resistance, (4) intersectional identities and oppressions, and (5) motherhood. For low- and zero-income Black women, the politics of survival encompasses the strategies they use to provide for their families. They all rely on cash transfer programs to provide food or other necessities for their families. They provide unpaid care to family members, including young children and older disabled children, and young children with health conditions. They engage in daily resistance by providing for their families even when they run out of monthly benefits. In this chapter, I argue that Afro-descendant women in Brazil and the United States actively engaged in these strategies of survival for their families and communities.

Patricia Hill Collins discusses the politics of survival as a form of Black feminism and resistance. She describes Sara Brooks, a domestic servant, as an activist due to her acts of resistance and her struggle to survive:

> To Sara Brooks survival is a form of resistance, and her struggles to provide for the survival of her children represent the foundation for a powerful Black women's activist tradition. Historically African-Americans' resistance to racial oppression

could not have occurred without an accompanying struggle for group survival. Sara Brooks's contributions in caring for her children and in rejecting the controlling images of herself as the objectified Other represent the unacknowledged yet essential actions taken by countless Black women to ensure this group survival.[1]

I believe the Black southern American aphorism "Tryin' to make it" best encapsulates the effort of low- and zero-income Black women social welfare beneficiaries. Although these women struggle financially, they employ the politics of survival through mutual and cooperative support of friends and family and participation in the informal economy to supplement their social welfare benefits: selling outgrown children's clothes, depleting their savings accounts, making partial payments, accepting money from family members, or painting nails and doing hair to earn extra income. These survival strategies demonstrate how they are "Tryin' to make it" and survive from month to month and day to day.

Many Black feminists have emphasized narratives and have included the voices of Black women in their work.[2] Léila Gonzalez is widely cited for her Black feminist work and her concept of Amefricanidade, which acknowledges the role of African and Black history in the cultures of Latin America. As Claudia Pons do Cardoso notes, Gonzalez's notion of *pretogûes*—the combination of *Preto* (Black) and *Portugues* (Portuguese)—acknowledges the influence of African languages on the colonial language of Brazil. Brazilian Portuguese is Africanized just as Spanish is Africanized in other Latin American countries. Gonzalez claims that certain consonants did not exist in African languages, and when enslaved Africans arrived in Brazil, they changed the colonial language.[3] Indigenous and Black feminists suggest that language can be used as a form of subversion, so it is important to consider Black women's voices and their use of language. In Brazil, the "l" might be omitted in some words (saying *fiha* instead of *filha*), other words were shortened (saying *tá* instead of *está*), and sometimes the "s" was not pronounced in plural words. This use of nonstandard language was also present in the United States sample. For example, the "s" might be omitted from plural words, some words were mispronounced, and verbs could be used improperly or entirely omitted. In the United States, some scholars refer to this language as Ebonics or Black English. I wrote this book in English and translated the Portuguese interviews of Afro-Brazilian Bolsa Família beneficiaries. Using a Black feminist framework, I chose to include the original voices of low- and zero-income Afro-descendant women.

Black feminism and Black feminist writers also consider everyday experiences of Black women.[4] Some of these experiences involve their intersectional identities or intersectional oppressions. In "Nao vou Mais Lavar os Pratos" (I will not wash the plates anymore), the poet Cristiane Sobral discusses a woman who is no longer satisfied fulfilling a gendered role as a wife.[5] This sentiment is present in some of the interviews. One Brazilian woman discussed how horrible her ex-husband was, and another chuckled and said she is married but her husband lives in another house. Black feminism includes women claiming their independence, discussing their everyday lives, and violence against Black women. A respondent in Chicago mentioned how her boyfriend "roughs" her up but does not do the same with his male friends. All of these experiences are important to Black feminism. Challenging machismo and sexism and violence are experiences of Black women, including marginalized Black women. My analysis includes the interaction of sexism, classism, and racism, and points out acts of resistance and empowerment. As Djamila Ribeiro notes, empowerment is not individual but collective.[6]

Beatriz Nascimento, Keisha-Khan Perry, and Kia Caldwell have all written about the various ways Black communities mobilize to resist oppression and, in particular, the important role Black women play in this mobilization.[7] *The Politics of Survival* continues this tradition but focuses on social welfare beneficiaries' everyday survival as a form of resistance rather than on formal organizing. Black feminism includes Black feminist academics but also women who may not view themselves as feminists but who engage in Black feminism in their everyday lives.

SURVIVAL IN BRAZIL

In Brazil I asked the women this question: Has it ever been difficult to make ends meet even receiving Bolsa Família? In Salvador, 93 percent of the women said it has been difficult to make ends meet even when receiving Bolsa Família. In São Paulo, 100 percent of the women said it has been difficult to make ends meet. In São Luis, 92 percent of the women said it has been difficult to make ends meet. If women responded yes, the follow-up question was, "What did you do?" The most common strategies of survival were working odd jobs such as house cleaning or painting nails (51 percent), financial support from friends and family (31 percent), and partial payments and budgeting (8 percent) (figure 1.1).

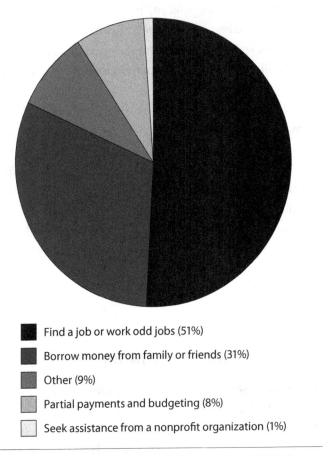

■ Find a job or work odd jobs (51%)

■ Borrow money from family or friends (31%)

■ Other (9%)

■ Partial payments and budgeting (8%)

□ Seek assistance from a nonprofit organization (1%)

FIGURE 1.1 Strategies for survival when facing financial difficulties in Brazil.

Source: Author's own data.

Work and Odd Jobs

In Brazil, 51 percent of women mentioned working at a day job or performing an odd job such as painting nails, doing hair, or house cleaning. The women were committed to their families and engaged in resistance by sustaining their families through participation in the informal economy. Many women paint nails at their homes, which enabled them to stay home while earning extra income. A thirty-nine-year-old dark-skinned *Parda* woman who did not complete middle school in São Luís stated, "I was desperate when this happened, but I always do house cleaning to help with my bills. I always lack things so I prioritize other things." This respondent worked odd jobs and also prioritized the bills she pays, another strategy women use. Women with various life circumstances continued working odd jobs to earn extra income. In São Paulo, a thirty-three-year-old dark-skinned Preta married mother of two who was pregnant had completed high school and continued to do odd jobs to provide for her family stated, "Yes, even receiving the Bolsa. The Bolsa offsets costs. . . . Oh I don't stop. I'm always doing something, doing odd jobs here, doing odd jobs there. I don't stop. . . . I'm pregnant. I'm *always* doing something to help the income" (emphasis added). Afro-descendant women are often the main caretakers of their families, and societal expectations and stereotypes of them as people who have the ability to work tirelessly can have an impact on their physical and mental health. Put more clearly, the thirty-three-year-old woman in São Paulo admits that she is always working. Throughout the Americas, Afro-descendant women do not have time to sufficiently rest because of societal and community expectations. In addition, experiencing discrimination takes a toll on one's health. Martins, Lima, and Santos found that women who have faced racial and gender microaggressions are more likely to have worse levels of mental health and self-esteem.[8] Racial identity or identification with blackness moderates the impact of microaggressions on mental health, and higher self-esteem mitigates the impact of these microaggressions on general health. These general findings are not restricted to Afro-descendant social welfare beneficiaries, who also face class-based microaggressions. In later chapters, I discuss their experiences with discrimination. In all cases, tireless working coupled with experiences of discrimination is detrimental to women's health.

Relying on Family and Friends

In Brazil, 31 percent of women mentioned financial support from family and friends, and 56 percent specifically mentioned relying on mothers or mother figures such as a stepmother. Only 11 percent mentioned fathers. When mentioning a specific family member who assisted financially, beneficiaries were 5.1 times more likely to mention mothers or mother figures than fathers. The reliance on mothers highlights the expectations of mothers. As Cláudia Cardoso argued, Black women play a central role in Black Brazilian communities. My study of Afro-descendant women social welfare beneficiaries demonstrates that women most often provide the support system for low-income Afro-descendant mothers and their families.

Bolsa Família provides relief for women, but some still need to rely on family members to make ends meet every month. A twenty-six-year-old light-skinned Negra woman with an incomplete level of high school who was the mother of one in São Paulo replied, "Yes, yes. . . . When I pay the bill and it is R$73 ($19.46 USD), and something else is R$30 ($8 USD) . . . it is difficult. I was working for a short time. . . . I left the company . . . and I turned around and started selling Avon. Then I pick up lingerie and bras to sell, and that's what I do. . . . If I don't have money, I borrow from my father. And that's how it goes." Although she sells Avon products and works odd jobs, she still has to borrow money from her father because the benefits from Bolsa Família do not cover all of her monthly expenses. A woman in Salvador received support from her brother, but he is now unemployed and is no longer able to help her. A dark-skinned thirty-one-year-old Parda woman in Salvador who finished high school responded this way:

> Yes. It was a little difficult because my brother was helping me . . . but my brother is unemployed. He's the one who supported me. He is my brother. But in this case now he's unemployed, so I'm just living off Bolsa Família and the cleaning I'm doing, so I earn two hundred and fifty a month ($66.67 USD).

Brothers, aunts, mothers, and fathers assist Afro-descendant social welfare beneficiaries with monthly bills. Family support is essential for these women and often, when women explicitly mention family members, they mention getting assistance from other women. A thirty-one-year-old light-skinned self-described Negra, Preta woman in São Paulo stated:

> Since I'm receiving a little, now it's my aunt who helps me with things for the kids. My aunt helps me, and there's my grandfather downstairs. . . . I don't work because my children have pneumonia. There is no way for me to work and leave them here with someone. So anyway this is the only recourse I have.

A forty-one-year-old dark-skinned Negra mother of two who did not finish middle school and resides in Salvador responded: "My family helps me. My mother, my sisters, my sisters-in-law, because I am separated and they help me with what I need."

In these examples, one woman has ill children, which makes it difficult for her to work; another is separated from her spouse so does not have spousal support, and her family members—all women (mother, sisters, and sisters-in-law)—stepped in to help her out. These examples highlight the important role women play in the lives of Afro-descendant social welfare beneficiaries. It is not that women exclusively are the family members who step in when they face hardships, but women are more likely to be named as part of their support system when they face difficulties.

In summary, women resist through survival in a number of ways. They rely on family, especially other women, work odd jobs, and budget or prioritize specific bills over others. It is difficult to make ends meet even while receiving Bolsa Família. A twenty-one-year-old dark-skinned Morena woman with an incomplete high school education who resides in São Luis stated, "Sometimes [it is difficult to pay bills]. I tried to divide the bills by only the necessary ones that I need to pay."

Racist and gendered tropes of Afro-descendant women as being strong powerfully shape society's perceptions of them. Although I argue that the politics of survival is a form of resistance, I acknowledge that the hypervigilance displayed by devoting all of their time and sacrificing their lives and happiness to the care of their children is unhealthy. An example is a twenty-six-year-old dark-skinned Negra single mother of two children who completed high school and resides in São Luis:

> No. I live in a support house. I do not pay light bills in this house. This money is exclusively for me to maintain my two children, but I prioritize only these five months because, like I said, milk is expensive. But in *terms of investment in myself, I do not think about this;* only food. I do not do anything else because my time now is only for my child. His health is not good. I only do what is certain. I do not . . . count on someone else (emphasis added).

Self-sacrifice and avoiding leisure time is expected of all women, but especially of Afro-descendant social welfare beneficiaries who are criticized if they spend money on caring for their bodies and their appearance. Cheryl Woods-Giscombe's study on the "superwoman schema" explores the role of the Black woman stereotype in diverse Black women's lives in the United States.[9] It had adverse effects on stress levels but was positively associated with maintaining family and community relationships. Some of the mothers in Brazil demonstrated this sacrifice as did some mothers in the United States.

SURVIVAL IN THE UNITED STATES

In the United States, 90 percent of beneficiaries in Chicago, 100 percent of beneficiaries in Milwaukee, and 88 percent of beneficiaries in Charlotte responded that it has been difficult to make ends meet. When it is difficult to make ends meet, the three most popular strategies used were relying on family and friends, working odd jobs, and seeking emergency assistance from nonprofit organizations. Other less mentioned topics were making partial payments, using money saved, and praying. Of respondents who said they faced difficult times, 24 percent sought assistance, 26 percent received financial assistance from friends and family, and 18 percent sought jobs or performed odd jobs (figure 1.2).

Respondents in the United States said that they often sought help from nonprofit organizations that offer assistance to low-income people or received food from food pantries. These interviews generally took place at nonprofit organizations, so it is not surprising that women in the sample overwhelmingly mentioned seeking help from these organizations. It is rather surprising,

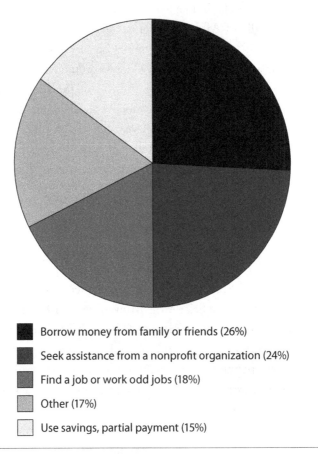

■ Borrow money from family or friends (26%)

■ Seek assistance from a nonprofit organization (24%)

■ Find a job or work odd jobs (18%)

□ Other (17%)

□ Use savings, partial payment (15%)

FIGURE 1.2 Strategies for survival when facing financial difficulties in the
United States.

Source: Author's own data.

however, that women receiving food assistance also went to food
pantries because their benefits were not sufficient to provide
the food required by their families. Some women sought assistance in the time between the loss of one job and the beginning
of another. A thirty-one-year-old dark-skinned self-described

Black, African American mother of two in Milwaukee who had some college education explained her need for assistance:

> Like now, that's why I'm here. . . . I just lost the job but I gained one, but I don't start until the third so I'm not going to be able to pay my rent. So I was seeing if they helped me with rent . . . and that's why I'm here because I'm going through a little hard time right now. . . . I'm just seeing if they could help me. If no, I *gotta do what I gotta do* (emphasis added).

A thirty-eight-year-old single Black woman college student in Chicago explains her strategy:

> *Deal with it.* I just deal with it because I think at the end, it wouldn't be nothing I could do. So I ain't gone mope and cry about it. . . . Sometimes I go to food pantries . . . because that helps a lot too. If you go to different ones on a certain day that help. I'll probably go do that today (emphasis added).

A fifty-two-year-old light-skinned African American mother of two with an associate's degree who resides in Charlotte agrees:

> Oh yes. Yes definitely. . . . I've gone to [name of nonprofit] here in Charlotte, and I've gotten financial help to pay for my bills. As far as food, before I was approved for food stamps, I would go to some of the self-referral food pantries. I'm very resourceful. I always have been. So I just would go on and see what I could do. Most of the time I would borrow the money from someone until my next paycheck. Or I would go to [name of nonprofit], and that's a big process because then I have to take a day off of work, because you have to go in the morning and you have to sit there all day until they call your name. And then they take the people

who are cut off first, then the people who have a shutoff notice . . .
so . . . you have to make sure you have all your documentation. . . .
It's a lot of stuff that you need to make sure that you have, but
you do what you have to do (emphasis added).

These women seek assistance for food or assistance to pay rent
when they fall on hard times, and none of them make excuses.
When faced with difficulties, they face them head on, stating
that they "deal with it," or "do what you have to do."

Family and Friends

Seccombe noted the important role of extended family for the
African American social welfare women beneficiaries in her
study.[10] In my study, for those getting assistance from family or
friends, 27 percent mentioned seeking help from their mothers
or mother figures such as a child's father's mother (figure 1.3),
with only 5 percent seeking help from their father or a father
figure. Women are 5.4 times more likely to admit seeking help
from their mothers or mother figures than fathers or father
figures. This difference speaks to the expectations of mothers
and the defining features of Black motherhood. Black motherhood responsibilities continue even to providing help for adult
children. One beneficiary lovingly refers to her mother as her
best friend. This loving relationship between Black women is not
present in popular media in which Black women are portrayed
as bad mothers. In *Re-Imagining Black Women*, Nikol Alexander-
Floyd explores the idea that stereotypical images of Black women
are political and not only impact society but also inform policy.[11]
Low- and zero-income social welfare women beneficiaries rely
on other Black women, often their mothers, to assist with caring

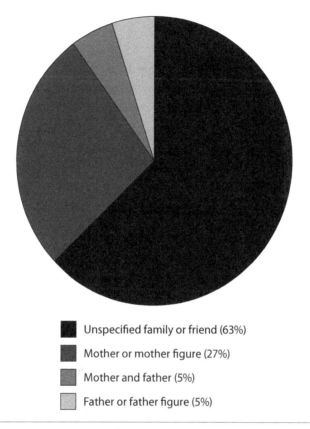

Unspecified family or friend (63%)

Mother or mother figure (27%)

Mother and father (5%)

Father or father figure (5%)

FIGURE 1.3 Reliance on family member or friend during emergency.
Source: Author's own data.

for their families financially and in some cases providing child care. Unfortunately, the media is less likely to show these positive images of Black mothers.

Some women are assured that they will have support from family members, but others may hesitate to ask family members for help. A twenty-eight-year-old African American single mother of five with a high school education who resides in

Chicago explained how it felt to need her mother's support during a difficult time.

> Yeah. Before I started working, well before I went back to work. So it's like, "Okay this is something new." It throws you out of whack because you're used to working and being able to cover where your SNAP or your . . . WIC doesn't fall into play. But it's . . . very hard. It's hard. My mom is my best friend, so I fall on her. I don't like doing it, but she understands; she understood then because I wasn't working, I wasn't able to work. So once I went back to work, everything went back to normal. It's like okay, my regular routine, going to work, being able to cover my bills, and then I just pay her back once I got the chance to.

A thirty-one-year-old dark-skinned African American single mother of five with some college education who resides in Chicago has received assistance from family and friends but does not like relying on others. She cuts back on expenses buying inexpensive food in an effort to save money:

> I've had a lot of help from friends and family. But I know that, for myself, I like to not depend on people because I have to be a responsible adult and also, set an example for my children. So, I make my bills my priority such as the roof over our head, electricity, and whatever else that may come with where we're living. If we have to just stick to eating noodles every night . . . I'll just make sure that our basic needs are met. It wouldn't be a thing of me focusing on us eating *steak or lobster tails* or anything like that. I'll just make sure that I take care of priorities. Then whatever's left, I'll make do with whatever I have.

This respondent is aware of the dominant myths that social welfare beneficiaries buy and eat expensive foods. She challenges the stereotype that beneficiaries are wasteful spenders, admitting that she feeds her family noodles to make sure she stays on budget. Although she has to ask family and friends for assistance, she remains frugal with her purchases.

A twenty-eight-year-old Black, African American single mother of three with a high school education who resides in Chicago relies on her mother for child care. She says that it has been very difficult to pay bills: "Yeah, very difficult. . . . Because now, like I said, I got two nine-month olds. And I don't really have like child care. . . . Honestly like my mom, she just, she help me out when she can. . . . Yeah, my mama help when she can."

Women with larger families may not receive enough aid to cover the costs of food for their families. This is evident in the experience of a fifty-four-year-old dark-skinned Black, African American married mother of seven who has a high school education and resides in Charlotte: "Yes. It have been difficult to make ends meet with what the government give us, and it's not accurately based on enough for the family. We have to go out with other members of the family and borrow money or even work harder or longer hours."

Families play a vital role in providing assistance when women are in a bind. Most women mentioned family and friends generally, but those who mentioned specific family members were more likely to mention mothers than fathers.

Jobs/Odd Jobs

Women exercise agency and resistance by engaging in formal work and in the informal economy, doing odd jobs to make ends meet. Moreover, they use material resources such as their own vehicle to run errands for others to earn money. In the United States sample, 18 percent of the women mentioned finding a job or working an odd job when it was difficult to make ends meet. These odd jobs included running errands for people, doing hair, grocery shopping for others, making clothing, or babysitting. Part-time work or work in the informal economy is an option for some, but it is not an option for all women.

A thirty-nine-year-old single mother of four did not wish to claim a racial identity, explained that she has two associate degrees and resides in Chicago and described some of the odd jobs she had done:

> It's difficult right now; do whatever I can. Anything. I don't do anything, I won't steal or anything like that. But I ask some people, or, I go do some favors, like take somebody to the store. Go to the store for them, stuff like that, babysit kids, braid some hair. I do something to help me meet my ends.

A twenty-six-year-old dark-skinned African American single mother of two who has a high school education and resides in Milwaukee explains the errands she runs to earn money:

> Yes. I normally ask my mom and sister because I do odd jobs. It's basically like I'll go to the store for my mom sometimes. Go grocery shopping for her sometimes. Once I had a vehicle. She'll reimburse me gas money. If I have gas in my vehicle already, I use that money to buy my kids whatever they needed.

A thirty-one-year-old dark-skinned African American single mother of one who has a GED and lives in Chicago stated, "Of course. I really prayed about it, to tell you the truth. But other than that . . . I go get a job. I have a job, so I was just on maternity leave. I'm a *worker*." Her identity as a worker defies stereotypes but is also reminiscent of the socially respectable category of worker present in Brazil, especially among low-income people.[12] In Brazil, people often use this category to justify why Black people should not be executed or harassed by police officers and death squads. In the United States, this Afro-descendant social welfare beneficiary identifying as a worker is also meant to justify why one should be treated well and not stereotyped. Although this woman is on maternity leave, she felt compelled to let the interviewer know that she is dedicated to labor.

Some women do not have the opportunity to work part time or full time or engage in informal labor due to a disability. A forty-seven-year-old dark-skinned Black single mother of three with a college degree who resides in Charlotte described how she feels:

> Yeah. Yeah, um, I've gotten to the point basically everything considered pleasure has been cut out of my life. Um, right now I'm barely making it, trying to keep the internet in becuz I need the internet to be able to do the classes that I was doing . . . between going to the . . . Goodwill, . . . do[ing] the classes and come back home and practice the stuff that they tell us we have to practice, online ya know. It's like I had to take a little bit of my light bill money in order to keep the internet on, and ya know normally I would not do that. I been tryna take and get myself back together cuz I can't work standing up. I barely can stand two hours. I can't lift more than so many pounds. . . . I still need surgery on my arm but becuz of Medicaid you know they say I have it but at the same time, when I talk to the caseworker they say that I'm not supposed to have it, ya know? And it's so many people telling me so many different things, I'm even scared to use it even though I've been told by the doctors that I can use it unless they say otherwise.

This mother has limited options in the formal or informal labor market because of her disability. Although she needs surgery, she is not confident that it will be covered by Medicaid. She prioritizes her bills to make ends meet. In addition, she takes care of her adult son who is also disabled. Although she is not paid as a caretaker, she is engaged in this daily labor even though she herself is disabled.

"Mother labor," which can be strenuous, takes a toll on Black women. But society expects this labor from women. Black women are also burdened with the strong black woman trope, and women who do not fulfill this role are viewed as lazy. Policy makers who advocate for social welfare beneficiaries to work should consider the complicated lives of women, especially low- and zero-income Afro-descendant women.

Saving, Budgeting, and Partial Payments

Some of the other survival methods women undertake are saving, budgeting, partial payments, and cutting back on food or energy expenses. A sixty-six-year-old Black, African American divorced retired mother of three who has a college degree and resides in Charlotte articulates the difficulties for older people on a fixed income when energy prices are high:

Yes it's difficult to pay bills and make ends meet but when we have to cut back on things um you know especially in the winter. The heating bill is exorbitant because the Duke Energy here um you know if you only got one heating source so then you know they run the rates up whatever they want it to be, so in our case, you have to turn the thermostat down. It helps [if] maybe you have a small heater in the area where you're sitting so it's not to raise it. I have gone to, don't really like it, but doing more micro-waving. . . . I've also started using the George Foreman Grill. . . . Where I'm living, normally in the winter months it's rarely that I'm going to get an electric bill under $200 so that means that . . . having the Food Stamp benefits, the good part of that, is I know that I will get some food for the month and be able to go to the grocery store. But if I wasn't getting what I'm getting, then it would almost be like, okay, we're going to not buy as much food because I have to pay this high light bill that comes during the winter time.

Although this woman receives SNAP benefits, the high cost of electricity makes it difficult to pay bills. She uses an electric grill to cook and, against her preferences, microwaves food during the winter months.

Women also mentioned budgeting, and some have to pri-oritize bills or make partial payments. An example of making a partial payment is expressed by a forty-three-year-old African American WIC beneficiary with an associate's degree who is a single mother of one child and resides in Charlotte:

I had to do a budget. And sometimes if a bill was due, I would pay a certain portion, and then pay the other portion. Especially when I did start back working and I had to put him in day care. Because, for his first year I was home. And once I graduated college, I had to go back to work, put him in day care, and that's when the struggle began. Because, day care's very, very expensive. And then, if you try to get assistance with it, everybody else is getting assistance. So you've got to be placed on a waiting list.

Another woman prioritizes bills when income is not sufficient to pay more than one bill. A forty-year-old dark-skinned single

Black mother of six in Charlotte who did not complete high school explains this practice:

> I take the one bill, and I pay the other bill. We call it robbing Peter to pay Paul. And that's usually the scenario with a lot of people that I know. My mother; I learned it from the best. Yeah. So that's what I usually do. If I don't have enough, I'm usually not so far behind. I try not to get so far behind that I have to go to the [nonprofit organization] . . . I try to go probably once a year. Like if I just got to, you know? But when I have a job, I'm fine. I have the income. It's not a lot but it helps. So that's why I just gotta go to work. Even though it's not that much money but it helps. . . . But I got lights, gas, water, cable, you know, rent, there's just a lot. And so I have more bills than I do money all the time. That's just the way it is. We make it fine. I try not to complain. My two children are disabled. They get SSI. I make it work with that and my work check.

Low- and zero-income Afro-descendant social welfare beneficiaries sometimes find it difficult to pay monthly bills. In the U.S. study, these women humbly seek assistance from nonprofit organizations and family members when they face difficulties. Mothers step in to provide assistance to adult children who are also mothers, thus demonstrating what motherhood looks like among Black women. It does not end once a child is an adult, and in the case of low- and zero-income women, mothers must meet financial or child care obligations to assist their adult children who are also mothers. Afro-descendant social welfare beneficiaries also have a range of skills and do odd jobs to bring in cash that can be used for monthly bills. Many of these beneficiaries are mothers with children, and some of them care for special needs children. Women budget and save money, but savings are quickly depleted when emergency situations arise. Budgeting commonly means making partial payments. These women defy stereotypes as luxury spenders as they seek to feed their families, keep the lights on in their homes, and avoid homelessness. Sadly, some women cut out leisure expenses and focus solely on basic necessities. They sustain their families often through family and community support.

The attitudes these women have expressed—"having to do what they have to do" or refusing to "mope and cry"—and the actions they take are forms of resistance to the dominant structures based on racism, sexism, and classism. The goal of Black feminism is to challenge and eliminate these dominant forms of oppression, and these women challenge and defy these forms through their daily actions of survival. Although some women may feel disempowered when relying on family for emergency assistance, others are empowered knowing that they can rely on close family members. Some exercise agency by seeking emergency assistance only as a last resort. They maintain independence by doing odd jobs, and they are empowered by their skills and resourcefulness, which enable them to provide for themselves and their families.

SUMMARY

Afro-descendant women SNAP, WIC, and Bolsa Família beneficiaries resist the gendered manifestations of white supremacy through their everyday strategies and efforts to survive. The experiences of these women more broadly mirror experiences of poor women who face separation or divorce. However, colorism plays a role in disadvantage, and what is distinct is that many Afro-descendant women are single and are dark skinned.

In Brazil and in the United States, poverty has a color, and it is a dark color. Black women with darker skin colors have lower marriage rates regardless of educational attainment.[13] Single mothers have fewer financial resources than people in heterosexual or homosexual partnerships who tend to have more than one income. Afro-descendant social welfare beneficiaries find their benefits useful, but they still need additional funds to meet monthly expenses. Afro-descendant women in Brazil and in the United States practice survival tactics such as relying on family, making extra money through odd jobs, and seeking emergency assistance from nonprofit organizations. Relying on nonprofits was more common in the United States than in Brazil. Some women in São Paulo received help from CRAS, but they did not mention it when discussing what they do when faced with financial difficulties. Some women admit they are always working or do not engage in leisure activity. In this way, the strong Black woman trope exists in both countries, and it can be detrimental to Afro-descendant women's health.

2

SUPPORT OF SOCIAL WELFARE PROGRAMS, STIGMA, AND RESISTANCE

"An unbelievable fact: our Minister of Citizenship made a survey of three thousand families that receive Bolsa Família. He considered the kids from zero to three years old. These kids were followed for a while. It was concluded that the intellectual development of these kids, children of Bolsa Família, was equivalent to one-third of the world average," says Bolsonaro.

—Agencia Estado, Correio Braziliense (translated by author)

In the spring of 2017, the newly elected president met with members of the Congressional Black Caucus. During that meeting, one of the members mentioned to Trump that welfare reform would be detrimental to her constituents—adding, "Not all of whom are black," according to NBC News. The president was incredulous. "Really? Then what are they?"

—Ryan Sit, *Newsweek*, January 12, 2018

SOCIAL WELFARE BENEFICIARIES' OPINIONS AND PERCEPTIONS OF SOCIAL WELFARE STIGMA

Deep-seated stereotypes about social welfare beneficiaries persist in Brazil and the United States. In the epigraph, Brazilian President Jair Bolsonaro misleadingly cited a study that reaffirmed his own stereotypes of Bolsa Família beneficiaries. Similarly, then President Trump cast social welfare beneficiaries as unequivocally Black, despite the fact that most are white. Underscoring the implications of such racialized misrepresentations, Layton and Hancock have shown that the proliferation of negative stereotypes of social welfare beneficiaries has the power to reduce public support for these programs.[1] In this chapter, I focus on Afro-descendant women's perceptions of differential treatment of social welfare beneficiaries. Hunter and Sugiyama detail the literature on whether conditional cash transfer programs empower or stigmatize beneficiaries.[2] In terms of empowerment, they are interested in whether beneficiaries have a sense of agency and feel included, or whether they feel stigmatized and monitored by the state and are treated poorly by state agents, such as social workers. As Hunter and Sugiyama observe, scholars like Mettler and Stonecash believe that welfare program requirements in the United States can bring about dignity insofar as these programs incorporate citizens and provide assistance, but they can also lead to isolation.[3] Other scholars, like Soss, Fording, and Schram, believe that eligibility requirements are problematic because they subject beneficiaries to continuous monitoring. Conditional cash transfer (CCT) beneficiaries in Brazil have generally expressed empowerment with respect to their participation in welfare programs.[4] In their study of men and women beneficiaries in northeastern

Brazil, Hunter and Sugiyama found that 75 percent of beneficiaries said they were proud to participate in Bolsa Família. However, most scholars ignore the specific experience of Afro-descendant women.[5]

Paying exclusive attention to issues of class and whether Bolsa Família empowers or stigmatizes through a race-neutral lens is a missed opportunity. I examine the intersectional stigma Afro-descendant women beneficiaries face along multiple axes. Women beneficiaries may feel empowered to the extent that the financial support enables them to provide resources for their children—food and clothing in Brazil and food in the United States—but they may still face stigma because of prevailing stereotypes of social welfare beneficiaries. These misrepresentations are rooted in classist, racist, and sexist stereotypes of Afro-descendant women. I found that Afro-descendant women in both countries do feel a sense of empowerment through welfare participation, but they also face stigma and discrimination due to the prevailing stereotypes of poor Black women. Furthermore, these women engage in Black feminist practice by resisting and challenging stigma. Rather than offering a race-neutral analysis, I ground my analysis in the theoretical and practical framework of Black feminism, which is centered around Black women and Black motherhood.

In the United States, the stereotype of Black women as welfare queens dates back to the Reagan administration (1981–1989), but this misrepresentation only became prevalent and politicized in Brazil during the 2014 presidential election. Scholars, print media, and social media platforms drew attention to the relationship between voting and Bolsa Família beneficiaries. Memes of Black women Bolsa Família beneficiaries that stereotyped beneficiaries as being lazy circulated on social media. Women were shown wastefully spending their money, and other memes portrayed women as depending on Bolsa Família instead of finding meaningful employment. Journalists focused on whether progressive politicians received more votes in regions or municipalities with significant populations of Bolsa Família beneficiaries. Similarly, academics debated whether Bolsa Família was a form of clientelism. And some scholars correlated the Bolsa Família program with voter support for Lula, which suggests some support for the clientelism argument.[6] Other scholars have cited a change in the socioeconomic composition of Lula's supporters from 2002 to 2006 as evidence to the contrary. Lula received less support from wealthy voters in 2006[7] because wealthy voters migrated to the opposition party and transformed the composition of his voter base. Beneficiaries have often been the topic of discussion, but these debates and discussions do not include the opinions and voices of beneficiaries, especially Afro-Brazilian women beneficiaries. Without the voices of these women, these debates and discussions effectively stereotype and silence them.

THE IMPORTANCE OF UNDERSTANDING STIGMA AGAINST SOCIAL WELFARE BENEFICIARIES

An understanding of stigma against social welfare beneficiaries is important because people who believe in stereotypes are less supportive of these programs, and negative media portrayals depress support among policy makers.[8] The Covid-19 pandemic highlighted existing inequalities and has shown the need for social welfare and government aid for low-income people. All Black women become the living embodiment of this stereotype and suffer from stigma. Social welfare beneficiaries' feelings of stigma depend on their belief that reliance on social welfare means they lack personal responsibility,[9] and social welfare beneficiaries have lower psychological well-being than those who do not receive social welfare assistance.[10] Women manage stigma in a number of ways. Seccombe found that some deny stigma, some distance themselves from other beneficiaries, some acknowledge the role of structures in society that lead to their situations, and others focus on motherhood. Seccombe acknowledges that some frameworks of motherhood are inappropriate for Black women because the notion of motherhood is far more expansive historically among Black Americans than among white Americans.[11]

In studying Black women in Chicago who receive Aid for Dependent Children, Robin Jarrett found that women generally challenge the culture of poverty myth that they have different values than nonbeneficiaries.[12] Women want to work, but child care costs, a lack of transportation, and a lack of jobs with a living wage prevent many from working. As a coping mechanism, some women focused on being good mothers. Motherhood became an identity that allowed women to manage the stigma of being social welfare beneficiaries. In this chapter, I am interested in how these women perceive discrimination or stigma against beneficiaries. I asked whether they have felt judged or treated differently, which covers both stigma and discrimination. If Afro-descendant women perceive stigma, what are their experiences? If they do not, do they rely on any of the mechanisms found in Seccombe's work? Black feminism examines the intersection of race, class, and gender, but it also examines the everyday ways in which Black women resist these structures of oppression.

I begin by examining U.S. women's responses to what they think of SNAP/WIC and whether these programs helped them, and in Brazil I analyze how women use their monthly Bolsa Família stipend. These responses dispel the stereotypes about how women use their benefits and reveal their lived realities: health challenges, budgeting for other bills, the challenges of being unemployed, and how they are empowered. My focus on Afro-Brazilian women enables me to analyze whether Afro-Brazilian women are empowered in the same way as CCT program beneficiaries more generally. In Brazil, the stipend is not limited to food and can be used for school supplies, medicine, and bill payments, although beneficiaries often spend the most on food. Second, I examine whether Afro-descendant women receiving social welfare benefits believe that they are judged or treated differently than other people.

IS SOCIAL WELFARE A LUXURY OR A BASIC GOOD IN THE UNITED STATES?

In this section, I analyze responses to the interview questions regarding Afro-descendant women social welfare beneficiaries' opinions about SNAP and WIC programs and whether they are helpful. The questions asked were "What do you think of SNAP/WIC?" and "Has SNAP/WIC been helpful to your family?" I analyzed these questions together because the interviewer sometimes forgot to ask one of the questions and respondents often gave one-word answers such as "yes." The United States and Brazil samples are discussed separately. Their responses highlight that women find these programs helpful, budget monthly to ensure they have money for other bills, and dedicate themselves to caring for family members. Budgets are tight, and these women rarely have extra funds for lavish spending, as critics of these programs would like people to believe. The responses here add important context to the struggles women face in honoring their family obligations.

The Importance of Food Assistance

In the United States sample, 98 percent of women found SNAP and WIC programs helpful. From this group, a subset (23 percent) found them useful but mentioned room for improvement. Some suggestions of room for improvement were increasing the benefit due to food being expensive and increasing the benefit for working or underemployed people. Only 2 percent did not find these programs useful.

Figure 2.1 is a word cloud that represents the most frequently mentioned words regarding food assistance: *WIC* (66), *family* (23), *SNAP* (51), and *food stamps* (21). Positive words were used 101 times, and they include *beneficial* (13), *good* (26), *helpful* (35), *great* (15), and *love* (12). The words *children* (21) and *family* (23) were often used, indicating respondents' commitment to family and children. The main themes were health issues or disabilities, managing monthly budgets, a desire for healthy options, and empowering women. Some women mentioned their own or their children's health issues. Words indicating sickness or health included *disabled* (2), *disability* (2), *sick* (1), *illness* (1), *diabetes* (1), *cancer* (1), *health* (3), and *autism* (1). Some women were out of work due to health issues such as cancer or a disability, and other women had disabled children for whom they were the primary caregiver. In 2018, 46.6 percent of SNAP households had at least one person with a disability.[13]

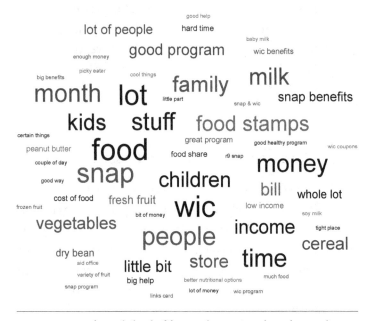

FIGURE 2.1 A word cloud of frequently mentioned words regarding SNAP/WIC programs in the U.S. sample.

Nearly half of all SNAP households include a disabled person, so it is not surprising that these women mentioned disabled people. However, Afro-descendant women are more vulnerable to the social determinants of poor health—including racism and sexism. As Collins notes,

> Within African-American communities, women's innovative and practical approaches to mothering under oppressive conditions often bring power and recognition. But this situation should not obscure the costs of motherhood to many Black women. Black motherhood is fundamentally a contradictory institution. African-American communities value motherhood, but Black mothers'

ability to cope with race, class, and gender oppression should not be confused with transcending those conditions. Black motherhood can be rewarding, but it can also extract high personal costs.[14]

In some households, poor Black women are sick but are still obligated to care for others. Also, some of these women are caring for children with health issues, and food aid may not be sufficient to accommodate the special diets required for their children.

Disability and Health: Social Welfare Beneficiaries and Their Children

Afro-descendant women social welfare beneficiaries face a number of challenges, including their own health illnesses as well as those of their children. Illness and sickness make full-time employment challenging. In general, African descendants in the United States are less likely to have positive health outcomes than whites. For Black American women, this problem is exacerbated, and these disparities largely exist regardless of socioeconomic status. Feminists such as Mikki Kendall advocate that basic issues such as health and food should be mainstream feminist issues for this reason. Black feminists have always focused on basic needs because of the precarious nature of Black life in the United States. As Chinn, Martin, and Redmond note, Black women have higher poverty rates and higher unemployment rates than their white counterparts. However, they are more likely to be single parents, which means they have fewer resources and more dependents. In addition, Black women are more likely than white women to suffer from chronic conditions such as anemia, obesity, and cardiovascular disease.[15] The health challenges of Black women in the general population are compounded by poverty and exacerbated by conditions rooted in structural racism and sexism. Food assistance helps these women feed their families even when their own bodies limit their ability to work.

The women in this study described the health challenges they and their dependents face, and they explained how social welfare benefits assist them. A forty-seven-year-old dark-skinned single Black woman with a college degree who resides in Charlotte had this to say:

> I understand what they saying about you know, if you able to work and some of the requirements and all. But I think the way it's set up, some people that need the help don't always get the help, or the amount you get is not always enough to help you make it through the month. And I know this is a supplement but . . . when you got disabled people in the household and you can't make it yourself because you already, you know sick and can't find work . . . that makes it even harder tryn'a feed two big grown people off that little bit of money.

A fifty-one-year-old light-skinned single Black woman with some college education who could not work due to cancer and has a pending disability claim who resides in Charlotte explained how important this assistance is for her:

> [It is] very beneficial, uh, especially for those in need. . . . I didn't anticipate on being on this program but because of my health reasons and the job situation then, yeah. . . . It's very beneficial. Now at the time, when I was working, I could have been eligible for it, but I did not take the opportunity to . . . explore that at the time because I was working. So I didn't feel like, I felt like if I did something, as far as taking it from someone else that

really needed it, then that would have shown where my integrity was. But now I'm really in need of it so yeah it has been very beneficial.

A thirty-eight-year-old Black woman with some college and three children who resides in Charlotte described how her children's health issues require more than what SNAP benefits provide:

> Um, I think it's really good . . . especially for me. . . . My family's a little different because I have children that have health issues [so] that we can't go to food banks. . . . Although it's good, it's still kind of limited for my situation. . . . My daughter has autism but she has an eating disorder; sensory processing, and so she can only eat certain things and she can only take medication with applesauce. . . . We have to shop separately for her and then my son who has been out of school for two weeks straight, bleeds inner rectally so I have to shop separately for him so all of that adds up. But that . . . medical [and] food costs; it's not covered in SNAP benefits.

A forty-year-old Afro-American divorced mother of seven and grandmother of one with an associate's degree who resides in Charlotte also commented on one child's needs:

> I feel that it's helped a little bit. It really has as far as me being able to buy the food and go into the grocery stores and buy the things that my child needs. I have one child that has severe illnesses. I can't afford to feed her . . . properly because she has borderline diabetes. The money that I receive does not allow me to buy organic, or the things that she needs because the cost of it is so high. So, somebody is suffering.

Not only do Afro-descendant women suffer from chronic conditions, but some of these women also have children who suffer from illness. These illnesses prevent them from eating inexpensive grocery store foods that often contain additives and have high amounts of sugar. It is a fine balance to provide healthy food when that food is expensive. The forty-year-old woman in Charlotte admits that her borderline diabetic daughter suffers because she cannot afford more costly, healthier food. Some farmers' markets in Illinois, Wisconsin, and North Carolina accept SNAP cards as payment, but not all cities in these states accept SNAP. The USDA Food and Nutrition Service provides lists of farmers' markets that accept SNAP by state and by month.[16] However, to reach these markets, beneficiaries also need access to transportation, and it is not clear how accessible these markets are to where beneficiaries live. In addition, beneficiaries need to make it to these markets on days when they are open (usually Saturdays); this is a potential scheduling and logistical challenge, especially in contrast to grocery stores that are open every day.

Social Welfare Frees Money for Other Bills

These women budget monthly and explain how food aid frees money for them to pay other bills. Darity et al. found that wealth disparities are not caused by families having poor financial management skills.[17] In fact, Hamilton and Chiteji's study found that the Black savings rate is not lower than whites; and when controlling for income, Gittleman and Wolff found that Blacks have a higher savings rate than whites.[18]

Low- and zero-income Afro-descendant women who receive Electronic Benefits Transfer (EBT) cards pay their bills based on the time of the month they receive aid (such as SNAP). A thirty-nine-year-old dark-skinned woman who has a monthly income of $720 and resides in Charlotte explains her strategy:

> You go from trying to save money to buying a place to live and pay your bills, and you're having hot dogs almost every other day, or peanut butter and jelly. When you finally get your EBT card, you can say, "Okay, well, we're going to have chicken and pork chops." . . . I have four children, and I don't always have to say no, because now I have just money to focus on food, which is why it's helpful for my whole family.

A twenty-four-year-old dark-skinned unmarried African American mother of one with an associate's degree who lives with her partner in Chicago appreciates her SNAP benefits:

> Yeah. They have. They have. We're able to keep food in the house. I live with my mom and she's on disability, so she's not getting like a check every two weeks or every week or nothing like that. . . . I work for home health care, so we don't get a lot of hours. Our paychecks aren't really that big. What I make goes to her and bills or whatever, so [SNAP benefits] . . . come in handy for the food part.

Empowerment

Many of the women (98 percent) were empowered by their ability to provide food for their families. Of this group, 3 percent were empowered by learning healthy eating habits or because they were able to assist people beyond their household. A thirty-one-year-old dark-skinned single mother of four with an associate's degree who resides in Chicago explains this benefit:

> To me, personally, it comes in handy. Regardless if you have a good income, regardless if you getting food stamps, it actually comes in handy. Cause when you don't have the money to go get the milk, you've got these coupons. Ah, I got these coupons last month, I can go use them. They comes in handy. It's worth it. Regardless . . . whatever you make, everyone should, if you [are] pregnant or expecting they should get it. It's a good program, especially if the kids turning four . . . cause when I had it with my daughter at first they stopped it at five, at four, now it's five. Its added an extra year. It's healthy; [a] good healthy program to have. It teach you, it teach your kids how to eat healthy. What should be portioned off, what they need as infants all the way up until now. It's a healthy, good healthy program.

Room for Improvement

Although women appreciate WIC and SNAP, some believe there is room for improvement such as offering healthier options and increasing the amount for working women. Some women desire healthier options such as organic food because of their children's health conditions or illnesses. A thirty-nine-year-old dark-skinned single mother of four with an associate's degree who resides in Chicago had this to say:

> I think SNAP is, and WIC, they both are, they both are good for our people, but the products that WIC, the formula . . . changed . . . [They] have those whatever ingredients they have in there, that give kids ADHD and things like that. They need to

take all the harsh stuff out, and make it as close to breast milk as possible for people who can't breastfeed.

A thirty-one-year-old dark-skinned African American mother of five with some community college education who resides in Chicago suggested these improvements for WIC:

> I think there is room for improvement in the sense of offering better nutritional options. For example, instead of just cow or soy milk, to offer almond, or rice, or other options, or to expand the variety of fruits and vegetables. It's extremely limited on fresh fruits, but extremely readily available on canned. So, they are offering more of the frozen fruits, which is fine, but it would be nice if they would offer organic and broaden the fresh fruits and vegetables.

A twenty-three-year-old dark-skinned Black, African American single mother of one with some college who resides in Chicago echoed some limitations of the WIC program:

> Yeah. Well, the WIC helped my family, because . . . if I don't have any money to get what I need to get, they there to be a backup plan for me to get what I need to get . . . if it's an emergency. It's basically for emergency. . . . Say, for instance, I run out of SNAP for today, I get in there, it's gone tomorrow, with grocery shopping. The month not even over yet and I ran out of food and I don't get it until next month. You only get SNAP once a month. So it's like, "Dang, what I'm going to do?" So now I got to depend on WIC, you know, and just, I don't know. WIC is just kind of hard to accomplish, because . . . it's only really milk that most people use. You can't just say, oh, this going to help me eat, because it's not. It's not really nothing. It's a healthier way and there's less products, so that's why.

A twenty-seven-year-old African American single mother of two with a high school education who resides in Milwaukee explained how a lack of transparency affects her ability to budget:

> Sometimes I have to feel like, you know . . . as far as the SNAP, . . . when they decreased the stamps . . . [saying] "Oh, you make a dollar or two more than your last pay period." But they fail to realize that two more dollars [of income] is still like basically you're at the same income. So they take like $50 or $60 or however much they want. Then it's like sometimes they do it without even giving you a letter or notifying you. So when you get your benefits, you're thinking it's this and it's not. So now you . . . got yourself in a hole because . . . you already made your budget for that month. So you're like, okay, I know for sure I'm going to get this $359. So I don't have to worry about it around this time.

In the United States, women find social welfare benefits useful because they help them care for their children. In some cases, mothers are disabled or caring for ill children and are unable to work. These benefits help them provide for their families. To receive WIC, women must meet the poverty guideline requirements and also be at nutritional risk. A number of women mentioned their satisfaction with the ability to buy fresh fruits. Some women were dissatisfied with the limited organic foods in lieu of canned foods, especially those with ill children. Yet women generally find these programs useful. They budget and are able to use available cash for bills when using these programs to buy food.

AFRO-DESCENDANT WOMEN'S OPINIONS ON BOLSA FAMÍLIA

In the Brazil sample, 99 percent of women found Bolsa Família programs helpful, but 8 percent found these programs only a little useful or mentioned that the amount provided was small when compared to the cost of gas or diapers. Variations on the word *help* were used 181 times, indicating the tremendous impact of Bolsa Família in the lives of Afro-descendant women in Brazil. The word *children* or *child* was used 39 times and *family* 8 times. Mothers often mentioned providing for their children, and at least six women mentioned the difficulty of providing as a single mother. Unemployment was a central theme, and women spoke about themselves being unemployed or their spouse being unemployed. Figure 2.2 highlights some of the words frequently mentioned by Afro-descendant women when discussing the Bolsa Família program in Brazil.

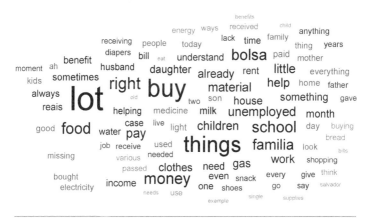

FIGURE 2.2 A word cloud of frequently mentioned words regarding the Bolsa Família program.

The Financial Hardship of Unemployment

Women mentioned unemployment twenty-four times when answering the question, "What do you think of Bolsa Família?" and "Has Bolsa Família been helpful to your family?" Unemployment poses a challenge to the potential benefits of Bolsa Família. Although I discuss unemployment in terms of economic remuneration for work, the women in this sample are mothers and are also engaged in labor or work caring for their children. Many feminists have noted that this difficult and unpaid labor often goes unnoticed and is expected of mothers. Women spend hours caring for their families, but this work is not properly captured in the statistics regarding unemployed people. The unemployment numbers are high for the social welfare beneficiaries in this sample, but we must consider the high percentage of these women who are engaged in the unpaid labor of caring for their children. Despite stereotypes that Afro-descendant people do not want to work, these women often do odd jobs to earn extra income.

Some women have husbands who are also unemployed. In response to this question, twenty-one women said that they were unemployed (*desempregada*). However, I believe there is a sexist bias in referring to these women as unemployed; "unpaid caregivers" more accurately reflects the labor of these women. In fact, in the Salvador sample, 65 percent are unpaid caregivers, and 35 percent are formally employed. In São Paulo, 77 percent of women in the sample are unpaid caregivers, and 23 percent are formally employed. In São Luis, 19 percent are engaged in formal work, and 81 percent of women are engaged in unpaid caregiving work. Afro-descendants are more likely to be unemployed than whites. In 2017, of the 13 million people who were unemployed, 63.7 percent were Afro-Brazilians.[19] Given this historical trend and the fact that the women in this study qualified for Bolsa Família, it is not surprising that they mentioned unemployment as this Forty-one-year-old light-skinned Parda mother of one who resides in São Paulo did:

> It is for my son. His father does not work. It's hard to get a job; he hasn't been offered one. He is a metallurgist and only does welding. He doesn't earn a very good income, maybe 200 ($53.33 USD), 300 ($80 USD), sometimes 200 reais a month because he's a welder. I'm unemployed. I've put in applications but have not been called back yet.

A dark-skinned woman who resides in São Paulo added: "At the moment it helps me a lot because I am unemployed. It helps me a lot with bills because I pay rent, electricity. Bills are very high."

A forty-three-year-old light-skinned Parda single mother of two children who resides in Salvador praised the flexibility of the Bolsa Família program:

> At the moment I find myself unemployed, my husband as well. At the time my boy was a newborn, and sometimes we needed to buy diapers . . ., medicine, medication, and we used this money for that. Later he went on and grew up. Today he goes to school. It's good. . . . Although at school they give lunch, but sometimes the children don't like it so we buy it! And it also helps in terms of energy because . . . it was very expensive. It was 150 reais ($40 USD). It went up to 170 reais ($45.33 USD) and then I found out that whoever had a benefit had a right. At COELBA you have to call . . . there to get a discount on your electricity bill. So when I managed to register, one year later today, my energy receipt comes to 28 ($7.47 USD), 35 ($9.33 USD), or 70 reais ($18.67 USD).

These interviews reveal that Bolsa Família plays an important role in supporting women and their families who are struggling because of unemployment. Some women or spouses applied for jobs, and while they wait for interviews, Bolsa Família ensures that they can provide food for their families. The participant in Salvador mentioned a program that helps with lowering bills, and Bolsa Família helped this family provide medicine and diapers.

Empowerment and Dignity with Bolsa Família

In this section, I examine the purchases Bolsa Família beneficiaries make. A racist, sexist, and classist meme circulated on social media in 2014 that purported to show an Afro-Brazilian woman "without Bolsa Família" and the same woman "with Bolsa Família." The second woman boasts all of the accouterments and accessories that the woman without Bolsa Família notably does not have: fancy glasses, colored contact lenses, straightened hair, and even what appears to be a different nose, presumably from a nose job. The meme intended to show the woman dressed and looking better as a result of Bolsa Família; however, this racist and sexist trope perpetuated the idea that Afro-Brazilian women spend their welfare money on themselves "wastefully," buying better clothes, going to the salon, and otherwise improving their appearance. Of course, Black feminists do not critique Black women of any income level for practicing self-care, and they are aware that poor Black women who engage in self-care are unfairly criticized.

The 120 participants in my study in Brazil tell a very different story: Bolsa Família stipends are only enough to provide

TABLE 2.1 FREQUENCY OF WORDS USED IN RESPONSE TO
HOW BOLSA FAMÍLIA HELPED PARTICIPANTS

Word	Frequency
help/helped/helping/helps	181
Lot	98
Food	37
electricity/light/energy	26
(school) materials	23
Children	22
clothes/shoes	22
Snack	19
Gas	19
Milk	13
Rent	12
Bills	10
Medicine	8
Diapers	6
single/alone	6
Bread	5
Notebook	4

for women's households. Bolsa Família expenditures are not restricted to buying food, but the women interviewed mainly spent their money on necessities for their household. Table 2.1 lists the items most often mentioned by interviewees. Although these stipends are fairly small, they allow women to purchase school supplies, clothes, and food for their families. As Hunter and Sugiyama's findings confirmed, by doing so, these women are able to live with dignity. A twenty-six-year-old dark-skinned woman with no income who graduated from high school and received 202 reais ($53.87 USD) in São Luis was very emotional and began crying during her interview when answering the question. She stated, "Well, in my case it helped a lot because I was unemployed, and it was just me and my two kids (started crying); so when it came, it helped a lot." A thirty-two-year-old dark-skinned woman with some college education in São Luis received 39 reais ($10.40 USD), and she stated: "It arrives at the right moment. Sometimes I did not have anything to eat. I separated from my husband so in the moment that I got it, God gave me this benefit, it was gratifying. I buy things for school, food . . . bread, butter, milk." Despite her separation, with the help of Bolsa Família she was able to provide school items for her children. One woman mentioned being unemployed and another was separated from her husband. Both of these women experienced hardships that are difficult, especially for mothers. These women were extremely grateful and were empowered because they could provide for their children. Being able to provide for their children gives women in extremely vulnerable economic situations a feeling of dignity.

In my study, Afro-Brazilian women found Bolsa Família to be helpful in enabling them to provide basic necessities for their children. Hunter and Sugiyama also concluded that women were empowered, but they did not believe the women were stigmatized.[20] I believe this difference is due to differences in our study samples. Their study included men and women whereas my study participants were all Afro-Brazilian women. Ignoring the intersection of race, class, and gender leads to a race-neutral analysis. In the next section, I discuss perceived stigma and discrimination against social welfare beneficiaries.

DISCRIMINATION AGAINST SOCIAL WELFARE BENEFICIARIES

Afro-descendant women in both the United States and Brazil recognized discrimination against social welfare beneficiaries. An astounding 85 percent of participants in São Luís perceived discrimination against Bolsa Família beneficiaries, compared to 69 percent in São Paulo and 57 percent in Salvador (table 2.2). In the U.S. sample, 55 percent of respondents in Chicago perceived discrimination against social welfare beneficiaries, compared to only 39 percent in Milwaukee and 30 percent in Charlotte.

The welfare queen stereotype was popularized by Reagan-era conservatives in the 1980s, and high-profile political moments since then have brought this stereotype back into the headlines. In 2012 Newt Gingrich made headlines when he claimed that President Barack Obama was the "welfare president," and in 2018 President Trump expressed shock at the observation that

TABLE 2.2 DISCRIMINATION AGAINST SOCIAL WELFARE BENEFICIARIES AND SKIN COLOR DISCRIMINATION BY CITY

City	Discrimination Against Social Welfare Beneficiaries (%)	Skin Color Discrimination (%)
Salvador	57	28
São Paulo	69	72
São Luis	85	48
Milwaukee	39	69
Charlotte	30	74
Chicago	55	67

welfare beneficiaries are not mostly Black. Despite the persistence and recirculation of the welfare queen trope, most Afro-descendant women in the Milwaukee and Charlotte samples did not perceive discrimination against SNAP/WIC beneficiaries.

This finding stands in contrast to discussions regarding skin color, for which Afro-descendant women beneficiaries in the United States more easily perceived racial discrimination. Although respondents differed in their perception of the reasons for discrimination, a majority of women in four of the six cities agreed that there was stigma or discrimination against social welfare beneficiaries.

STIGMA AGAINST SOCIAL WELFARE BENEFICIARIES IN THE UNITED STATES

Misrepresentations and stereotypes of social welfare beneficiaries are deeply rooted in paternalistic ideas and efforts to control Black women's bodies. Efforts to control Black women's bodies through sterilization lasted well into the 1970s in the United States, long after emancipation. Poor Black women were sterilized from 1929 to 1974 in North Carolina. Methods of controlling Black women's bodies today are the result of interlocking systems of domination that stereotype Black women as unfit mothers who live beyond their financial means.[21] In this study, social welfare beneficiaries perceived stereotypes include laziness, wasteful spending, and the idea that women have babies to receive more benefits. These controlling images and interlocking systems of domination based on class, race, and gender convey the idea that the women are not deserving of the human right to food.

A contemporary example of the attempt to control poor women's bodies was a proposal in the United States to tie Norplant, a type of birth control, to receiving welfare benefits. In the early 1990s, more than twelve states attempted to pass bills that would have given financial incentives to women on welfare to use Norplant. Norplant is a silicone capsule placed in the arm that can only be removed by a doctor. In this way, these women could be monitored. The birth control was to last five years. Other proposed bills required social welfare beneficiaries to risk losing their benefits if they did not take Norplant.

STIGMA AGAINST SOCIAL WELFARE BENEFICIARIES IN BRAZIL

The most prevalent negative stereotypes women in Brazil mentioned were perceptions of laziness and misconceptions that women would intentionally have children solely to receive social welfare benefits. People also use degrading terms such as Bolsa Misery to capture the widespread idea that these women live in miserable conditions and therefore need the stipend. Some of the frequently mentioned words by Brazilian social welfare beneficiaries were *people*, *Bolsa Família*, *children*, *a lot*, *lazy*, and *government* (figure 2.3). Participants were often referring to others—these were not their own perceptions.

"A Lot" of Women Have Children to Receive Bolsa Família

Respondents mentioned that "a lot" of people hold stereotypes about Bolsa Família beneficiaries and that these people believe

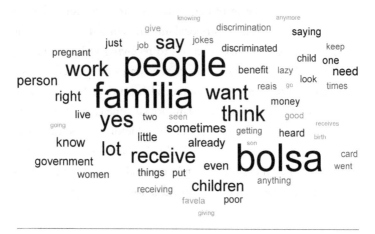

FIGURE 2.3 A word cloud of perceptions of Bolsa Família beneficiaries in Brazil.

that "a lot" of women have children so they can receive Bolsa Família benefits. A thirty-three-year-old Negra single mother of four with a high school education and a monthly income of $254.40 USD who resides in Salvador stated the following in her narrative:

> Yes. A lot. Because some people have heard that women want to keep giving birth to receive Bolsa Família, and that because of Bolsa Família, people no longer want to work. [People say] these things—that the government keeps giving away free money [and] that the people don't want to do anything else.

In the Brazilian sample, 16 percent perceived stigma or discrimination against Bolsa Família beneficiaries due to the stereotype that women have children in an attempt to receive benefits. This stereotype does not consider the sacrifice mothers make in the process of mothering and taking care of their children.

In fact, this misperception of women as actively seeking to have children aligns in some ways with the persistent jezebel stereotype that hypersexualizes Black women and promotes the idea that they are always sexually available. At the same time, such representations cast these women as irresponsible members of society. Women in this study discussed, understood, and responded to the stereotype that women have children to receive social welfare. A forty-three-year-old dark-skinned self-identified Negra woman who resides in Salvador acknowledged hearing this misstatement often:

> Yes, because sometimes there are other women who have several children and . . . I see a lot of people saying, "Oh, they have a lot of children, because there is Bolsa Família and they can get it. That's why they have so many children."

A thirty-two-year-old dark-skinned self-identified Negra woman with up to two minimum family salaries ($508.80 USD) and an incomplete college education who resides in São Luis found some humor in this mistaken assumption:

> Yes, like [a] parasite, dependent, thief (laughs), [they] don't want to work, [they] only want to receive Bolsa Família money. Now sincerely, it's in the heads of a lot of idiotic people, you know? There are places; there is a municipality here in São Luis called Belagua, have you ever heard of it? Belagua is in the interior of São Luis that has the lowest income per capita per person. It is in the interior and most poor in Brazil. . . . I think the maximum they can receive for each child is the same as someone that has ten [children]. I think that it is only 200 ($53.33 USD) or 300 ($80 USD) [reais], right? Even so, a person who has five children is [not] going to do it for two hundred and a few reais.

A thirty-four-year-old dark-skinned Negra woman who resides in Salvador echoed the ignorance of people who hold this view:

> Not me, but I've seen people comment. They say, "you don't work, you don't do anything; you give birth every year because you have the Bolsa Família benefit," and actually, it's not like that. . . . I think there are people who are lucky enough to receive like, let's assume 500 ($133.33 USD), 400 [reais] ($106.67 USD). . . . In my case, as I have two [children], I receive 78 reais ($20.80 USD), but there are people who have more children and receive less. I think that discrimination is [the idea that] women get pregnant just to receive Bolsa Família. I think this is ignorance because when you get pregnant, you get pregnant. If the woman kills the child or throws it in the trash, everyone talks, but if she gets pregnant and keeps her child, it's great. Nobody else gives food; she gives food [to her child].

A forty-one-year-old dark-skinned Negra single mother of two with an incomplete middle school education who resides in Salvador responded this way:

> Many say that Bolsa Família has brought more children in the world because nowadays there are many women who are having children because of Bolsa Família. Most of them are getting pregnant . . . they don't even want to go to work anymore, because of Bolsa Família. I know a lot of people where I live who nowadays don't want to work anymore because of Bolsa Família.

A thirty-one-year-old light-skinned Parda single mother who resides in São Luis said, "Yes. Because a lot of people think we had a child on purpose because we want to receive the benefit. . . . They have these jokes."

These women, who know the cost of food from experience, recognize that Bolsa Família financial assistance is not enough to offset the costs of providing for that additional child. Although most participants discussed other people's perceptions, in rare cases, such as the forty-one-year-old woman in Salvador, beneficiaries believed the stereotype that women have children to receive benefits. In fact, women are aware that discrepancies in the amount women receive, lead to some women with more children receiving less money than women with fewer children.

Scum of the Poor

The "lazy mother" stereotype is tied to gendered and racialized stereotypes of Afro-descendant women. In the study sample, 33 percent of Bolsa Família beneficiaries were aware of the stereotypical view of beneficiaries as lazy. This pernicious stereotype does not consider the costs associated with formal employment. Moreover, women beneficiaries may supplement their benefits through formal employment or rely on informal means of employment. Some Bolsa Família beneficiaries, like this fifty-eight-year-old dark-skinned Negra divorced mother of five who completed high school and resides in Salvador, talked about the lazy mother stereotype:

> Yes, Yes. We are called *scum of the poor*, dependent, lazy, that women make children to receive the Bolsa Família. . . . There are elderly people in the program too, but people can't see, they don't see [that] and they talk about what they don't know (emphasis added).

Women also receive the brunt of degrading terms. An eighteen-year-old light-skinned Parda single mother of one who did not complete middle school and resides in São Luis reported this: "Yes. Because a lot of people think that we receive a "Bolsa Misery." I've already heard a lot of people say that we receive this because we do not want to work." People often refer to Bolsa Família as Bolsa Miserable (Bolsa Miserável) or Bolsa Lazy (Bolsa Preguiçoso). The words *miserable* and *misery* were mentioned six times. Women often mentioned outsiders using these degrading terms but noted that sometimes family members also degrade them. A forty-one-year-old light-skinned Parda woman who resides in São Paulo explained how it felt when her own family members criticized her for receiving Bolsa Família assistance:

> Yes, I've been discriminated against, called starving, miserable, because I didn't have anything to eat at home. My husband had it [Bolsa Família], but he said he didn't have it. . . . But it wasn't a very big offense, because for those in need, it's not a misery, it's a help. And they said I was starving, that I was miserable, that I didn't have all these things. My family. I won't mention them by name, but it's my own family; outsiders too. But family is worse. . . . But it hurts even more from the depths of the heart when it's blood, family.

Resistance and Empowerment

Rather than passively receiving these derogatory comments, these women often spoke back against the criticism and condescension. Some women felt empowered because they could buy necessities for their families. In Brazil, three women explicitly resisted stereotypes by addressing people who complained about them receiving Bolsa Família or who they felt discriminated against them. However, other women said that Bolsa Família was something they were entitled to or had a right to receive. I argue that this perception of a right or entitlement is a form of empowerment, which can be seen in this statement by a thirty-nine-year-old light-skinned Negra woman who resides in Salvador who was applying for Bolsa Família:

> There was a time when a woman said that when I went to get the Bolsa Família, right? . . . I went to get the Bolsa Família . . . then the little paper came out saying it was blocked. Then she said, "Anyway, a woman like this, instead of working, is using Bolsa Família." Then I said, "My love, if you're thinking it's wrong that I'm coming to take something that's to my benefit, that's your problem." She said . . . "unfortunately, it's blocked so she's going to have to work to try to raise her children instead of being on Bolsa Família." I told her, "If you think that way, okay." I took it and left her talking.

This woman responded to the person who gave her a hard time by proudly asserting her right to the benefit. In a similar fashion, four other women also discussed Bolsa Família as a right. These women understand Bolsa Família not as something shameful but rather as something the government *should* be providing to support their livelihoods.

In Brazil, Afro-Brazilian women beneficiaries are aware of the stereotype of laziness and the perception that they have children just so they can receive the Bolsa Família benefit. They are also aware of the stereotypes that humiliate and degrade them. Contrary to these perceptions, some of these women are employed, and others have applied for jobs. When they experience stigma, some respondents resist by addressing people directly in the moment; others spoke about their right to Bolsa Família during their interviews. Yet nearly all these women exhibited a sense of empowerment through their participation in Bolsa Família, and they acknowledged that the financial support helps them buy basic necessities for their families.

STIGMA AGAINST SNAP AND WIC BENEFICIARIES IN THE UNITED STATES

The most common stigmas social welfare beneficiaries in the United States encountered were the stereotype of laziness and criticisms that they heard in grocery stores. Some women beneficiaries also pointed to popular stereotypes that social welfare beneficiaries are addicted to drugs, as this forty-seven-year-old dark-skinned Black single mother of three who has a bachelor's degree and resides in Charlotte explained:

> You know . . . I've heard females say, "Oh, if you on food stamps, you this and you that." Now I know it may have sounded like earlier I was making a judgment call when I said what I said about um some people, some females don't want to get off they butt and get a job and all that; depending on the system. But, see, I'm sayin' that based off what I've heard some women come out they mouth and . . . based on the fact of seeing people on crack and all and stuff. Judging somebody just becuz oh you just see them with a SNAP card, that's different. You know what I mean. Hey people got an opinion. I'll just say it, you know. Yep. I base mine on morals and values.

However, most women focused on other people's perceptions. The most popular words mentioned in interviews in the United States were *people* (39), *card* (10), *SNAP* (51), *look* (2), *food stamps*

(21), *store* (13), *jobs* (13), *WIC* (66), and *work/working* (28). Women who mentioned a stigma against social welfare beneficiaries discussed experiences they had in the store and their experiences with judgments (often nonverbal microaggressions) from family members or strangers. They mentioned the looks people gave them when they used their SNAP cards. Looks and staring are meant to shame women using these benefits, and they telegraph the dominant racial, class, and gender narratives that circulate around welfare beneficiaries. When aware of these stares and the attendant hostility behind them, some women believe they have the right to this food assistance and resist by directly addressing people who are disrespectful.

Stereotypes of Laziness in the Land of Milk and Honey

In the United States sample, 8 percent of respondents perceived that people view social welfare beneficiaries as lazy people who do not want to work, and 25 percent of those women mentioned family members or friends who stigmatize them. A nineteen-year-old dark-skinned mother of three who self-identifies as Black, not African, has a tenth-grade education, and resides in Chicago explained it this way:

> Yes. Oh, yes, because people just feel like . . . they feel like just because you're on SNAP like you're trying to live off it. And some people that's not on SNAP, they cannot get WIC. . . . They upset about it because they feel like, "Why should they get it and we work? We work. Why should they get it and we don't?" But, to me, it's helpful. But it's really not a big help when you got a big family. So people just judge, and they be like, "People with kids just

trying to live off of WIC," when that don't even be the case for me because I'm trying to get off it. . . . I'm trying to work, find me a job, something permanent so I can be getting paid. It's helpful, . . . but who just want to settle for four hundred dollars a month? Who want to do that? You spend that in a couple days, four or five days. Who wants to settle for that? So it really pushes you. It really makes you want to work and just say, "I don't need this no more. I don't want to be on welfare anymore. I want to work so I can have more so I can take care of my family."

This respondent is aware of the misperception that women beneficiaries do not want to work, whereas she *wants to work* in order to earn more than what she receives through welfare. In emphasizing the fact that the program incentivizes her to work because the benefits are not enough to cover her family's expenses, she conveys a sense of self-empowerment in looking for work and a more permanent source of income. She would like more money to take care of her family, and she assumes potential jobs would pay a living wage that could help her accomplish that goal.

Other social welfare beneficiaries described how family or community members viewed them as being "lazy" and "undeserving." A thirty-three-year-old Black, African American married mother of five with some technical college education who resides in Chicago made this comment:

Judged me or treated me differently . . . I'm the, um, I'm the reason for jokes around my sister's family—her husband and stuff. He makes jokes because they're more well off than I am. But it's okay. I try to make light of it. . . . They'll say some things . . . "Let me get some of that." Well, you've got to qualify. You've got to be poor like I am, if that's what you want to do. But it's just them. I'm used to it.

A twenty-nine-year-old dark-skinned African American woman with some college education who resides in Charlotte explained her observations this way:

> Yeah . . . The looks in the store, I get looks, but people in my community, those are the actual persons who, who verbally speak on it and a lot of times, they not gonna say it in your face, but like I know they like, "Chile, she get food stamps, you know, um, that's why, that's why they eatin' good or you know." It's in that community they look, wouldn't really say it but uh in the grocery store you know you got that card people look, they ain't gone say nothin'. But the, uh, yo', yo' peers in your community when you make them upset. Yeah it'll come out how they really feel . . . and they can be gettin' it too. . . . A lot of times, people, people really do need food stamps, but like I told you, you get you a little piece of job, they take those away. . . . And I pay taxes just like everybody pay taxes. I don't think I'm owed it [welfare], but I appreciate it. I don't want to be on it forever, but at this time right now I do need it and I appreciate it. . . . I know in other countries they would love to have something like this.

A twenty-nine-year-old African American mother of two who has a high school education and resides in Milwaukee recognized subtle microaggressions from friends on social media:

> I got a couple of friends who feel like they better than me because they don't get food stamps, and I do. So like, I, like, you know how, you put comments, you read the comments on Facebook and stuff, and like, you know when somebody's talking about you, but they not directly talking to you, but they making comments and you know it's about you, because the comment that they making is identifying with what you going through? Like, yeah, I've

been discriminated against before for receiving food stamps. Like, you would be like, well, why can't you get up and work, instead of receiving food stamps? Like, I do work. That's why I only get $140.

Women beneficiaries are often seen as lazy and undeserving even when they are employed. The actual experiences of these women dispel these misperceptions of laziness and being undeserving. Indeed, the women who do work often receive fewer benefits than they would receive if they were not employed. In addition, these women do not believe these benefits are owed to them in any sense, but they appreciate the financial help they provide in the context of their need. Furthermore, unemployed women beneficiaries expressed a sense of guilt for not being employed, and some have hopes of gaining employment. The right to food is very little to ask from a society that provides few opportunities for Black people in terms of employment and education.

Shopping Experiences

Unlike their Brazilian counterparts, respondents in the United States received criticism, were judged, and experienced verbal and nonverbal microaggressions in public places. In grocery stores, women often had hostile, derogatory, or otherwise negative interactions with cashiers and other patrons. The effect of the interactions, attitudes, and treatment these women beneficiaries experienced were described by this fifty-eight-year-old Hebrew Israelite married woman with no children who has completed high school and resides in Charlotte:

Well, I have been kind of looked at kind of strange in the line, in the grocery line, maybe because I pull out a food stamp card and they have to pay with they credit card, but they pay in cash or something. Yeah, you get those feelings and vibes from people. And sometimes you feel really ashamed. You don't even want your card to show up when you're pulling out your driver's license or something. You're kind of skeptical around certain people because you don't want them to see your little red, white, and blue card, that you get food stamps. You just don't want them to know, because sometimes they looking like they doing so good. You feel bad.

This comment from a fifty-two-year-old light-skinned African American mother of two who resides in Charlotte sheds insight into the nature of spatial segregation and racial hierarchies in Charlotte specifically, but also on American cities generally:

If they did, I didn't care. Really, I'm trying to feed my family. It don't matter to me. I may have had a little bit when I've gone to grocery stores. At Publix you get a look. When you're in South Charlotte, you get a look. I remember me and my daughter were in Publix, and this was a couple of years ago. And I saw the little white girls looking at my daughter, like, "What is she doing here?" When you go to SouthPark Mall [an upscale shopping center in an affluent, predominantly white part of Charlotte], I get the same thing when I go to Publix. When I have my food stamps, what you think I care, I don't care. I'm *taking care of my family* and wouldn't let it bother me. You get a lot of that in South Charlotte. If you're in a store . . . it's like "what are you doing here?" And you can tell that you don't have to say a word because I read people very well, so you don't have to say anything. It's the way you act. It's the looks on your face. The way—just the way you looked at. You feel like. . . . It doesn't bother me though. I go where I want to go [emphasis added].

Well aware of the racialized, segregated spaces in the city, this respondent chooses to shop at a Publix in this wealthier, predominantly white neighborhood. Although she experiences stigma, this does not stop her from what she understands is her motherly duty to take care of her family. In frequenting these spaces with her daughter in spite of the verbal and nonverbal hostility she might encounter, this woman is teaching her daughter that they have the right to access different parts of the city and are not limited to the predominantly Black areas. She is modeling for her daughter a right to assert belonging—even in those spaces where Blackness and poverty are openly stigmatized.

A forty-three-year-old African American single mother of one who has an associate's degree, a monthly income of $2,000, and resides in Charlotte feels empowered, and she rightfully claims that she is entitled to food aid because she is going through a difficult time:

> When I was receiving food stamps, when I was pregnant with him, I didn't know that you could use food stamps at Sam's. And I went there one time, and this white lady was like, "Huh," because I would buy the big things of milk, the powdered milk for him. And the water, and all that stuff. I would buy my meat. And so, you know I had a lot of stuff in that cart. But when they asked me . . . and I, when I was like, "Yeah, it's food stamp." "Huh, yeah. Huh." I've been working since I was fifteen years old, and I am entitled to this because I'm having a hard time right now.

The issue of employment is complex; beneficiaries who do work often have low-paying jobs that fall short of covering their family's expenses.

Part-Time Pay for Full-Time Work:
Social Welfare Beneficiaries and Low Income

In "The Other America," a speech Martin Luther King Jr. gave at Grosse Pointe High School in 1968, King discussed how low wages make Black life difficult. He stated, "There are so many other people in the other America who can never make ends meet because their incomes are far too low if they have incomes, and their jobs are so devoid of quality. And so in this other America, unemployment is a reality and under-employment is a reality." He further discussed how this problem is pernicious among Black Americans: "Most of the poverty stricken people of America are persons who are working every day and they end up getting part-time wages for full-time work. So the vast majority of Negroes in America find themselves perishing on a lonely island of poverty in the midst of a vast ocean of material prosperity."[22]

Reminiscent of King's speech, Afro-descendant WIC and SNAP beneficiaries who work have wages so low that it is difficult to pay their bills. One study participant discussed the difficulties of paying for expensive food and shared her belief that everyone should have access to SNAP. She believes that people who post Facebook messages criticizing SNAP beneficiaries have been misled and do not understand the lives of SNAP beneficiaries. She painstakingly described how some people receiving SNAP are hard workers but do not make enough to provide food for their families. This thirty-nine-year-old dark-skinned mother of four who resides in Charlotte explained that SNAP provides necessary financial assistance for these women to survive:

> Oh, yeah. They'll say like, you have a couple of people be like . . .
> I heard a couple on Facebook, a couple of people talk about that

they pay for us to eat, because it's coming out they tax money. And they don't think it's right. Everybody shouldn't, you should get out there and work, and be able to survive for your kid and stuff. "You shouldn't be able to get food stamps." But in reality, you got people that's hard workers and sometimes it's still hard. Because when you [are] paying all these bills and stuff, a lot of us, we live to pay rent, uh to pay bills. Once all that stuff is gone, you don't have any money. Food is expensive, you know? It, it's [the] only thing you can really get that's cheap. If you [are] getting a pack of chicken or something that's not [expensive], but everything, food is expensive. So by that time, you . . . [are] not gonna have enough money to get food.

Fifty-three years after Martin Luther King Jr.'s speech, avoiding poverty still presents a challenge for Black people in some of America's urban cities. The poverty rate for Blacks in Milwaukee in 2018 was 33.4 percent compared to 7.1 percent for non-Hispanic whites.[23] Poverty is not a result of laziness. It is a structural condition mediated by racism and sexism that relegates Black women to particular occupational niches characterized by low wages. The median Black household income in Milwaukee was lower in 2018 than it was in 1979, and it has decreased by 30 percent compared to a decrease of 2.4 percent for non-Hispanic whites.[24]

Critics who stereotype Afro-descendant women as lazy fail to consider the complex realities of low wages and the financial strain imposed by the costs for mothers who require child care or need to provide care for homebound children with disabilities. These critics also fail to consider transportation costs to and from work. As Marc Levine finds, the Black poverty rate is 19 percent in Charlotte, 25.7 percent in Chicago, and 33.4 percent in Milwaukee. Blacks in Charlotte are 2.2 times more likely, and in Chicago 3.8 times more likely, to live in poverty than non-Hispanic whites. In Milwaukee, Blacks are 4.7 times more likely to live in poverty than whites.[25] These statistics lay bare the harsh reality of Black life in these three metropolitan cities. Social welfare programs provide much-needed support for low- and zero-income women who take care of their families and *survive* their particular contexts of racialized, gendered poverty.

In summary, women in both countries mentioned stereotypes such as the belief that women intentionally become pregnant and have more children so they can receive food assistance. More Brazilian women than U.S. women mentioned this stereotype. Women in Brazil and in the United States also mentioned the stereotype that social welfare beneficiaries are lazy. Women are aware of the difficulties of gaining employment that pay livable wages, and some who work in the formal and informal labor markets still need food aid because their wages are low. Poverty and unemployment affect Afro-descendants in Brazil and in the United States, which creates the need for and the societal duty to provide food aid.

RESISTANCE TO STIGMA AND DISCRIMINATION

Hunter, Patel, and Sugiyama and Mariano and Carloto found that social welfare beneficiaries in Brazil felt empowered through their participation in welfare programs.[26] Sugiyama and Hunter focused on conditional cash transfer beneficiaries, and not strictly on Afro-Brazilian beneficiaries, and Mariano and Carloto focused specifically on Afro-Brazilian women. Sugiyama and Hunter found that women are empowered as citizens by feeling integrated into society, and Mariano and Carloto found that

Afro-Brazilian women beneficiaries of Bolsa Família felt that they gained respect. Interviews with U.S. respondents revealed that the women felt empowered, and they pointed out that they learned about healthy eating through the program. In addition, in the United States these women revealed acts of resistance. Some women discussed how they resist or address stereotypes head on, escalating the issue to a manager when they were disrespected by a grocery store clerk or by directly responding to cashiers who mistreat or judge them. Some women expressed what might be characterized as a socialist position on welfare, advocating that everyone should receive social welfare in the form of food and health care. An example of this thinking around universal welfare was articulated by a thirty-nine-year-old dark-skinned mother of four who resides in Charlotte:

> If we're not having Medicaid, it's expensive to go out to the [doctor]. You go out there just to go to the doctor. That bill coming over a thousand dollars, just for you to sit in an emergency room. Who gon' have that much money to pay for bills? A lot of people be sick. A lot of people be dying. A lot of people [are] without food. So we need this type of stuff. *I feel like everybody should be able to get food stamps, or Medicaid . . . I feel like people that's working should be able to get it too, because we all fall short. We all need help"*(emphasis added).

This progressive "Medicaid for all" and "SNAP for all" thinking contrasts with the U.S. perspective that people experiencing financial precarity are to be blamed for their situation because it is the result of their own lack of effort or hard work. In the United States, challenging the individualistic position by claiming food assistance programs and health care should be available to everyone is a radical concept.

At least eight women discussed how they addressed disrespect or stereotypes by speaking up in stores, responding to Facebook posts, and shopping in high-income majority white areas of town. A thirty-year-old dark-skinned Black divorced woman with a high school education who resides in Charlotte addressed disrespect in a grocery store this way:

You know it's interesting, because as a customer, whenever you get your WIC items, you take them out, you put them on the belt. You're not required to sort them or anything. Now because I years ago worked as a cashier, I know how it feels (laughs) when you see those you know, but like I said they have the vouchers not the card, and it's like, oh, goodness. Okay we got to do all of this. So I always put them on the belt and actually organize them, the cheese, the fruits, everything. . . . I do that to help, especially if I have people behind me. And so um I had pulled my cart up to the register, and the sales associate, she goes, "Uugh! Huuh!" Turns her head and everything. . . . I said, "Okay, Good morning!" (laughs), and she was "Hiii" (unenthusiastically). And I had . . . put everythang up there nice like I always do and all, and she starts scanning and slanging my stuff. And I was like, Okay. I said, "Well, let's say you feel some type of way . . . because I've come here with WIC, . . . So let's get the manager over here, so maybe she can assist." And so, uhh, she was so outdone, and so then her manager came, and she was like, "Well, what's the problem?" And I said, . . . "I don't know what's going on here today." . . . This was at the Food Lion but, um, I'm not required to organize or anything. I said, "I even came with a smile. I told her it was WIC before she started so she didn't have to cancel any transactions, speeding through. . . . And I've gotten so much attitude," I said, "when I haven't done anything. If anything, I was trying to be helpful—more than I'm required to." And so, you know, I've had those situations.

A twenty-year-old dark-skinned African American single woman who resides in Charlotte tactfully addressed the cashier who stereotyped her as a SNAP beneficiary before she had even pulled out her card:

> Well, being that I just got on it [SNAP], I really didn't take it to an offense because we were in line and I was at Food Lion and I didn't have a lot of groceries, but I had like some snacks and stuff, and she was like, "Oh, I wish I had food stamps." But I'm like, "How do you know I have food stamps? You didn't even see me pull out my card." So I just told her, "Well, you better go get you some because they're giving them out for free, so you better go apply." But I don't care because, like I said, it's not set up for African Americans. It's set up for Caucasians.

In this encounter, the respondent resisted the microaggression from the cashier by speaking directly to the cashier in a playful tone. She was aware that Great Society programs such as social security and food aid were created to help whites, although Black women are stereotyped as welfare beneficiaries. A single thirty-nine-year-old dark-skinned mother of four with no income and an associate's degree who lives in Chicago advised a cashier that she did not have to speak so loudly: "'Are you using SNAP, are you using SNAP?' And I be like, 'Yeah, but you don't have to say that so loud, everybody don't need to know how I'm paying for my stuff.' Because they only can see it unless I show it to them."

A twenty-five-year-old African American mother of one with an associate's degree who resides in Chicago addressed a shopper who criticized her purchases by explaining that she was paying for most of her food with cash, not with her benefits:

I had someone in line at the grocery store. I bought $700 worth of food. I told you I get $221 in Link, so the rest I was paying cash. And I had someone like, "I know she did not just get all this food and pulled out a Link card." I'm like, "Okay, the rest of the food I do have to pay cash for. What's the difference?"

"You shouldn't receive any benefits if you can spend $500 in . . . cash."

"What does that have to do anything with you? I'm buying food for my house. What you buy for your house you buy, what I buy for mine, it's for mine."

And the crazy part is I literally had all the healthy food and good food. She had the junk food, but judged me. "Oh, well you have shrimp." Okay, I bought that with cash. . . . "You have crab legs." I bought that with cash. I buy certain items with my Link card like vegetables, fruit, uh, meats, healthy food. I feel that is what your card's supposed to go on, and then I spend cash on other items that I want.

In this interaction, the woman refers to Link, a state-run food aid program in Illinois. In the verbal exchange between the respondent and the customer who criticized her purchases, she resisted this woman's judgment by directly responding to the woman's remarks about her purchases.

These women beneficiaries are often employed or hold degrees in higher education, which illustrates the lived realities of Black women who fall squarely in the category of the working poor. These women must navigate the challenges of putting food on the table when employment is difficult to find or wages are low. In the previous examples, two of the women respondents have two-year associate's degrees, an indication of the low returns of education for Black women. The twenty-nine-year-old woman in Milwaukee and the thirty-nine-year-old woman in Charlotte articulated the difficulty of affordable food even for people with some higher education who hold formal paid jobs. The racial disparities in wealth also underscore the uneven returns on education in the United States. Whites with less than a high school diploma tend to have higher levels of wealth than Black households where the head of household has a graduate school education.[27] Income returns on a college education are also lower for Afro-Brazilians than white Brazilians, and Afro-Brazilian college graduates are 1.2 times more likely to be unemployed.[28] In the following section, I analyze why some women beneficiaries do not perceive discrimination or stigma.

"EVERYONE'S ON IT": SOCIAL CAPITAL AND DENIAL OF STIGMA

I don't think they treated me differently because, once again, I feel like everyone has SNAP and WIC. We all have the same thing . . . you know, it's like no one is treating anybody different at this point of life because everyone is on it. Everybody, so we're all in the same boat at this point.

—Twenty-six-year-old single mother of two who self-describes as Black, African American, has one year of college education, and resides in Chicago

In the U.S. sample, 10 percent of social welfare beneficiaries believed that everyone received food benefits, and they did not perceive any discrimination or associated stigma. Women in Brazil who did not perceive discrimination sometimes mentioned that there was no stigma because family and friends also receive these benefits. This form of denial may be the result of homogeneous networks and the isolated environments in which some of these women live. Seccombe believes that women who state that everyone around them is on welfare are providing evidence of the "culture of poverty" thesis: they feel no stigma because these women live in a separate culture that has different values.[29]

My analysis departs from the culture of poverty thesis because some women in my sample viewed their benefits as social capital. It is undeniable, however, that the segregated environments in which they live and interact daily also contribute to their worldview. Chicago has a segregation index of 75 percent, and Milwaukee has a segregation index of 79.4 percent. These segregation indexes are based on residential segregation of racial/ethnic groups. Low-income Blacks are even more isolated; they live in low-income neighborhoods within Black communities. Milwaukee has one of the highest percentages of high-income Blacks living in low-income neighborhoods. Only 24.4 percent of affluent Blacks (with a household annual income of more than $100,000) live in the suburbs. In Milwaukee, 90 percent of the Black population lives in the city center. In Chicago, middle-class Black neighborhoods are surrounded by low-income Black neighborhoods.[30]

Some study participants indicated that low-income Blacks tend to interact with other low-income Blacks even when they live in proximity to high-income Blacks. Despite the proximity of high-income and affluent Blacks to low-income Blacks, Afro-descendant women social welfare beneficiaries do not often come in contact with nonbeneficiaries. Less or no stigma is felt because they believe everyone receives these benefits. In fact, these beneficiaries may have opportunities to share their experiences of having benefits with family and friends, thereby gaining a type of social capital or social currency. Herbst and

Lucio found that Blacks in segregated neighborhoods had high levels of happiness and attributed these high levels to social capital and the networks they have within their neighborhoods.[31] Similarly, Afro-descendant women social welfare beneficiaries in the United States may share skills such as knowing how to successfully enroll in SNAP and WIC programs as well as how to budget so families have enough food each month. This knowledge in addition to the actual WIC or SNAP benefit may be a form of social capital and currency. Furthermore, Afro-Brazilian feminist Claudia Cardoso believes that Black communities practice collective behavior more than individualistic behavior, and women have an important role in these communities.[32] These women carry ancestral and collective knowledge, and women share knowledge in these mainly Black neighborhoods and in Black women's spaces. From this point of view, sharing news or knowledge about WIC or SNAP is not an alternative culture, as suggested by the culture of poverty thesis, but is part of the African cosmovision that Cardoso claims values the collective and is non-Western. One example of this collective thought was expressed by a participant in Charlotte who said she "paid it forward" by paying for a stranger's food with her benefits.

Many of the women who denied the stigma of social welfare said that social welfare benefits are common in their social networks, and others valued the idea that it is something that can be collectively shared. Women in this study who live in Chicago, Charlotte, and Milwaukee all commented on the idea that everyone receives SNAP or WIC. A forty-year-old dark-skinned Black mother of six who dropped out of high school and resides in Charlotte said this:

> I don't know. The Black community don't do that. Like my family and everybody, I know they get food stamps and Medicaid and

stuff like that. I know a lot of people just like me. So there's not, I don't know. I don't know how people on the outside look at me. As a working mother, as a food stamp recipient on Medicaid, with [name of daughter] as an SSI recipient . . . I guess I don't care. . . . That. . . . never happened to me before.

A twenty-eight-year-old dark-skinned single mother of three who identifies as Black, African American has a high school education and a monthly income of $474 and resides in Chicago shares this view:

> I don't think so. I mean, why would they? Shit. I'm only human just like everybody else. I'm just on SNAP. We know we gots to get SNAP benefits. A lot of people befo' [before] they start having money, is on SNAP benefits too. But I don't know. The answer is no.

And a twenty-three-year-old dark-skinned single mother of one who self-identifies as Black, African American, has completed high school, has a monthly income of $1,200, and resides in Milwaukee agrees: "No. No, because I mean it's a normal thing. They know it's a thing that's gone on in the world. I don't think so. Not for me at least."

A thirty-year-old dark-skinned mother of one who self-identifies as Cuban and African American, has no monthly income, has completed eighth grade, and is pursuing a high school equivalency diploma and resides in Milwaukee had a similar belief: "No, because I believe everybody do, in this day and age really. A lot of people get SNAP and WIC. You get WIC when you have a baby."

This fifty-one-year-old light-skinned disabled single mother of four children who has an associate's degree, a monthly income of $1,050, and resides in Charlotte shared her experience of being able to help others:

> No. If anything I've been asked to pay it forward. I was in the store and a man asked for some help. He didn't know who I was or what I had. All he knew is that he had his groceries paid for at the end of the day so it, it's helped me help someone else. Yeah.

Remarkably, the theme of "everyone receives it" did not come up as much in Brazil. In the U.S. sample, WIC is so normalized that at least one woman believed that WIC is available to all women when they give birth. In reality, women must meet certain poverty income requirements. In the U.S. sample, women social welfare beneficiaries whose families and friends in close proximity also receive benefits normalized receiving benefits, but this did not indicate a culture of poverty with different values. Instead, this common situation gave beneficiaries the opportunity to discuss shared experiences, and it allowed one woman to help a stranger.

SUMMARY

This chapter contributes to the literature on social welfare in Brazil and the United States by examining the ways Afro-descendant women social welfare beneficiaries perceive and experience stigma and discrimination. Despite encounters mediated by racial, class, and gender microaggressions, these women felt empowered in their participation as beneficiaries. They were able to provide food for their families, and the Brazilian beneficiaries were able to live a dignified life by providing clothes and school materials for their children.

When experiencing discrimination, women resist stereotypes and public humiliation in a variety of ways that resonate with intersectional Black feminist analyses. The perspectives offered by these Black women serve as an important reminder that Black motherhood includes poor women who face distinct challenges structured by race, skin tone, class, and gender. Many low- and zero-income Afro-descendant women are the sole providers in their households, and the women in both countries engaged in informal labor to sustain their families. Many also provide care for ill children, which prevents them from seeking full-time employment. These complex realities are captured in the words of the women who shared their day-to-day perspectives as welfare beneficiaries.

3

PERCEPTIONS OF CLASS, SKIN COLOR, AND GENDER DISCRIMINATION

I work in Northbrook, at Buffalo Wild Wings, and because they see this little black girl standing here behind this bar, they just [say] like, "Why the hell is she all the way out here?" And someone asked me, "Why you come all the way out here? . . . There's nothing in the city?" I said, "Whoa." "So why did you come here to drink?" Like, "Because I like it here." You get what I'm saying? So it was like, I was a little stunned. And I didn't catch it at first, until they kept driving on me. I said, "Because I like money, and I love a different atmosphere."... I always been a hustler, so I like to travel for my money (emphasis added).

—Thirty-one-year-old dark-skinned African American woman
who resides in Chicago

How do national myths shape Afro-descendant social welfare women beneficiaries' perceptions of classism and racism, and how are these myths rejected or reproduced in the United States and Brazil? The American myths of meritocracy and exceptionalism are rooted in capitalism. If you work hard and make a lot of money, you can move around freely wherever and however you please. Spending money as a consumer is how many Americans participate in capitalism and express their social class. And some marginalized populations, including African Americans, believe that their ability to consume protects them from experiencing discrimination. "Liking money" is part of the American identity. The myth of meritocracy is based on the premise that if you work hard, you will be rewarded with capital and resources and that everyone has an equal opportunity to make money. At the same time, however, the myth of American meritocracy provides a framework that justifies the circumstances of economically marginalized people—their lack of money is due to their own inadequacies and laziness. Some marginalized groups are aware of the structures that bar them from economic advancement, but others buy into the idea of American meritocracy.

In the United States, race overrides class in explanations of Black marginalization in society. In Brazil, the myth of racial democracy explains the lack of racial discrimination, and one's perceived class status is uncritically viewed as the main form of discrimination. When Afro-descendants in Brazil complain about discrimination, the question often asked is "What did the person wear?" Today Brazilians are more likely than in the past, to say discrimination is due to race, especially Black movement activists such as the Coalizão Negra por Direitos (Black coalition for rights), an umbrella organization of more than 180 Black movement groups. However, it is still less common for Afro-Brazilians to admit that they have experienced discrimination based on their race.

In this chapter, I consider three forms of discrimination that often intersect: class, race, and gender. Examining these three forms of discrimination will highlight whether Afro-descendant social welfare beneficiaries are treated the same way as the general population. The analysis of class discrimination is based on where one lives. In a study of Black and white social welfare beneficiaries in Florida, Seccombe found that some of the women acknowledged discrimination and stigma against people receiving welfare benefits.[1] And some also believed in stereotypes about beneficiaries even when they could not recall knowing anyone who fit the stereotype. Some had what Seccombe called an "individual perspective"; that is, personal responsibility determines one's station in life. Some beneficiaries also believed in the culture of poverty thesis, which purports that beneficiaries are part of a subculture with different values and norms than the larger society. These findings are similar to Layton's findings that some Bolsa Família beneficiaries in Brazil believe the stereotypes about beneficiaries, and these stereotypes depress support for the program.

There is evidence in Brazil and the United States that the myth of meritocracy or the individualist perspective have led some social welfare beneficiaries to believe that some women are undeserving of the program. This cognitive dissonance allows them to believe that individuals have agency over their own life and that their individual circumstances are a result either of personal failings or of personal merit. This is in direct contrast to the more progressive discourse of Brazil's leftist leaders who acknowledge the role social exclusion has played in society and who support social programs for a more equitable society.

Seccombe argued that women social welfare beneficiaries are similar to women who do not receive benefits in terms of valuing education and having dreams for their children. My study diverges from Seccombe's study because I focus solely on Afro-descendant women who receive social welfare benefits. I examine whether beneficiaries are aware of stigma against Afro-descendants, or against women, and whether they perceive stigma against their neighborhoods. Hunt et al. found that African American women in mainly Black neighborhoods are less likely to perceive racial discrimination than those in racially mixed neighborhoods.[2]

I am also interested in perceptions of gender discrimination. Do marginalized intersectional identities lead to a higher likelihood of perceiving skin color discrimination for those who perceive gender discrimination? In discussions of discrimination in the United States, all too often racial discrimination overshadows discussions of gender discrimination. Furthermore, when there is a focus on gender discrimination, the focus has been on Black men. As Crenshaw notes in the Anita Hill case, people came to Clarence Thomas's aid, and in the Tyson versus Desiree Washington case, people came to the aid of Mike Tyson rather than to the aid of the Black girl who accused him of rape.[3] Crenshaw's #SayHerName campaign, twenty-five years after her publication on intersectionality, proves that Black women's experiences are still overshadowed by the experiences of Black men and Black boys. The #SayHerName campaign was an effort to bring attention to cases of police brutality against Black women. Soon mainstream media began to pick up the case of Breonna Taylor, a Black woman killed in her apartment by police serving a no-knock warrant in Louisville, Kentucky. The case received attention due to the tireless efforts of activists to bring cases of Black women to the forefront. Needless to say, race continues to trump gender even within the Black American community.

Harnois found that Black and Latina women in the United States who experience gender discrimination in the workplace are more likely to perceive it as racial and ethnic discrimination.[4] Layton and Smith found that Brazilians with darker skin tones are more likely than those with lighter skin tones to perceive race, gender, and class discrimination. In addition, they found that women with darker skin tones are more likely to perceive gender discrimination.[5] In this chapter, I analyze poor Black women's perceptions of skin color, gender, and class discrimination to understand how they experience the world and whether national myths influence their perceptions. Do poor Black women buy into merit-based myths and capitalist thinking? Are they more perceptive of race-based discrimination and less perceptive of discrimination against economically marginalized people?

Studies on discrimination too often take a general approach[6] when studying marginalized groups and ignore the additional marginalization within these groups. Cathy Cohen describes the marginalization within marginalized groups as secondary marginalization.[7] Considering how race, class, and skin tone interact in two countries in the African Diaspora can reveal the intricacies of colorism and patriarchy. In addition, how national myths of American meritocracy and Brazilian racial democracy have influenced Afro-descendant women social welfare beneficiaries' perceptions of discrimination can be assessed. This work is based in Black feminism, which includes aspects of intersectionality but is centered on Black women, a key element of Black feminism. Furthermore, this work focuses on the perceptions of poor Black women in a comparative context. I am interested in systems of domination that are not country specific but that influence citizens from all socioeconomic classes who buy into specific national myths.

HYPOTHESES

The first hypothesis is that Afro-Brazilian Bolsa Família beneficiaries are more likely to perceive class discrimination based on neighborhood than on skin color, and that Afro-descendant women social welfare beneficiaries in the United States are more likely to perceive skin color discrimination than class-based discrimination. In Brazil, although the myth of racial democracy has been challenged in the academy, many Brazilians believe that discrimination is based on class rather than race because the population is racially mixed. In the United States, the myth of individualism and meritocracy is predominant even among Black Americans. Many Americans believe that education and working hard will lead to success and that class, race, and gender are not impediments to success. For African Americans, studies by Darity et al. and others debunk this myth, African Americans have lower levels of wealth and higher unemployment even when they have higher levels of education than their white counterparts.[8]

The second hypothesis is that Afro-descendant social welfare beneficiaries in Brazil and the United States who perceive gender discrimination are also more likely to perceive skin color discrimination. Layton and Smith found that dark-skinned Brazilian women were more likely than light-skinned Brazilians to perceive skin color discrimination, gender discrimination, and class discrimination. Diette, Goldsmith, Hamilton, and Darity found that lighter-skinned Black American women have a higher chance of getting married than their darker-skinned counterparts.[9] In general, discrimination increases as skin tones get darker among Afro-Brazilian Bolsa Família beneficiaries because Brazil is a pigmentocracy.[10] In the United States, I expect women with darker skin tones to have a higher chance of perceiving skin color discrimination because research has shown that income and marriage differences are based on skin tone.

DISCRIMINATION

Research on discrimination in Brazil and the United States has focused on Black professionals,[11] employment discrimination,[12] discrimination in families and communities,[13] and the impact of discrimination on health outcomes.[14] Lamont et al. found that Afro-Brazilians are more likely to perceive discrimination based on class rather than race, and African Americans are more likely to confront racial discrimination. Their research on Black and Brown Brazilian professionals demonstrates that they are often in workplaces or social spaces that are predominantly white. Black and Brown Brazilians in prestigious positions may be aware of their unique positions as the only Black or Brown person in their workplace or social environment, but this does not necessarily produce isolation from or inhibit friendships with whites.[15] Thus, it is possible that Black and Brown professionals are less perceptive of discrimination because they build relationships with whites. However, Figureido documents that Afro-Brazilian professionals are aware of stigmatization,[16] and Kopkin and Mitchell-Walthour found that Afro-Brazilians in less prestigious occupations are more likely to perceive discrimination than those in high prestige occupations.[17] In the U.S. case, Black professionals are also few in number in their workplaces and are often met with suspicion by their white colleagues.[18] Like Brazilian professionals,[19] they experience racial stigmatization when whites assume they are in lower status jobs.

Lamont et al. terms this stigmatization an "assault on worth." They also found that in Rio de Janeiro, middle-class Blacks and Browns are more likely than working-class Blacks and Browns to discuss incidents of stigmatization when asked about discrimination. In addition, working-class Blacks and Browns had a more difficult time attributing stigmatization to their racial identification or class.[20] However, Jennifer Roth-Gordon and Robin Sheriff found that racism is present in discourse and in quotidian practices in low-income neighborhoods where blackness is naturalized as negative.[21] Residents in favelas are aware that favela residents are viewed as criminals based on the language they use: the body is marked as Black through language and discourse. It is not known whether low-income people perceive discrimination because most studies have focused on professionals and working-class people.

RACIAL IDENTIFICATION AND SKIN COLOR DISCRIMINATION

In Brazil and the United States, people with darker skin tones face more discrimination. Ellis Monk's work showed a distinction between skin color and racial identification in Brazil. In fact, one's skin color tends to be a better predictor of education and income differences than one's racial identification. In addition, Monk found that in Brazil skin color is a predictor of occupational status and that those with darker skin are more likely to hold less prestigious positions.[22]

Silva and Paixão found that Blacks and darker-skinned people are more likely to admit that they have faced discrimination based on color.[23] In their study, 36.9 percent of Blacks and 10 percent of Browns said they had experienced discrimination due to their skin color, and 26.8 percent of those classified as dark-skinned reported discrimination compared to 8.2 percent of those classified as medium-toned and 6.6 percent of those classified as light-toned.

Those with darker skin are more likely to acknowledge racial discrimination, but the intervening factor of class, as measured by occupation, may influence perceptions of racial discrimination. Black women in Brazil who serve as domestic workers face both sexism and classism[24] and may be aware of racial discrimination, sexism, and classism in this lower status position. Similarly, in the United States, skin tone has an impact on experiences of discrimination.[25] Szymanski and Stewart's research focused on African American women and found that they faced both racism and sexism but that sexism was a more significant stressor than racism.[26] In summary, skin tone determines whether Afrodescendants in Brazil and the United States experience discrimination. In the Brazilian case, racial identification is associated with perceptions of discrimination such that Negros are more likely to perceive discrimination and darker-skinned women are more likely to perceive race, gender, and class discrimination.[27]

NEIGHBORHOOD DISCRIMINATION AND SKIN COLOR DISCRIMINATION

To operationalize class as a possible reason for discrimination, the survey question asked respondents if they felt discriminated against because of where they live. A subsequent question on skin color discrimination asked respondents if they had ever been treated badly because of the color of their skin. Results are mixed: respondents in Salvador and São Luis were more likely to perceive class discrimination than skin color discrimination, but there was only a 1 percent difference in São Luis. In São Paulo, participants were more than twice as likely to perceive skin color discrimination over class discrimination. This difference may be due to São Paulo having a larger white population than Salvador and São Luis. The population in São Paulo is more similar to the selected cities in the United States in which the Afro-descendant populations are in the minority. In Salvador, Afro-descendants are in the majority, and it is common for soteropolitanos (residents in Salvador) to say there is no racism because the city is majority Negro.

In the United States, Afro-descendant social welfare beneficiaries in all three cities were more likely to perceive skin color discrimination over class discrimination. Participants in Milwaukee were more than twice as likely to perceive skin color discrimination than class discrimination. This is a striking finding in a city in which Blacks are more than four times as likely to live in poverty than whites. To better understand how these women discuss class discrimination based on neighborhood, I have examined their responses in more detail.

Perceptions of Neighborhood Discrimination

Afro-descendant social welfare beneficiaries are aware of negative perceptions of their neighborhoods. Salvador has the highest percentage (73 percent) of respondents who perceived bias against their neighborhoods (table 3.1). Charlotte followed with 56 percent of participants aware of the negative perceptions of their neighborhood. I also examine high-frequency words mentioned in the interviews. In both countries, frequently mentioned words referred to types of communities that carried negative stereotypes. In the United States, "projects" were mentioned nine times; in Brazil, "favela" was mentioned twelve times. Projects are low-income housing units heavily subsidized in the United States. Respondents in Chicago most often referenced projects. Chicago was home to the Robert Taylor Homes, the largest housing project in the United States. At its height, 27,000 people lived in the Robert Taylor Homes, which were demolished in 2005.

**TABLE 3.1 NEIGHBORHOOD AND SKIN COLOR
DISCRIMINATION BY CITY**

City	Neighborhood Discrimination (%)	Skin Color Discrimination (%)
Salvador	73	28
São Paulo	31	72
São Luis	49	48
Milwaukee	29	69
Charlotte	56	74
Chicago	48	67

In Brazil, favelas typically refer to low-income neighborhoods in which families often build homes on top of existing homes because land is scarce. In both countries, housing projects and favelas are stereotyped as a haven for criminals and thieves and are viewed as dangerous.

Some of the most popular words mentioned in answer to neighborhood discrimination among social welfare beneficiaries in Brazil are *favela, thieves, drugs, dangerous, discrimination,* and *violent* (table 3.2). Women commonly spoke about how others perceived their neighborhoods. The word cloud in figure 3.1 shows commonly mentioned words in the interviews. It also shows how these words were used. In answer to the question, respondents generally discussed how others perceived where they live in negative terms. For example, the word neighborhood was mentioned forty-four times, which is no surprise because the question was asking about discrimination based on where one lives. The word *dangerous* occurs seven times and *thieves* nine times. Together the words *dangerous* and *violent* were mentioned

TABLE 3.2 WORDS USED IN NEIGHBORHOOD DISCRIMINATION RESPONSES IN SALVADOR, SÃO PAULO, AND SÃO LUIS

Word	Frequency
Favela	12
thief/thieves	9
drug/drugs	11
Dangerous	7
discrimination/discriminated	6
Violent	6
Poor	5
Palafita	4
Difficult	3
Marginal	3
Humble	3
job/employment	3
bandit	2
Interview	2

FIGURE 3.1 Word cloud of responses to being judged based on where one lives in Brazil.

thirteen times. Brazilian social welfare respondents are aware that people largely view their neighborhoods negatively. To give a better idea of how beneficiaries discussed these perceptions, I examined their responses.

Avoiding Poor Neighborhoods

Brazilian women social welfare respondents mentioned that friends and family members avoid visiting them because they believe these neighborhoods are dangerous, and they are fearful of visiting. Women recounted stories of strangers being shocked and surprised when the women identified their neighborhoods, and some people believed that residents of these neighborhoods were uneducated. In addition, Brazilian women social welfare respondents said that Uber and taxicab drivers try to avoid entering these neighborhoods. A thirty-nine-year-old light-skinned Parda woman who resides in Salvador said: "Yes, sometimes, when I have gone shopping for my mother, the taxi doesn't want to [bring me home] from the store." And a twenty-eight-year-old dark-skinned self-identified Parda woman who resides in São Luis had a similar experience: "Yes. I was in a location and caught a taxi and I said the neighborhood where I live. He said he doesn't enter there because it's dangerous. I had to go to a place that was much farther away, then go home."

A thirty-seven-year-old light-skinned Parda woman who resides in São Luis mentioned her family's response to where she lives:

> Until now no, but in familial social situations families discriminate because they say, "Oh, my God, I'm not going over there

because someone will rob me." My sisters [say this] because they live in a very noble place, but they think I live in a poor house.

And a twenty-three-year-old light-skinned woman who self-identifies as white and resides in São Paulo explained why her purchases failed to arrive at her home:

> Yes, the people who live outside Brasilandia . . . Relatives really call and say, "Oh where do you live? In Brasilândia? Brasilândia, Oh Mercy!" Then you are discriminated against due to the neighborhood you live in. Even when you make a purchase and you enter the address, it is not enough. It doesn't come because of the neighborhood.

It is an inconvenience when an Uber or taxi driver refuses to drive into a low-income neighborhood, and it may be hurtful to respondents when family and friends avoid neighborhoods. However, stereotypes of these neighborhoods also limit employment opportunities for these women. This is another area of prejudice the women identified.

Neighborhoods as a Threat to Employment Opportunities

Some Brazilian respondents mentioned that employers hold stereotypes about their neighborhoods. Considering the need for low-income women to work, prejudice against them because of where they live continues a vicious cycle of making it difficult to find work. Not working or bringing in income further marginalizes them. A twenty-two-year-old light-skinned woman

who resides in São Luis believes she was fired when her boss
found out where she lived:

> Yes, at the place where I worked, I was fired when they found
> out I was from Liberdade. When the boss found out I was from
> Liberdade, I feel like this was the reason she [fired me]. . . . When
> people know you live in Liberdade they make an ugly face.

Others reported not being considered for a job because of where
they lived. A twenty-three-year-old dark-skinned woman who
resides in São Luis was not considered for a job when she identified her neighborhood: "Yes. Here in Bacanga, it looks like a
center of marginal folks. For employment, they asked where I
lived, and when I said Bacanga, she was like 'Nossa.'" A fifty-
two-year-old dark-skinned Negra woman who resides in Salvador confirmed this experience: "It has happened several times.
There are places where you will have a job interview. When you
say where you live; when I say it is Calabetão, they are scared.
You [won't] be hired because of the neighborhood." In Brazil,
women were judged unfairly because their neighborhoods were
stigmatized. This prejudice from potential employees impinges
on job opportunities.

Afro-descendant women in the United States face similar challenges. In the United States, among social welfare beneficiaries,
the highest frequency words were *area, afford, projects, bad, rent, job,
rough,* and *low* (table 3.3). *Area* was referenced thirteen times, and
afford was mentioned eleven times. The *projects* were mentioned
nine times. A total of twenty-seven negative adjectives were used
by social welfare beneficiaries to describe these neighborhoods.
Social welfare beneficiaries in the United States were concerned
that when neighborhoods are negatively stereotyped as being "bad"
or "rough" it threatens their employment chances (figure 3.2).

TABLE 3.3 WORDS USED IN NEIGHBORHOOD DISCRIMINATION RESPONSES IN CHICAGO, MILWAUKEE, AND CHARLOTTE

Word	Frequency
Area	13
afford	11
Projects	9
Bad	8
Job	7
Rough	7
Low	7
work/working	5
Ghetto	3
scare/scared	2
Rent	2

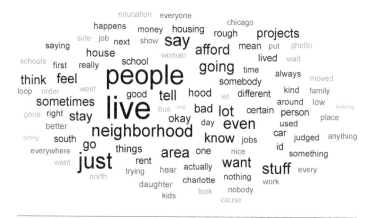

FIGURE 3.2 Word cloud of responses to being judged based on where one lives in the United States.

Neighborhoods and Residents as Violent

Neighborhoods where Afro-descendant social welfare beneficiaries live are viewed as dangerous places where one might risk being killed. One of the most often mentioned areas in the Chicago interviews were the projects. A twenty-nine-year-old light-skinned woman receiving WIC and SNAP who resides in Chicago said her own family won't come to her home in the projects:

> Yes, by my own family. They don't want to come down [here] because I stay in the projects. They feel like they are going to get shot or something. I mean I know they shoot everywhere in Chicago, but you can't just say that. . . . But yeah. They all treat me different. They don't want to come visit because I stay in the projects.

A twenty-eight-year-old dark-skinned woman who resides in Chicago defended her neighborhood:

> I grew up in Henry Horner projects and yeah. Oh yeah, even going to school, [people would say] "You still in the projects?" Yeah, so? [They would say] "It's rough over there." You know what I'm saying? It's really not. It's really a community. Yeah, it's rough. It's rough everywhere if you think about it. Stuff happens in the suburbs. Stuff happens in the projects. Stuff happens here. Stuff happens over there. It was rough everywhere. So yeah, I've been judged because I live in the projects.

This young woman says people stereotype her because of the community in which she lives. She believes all neighborhoods are "rough," be they in the city or in the suburbs.

Social welfare beneficiaries have experienced being viewed as violent when they were young people. A twenty-two-year-old dark-skinned Black woman who resides in Milwaukee claimed she was stereotyped as violent because she's from a Black neighborhood: "I attended South Milwaukee High School, so a lot of the kids were scared of me because I came from the north side. So, I remember one time I didn't hear something a kid said to me, and I simply said, 'What did you say?' And somebody was like, 'Ooh, you'd better not say it. She['s] going to beat you up.' I'm like, I'm not even violent."

In 2008, 6.1 percent of the state of Wisconsin was African American, and 69.4 percent of the state's population lived in Milwaukee.[28] Most Blacks in the city live on the north side. As a predominantly Black section of the city, the community is stereotyped and stigmatized. Afro-descendant women social welfare beneficiaries are also viewed as violent and uneducated. A twenty-nine-year-old dark skinned woman from Milwaukee who describes herself as African American, Native American, and Hindu remarked that she was stereotyped as uneducated based on her neighborhood: "They think that you live in a bad neighborhood, you [are] ratchet you [are] ghetto, you have no education, and then they find out that you have a college degree, and you actually have a job." This woman is aware that employment and a college degree do not protect Black women from being negatively stereotyped if they live in a "bad" neighborhood.

Employment Disadvantages of Neighborhoods

Like the Brazil sample, when U.S. employers are made aware of where these women live, they may become less likely to hire them. The zip code where one resides has an impact on employability.[29] Social welfare beneficiaries in Chicago and Milwaukee noted employer bias due to the neighborhoods in which they live. A nineteen-year-old dark-skinned woman who resides in Chicago had experienced this neighborhood bias:

> Yes, . . . with jobs when you're applying. Well, like, I was in this program, and this lady was trying to help me with housing. When I had talked to her, she was trying to make an appointment. Well, she made an appointment to come out to my house the next day. But once I told her where I live, she didn't come. She kept on telling me like, "I couldn't come today. I was sick, or whatever." And I'm like, "That's okay. Well, I'll see you tomorrow." She like, "Okay, I'll come around tomorrow," and didn't come. The next day come, and she didn't never show. So that's when I'm like, "She just probably doing that because of where I stay." She was probably scared to come around because she was a white lady. Like when you put down your address and stuff and then they go through your application and stuff. Sometimes they judge you off of where you stay and who you are, who they think you are.

This young woman is keenly aware of the bias employers have based on where a person lives, and this bias extends to judging the character of the person. This respondent indicated that the lady would be uncomfortable due to her neighborhood. A twenty-year-old who describes herself as "Black and Creole" and resides in Milwaukee stated, "Like, sometimes, like I don't put my zip code or my address when I'm applying for jobs cause sometimes, like I do feel like people look at my answers and be like, Oh, she from a bad area, then don't give me like an interview or a callback. I do feel that way." These examples show that poor Black women in the United States, much like women in Brazil, believe their employment prospects are shaped by stereotypes about people from their neighborhoods.

SKIN COLOR AND
GENDER DISCRIMINATION

Women in both countries acknowledged class discrimination. However, women in Brazil were more likely to acknowledge class discrimination over racial discrimination whereas women in the United States were more likely to perceive racial discrimination over class discrimination. I now consider gender discrimination. The Black Feminist Statement of the Combahee River Collective in 1977 includes this observation:

> Feminism is, nevertheless, very threatening to the majority of Black people because it calls into question some of the basic assumptions about our existence, i.e., that gender should be a determinant of power relationships. . . . Many Black women have a good understanding of both sexism and racism, but because of the everyday constrictions of their lives cannot risk struggling against them both.

Sexism continues to be overlooked in struggles over racial inequality, and I am interested in whether low-income Black women perceive sexism and racism.

In Brazil, political violence has brought attention to racism and sexism against politicians. Some high-profile cases are the assassination of Marielle Franco, threats against Congresswoman Talíria Petrone, and threats against Black trans woman city council member, Benny Briolly. Activists and Black feminists in Brazil and in the United States have long called attention to the role of racism and sexism in the lives of Afro-descendant women. In this section, I examine whether low-income Black women perceive the two and test my second hypothesis: Afro-descendant social welfare women beneficiaries in Brazil and the United States who perceive gender discrimination are more likely to perceive skin color discrimination. The interview question I asked was, "Do you ever feel like you have been treated differently because you are a woman?" I generated this hypothesis based on research that Brazilian women with darker skin tones were more likely to perceive racism, classism, and sexism[30] and that in the United States Black and Latina women who perceive gender discrimination were more likely to also perceive skin color discrimination.[31]

Rather than examining perceptions of skin color discrimination in opposition to gender discrimination among individual respondents, which Harnois refers to as oppositional, I considered individual respondents who perceived both gender discrimination and skin color discrimination. To test my hypothesis, I considered which respondents who perceived gender discrimination also perceived skin color discrimination and compared them to those who perceived gender discrimination but not skin color discrimination. In both cases, I include only respondents who perceived gender discrimination. There is strong support for my hypothesis in all the cities studied except Salvador, which had a relatively low level (29 percent) of social welfare beneficiaries who perceived both gender and skin color discrimination compared to those who perceived gender discrimination but not skin color discrimination (71 percent) (table 3.4). In the other cities the percentages of perceiving gender discrimination and skin color discrimination were higher than those perceiving gender discrimination but not skin color discrimination. With the exception of Salvador, those perceiving gender discrimination were more likely to also perceive skin color discrimination.

In general, Afro-descendant women social welfare beneficiaries are less perceptive of gender discrimination than skin color

TABLE 3.4 PERCEPTIONS OF GENDER AND SKIN COLOR DISCRIMINATION

	Perceive Gender and Skin Color Discrimination (%)	Perceive Gender but Not Skin Color Discrimination (%)	Total (%)
Salvador	29	71	100
São Paulo	76	24	100
São Luis	57	43	100
Milwaukee	78	22	100
Charlotte	93	7	100
Chicago	79	21	100

TABLE 3.5 GENDER AND SKIN COLOR DISCRIMINATION BY CITY

City	Gender (%)	Skin Color (%)
Salvador	15	28
São Paulo	58	72
São Luis	35	48
Milwaukee*	36	69
Charlotte	71	74
Chicago	63	67

*Included respondent who said maybe as a yes.

discrimination (table 3.5). However, the intersectional approach I used revealed that those who perceived gender discrimination were more likely to also perceive skin color discrimination. Therefore, poor Afro-descendant women social welfare beneficiaries are aware of the multiple marginalized positions they occupy through these identities.

GENDER DISCRIMINATION AGAINST POOR BLACK WOMEN

In this section, I examine the forms of gender discrimination Afro-descendant social welfare beneficiaries experience. Women participants in this study from Brazil and the United States discuss sexism at their places of employment and more generally in society as well as gender stereotypes that include criticism of young mothers. Some women acknowledge sexism within their communities or family, which demonstrates the secondary marginalization Afro-descendant women experience due to intersectional identities. Women perceive and critique sexism, sometimes saying that women can do as much as men. They also call into question differential treatment; one woman noted that her boyfriend is abusive with her but not with his male friends. Some of these Afro-descendant women engage in resistance, a key aspect of Black feminism. They resist sexism in individual ways, continuing to work in male-dominated workplaces and navigating spaces in which they are not meant to be. They also point to societal notions that dictate women should be at home.

Employment Discrimination

"Employment" was a high-frequency word in both countries. Women recalled being stereotyped at their places of employment or felt discriminated against when applying for jobs based on their gender. A forty-two-year-old dark-skinned woman who resides in Chicago expressed her opinion on this: "Yes, because I think some jobs think a woman can't do the job. But I think all of us women can do the job. You have certain jobs that treat you like that. I'm just keeping it 100."

A thirty-four-year-old dark-skinned self-described Black, African American woman who resides in Milwaukee recounted bias in promotions in the workplace:

> Yeah. Even at my last profession, where I was working . . . the men were getting promoted faster than me, even though I was a better worker than them. Even though I gave more time to the company, they still gave more money to the men.

And a twenty-seven-year-old dark-skinned African American woman who resides in Milwaukee found that other employees questioned her place:

> Half of the stuff men do, we can do that and more! Sometimes better. So, definitely been stereotyped many times for being a woman. Because I like picking factory jobs most of the time. Walmart is my main job, but I worked a lot of factory jobs so I always got that, "What is this little skinny, little pretty girl doing here? What's she going to do? Do I have to work with her? I can't work with dudes?" I'd be like, "okay."

These women are aware that they are underestimated and underpaid in their jobs. Yet some continue to work in male-dominated jobs, such as the factory worker who was not intimidated by being outnumbered by her male peers. In fact, some of these women are convinced they can do the same work as men with better results.

Stereotypes About Women's Role in Society

In both countries, women are stereotyped. Some of the stereotypes that prevail are that women should not work and should be at home cooking or taking care of children. A thirty-five-year-old dark-skinned self-identified Negra woman who resides in São Paulo spoke about this: "People say, 'women should be in the kitchen.' . . . When she works, they say, 'Why are there women here? They should be at home.'" A twenty-eight-year-old self-identified Negra woman who resides in São Luis confirmed this stereotype: "People think that it is because you are a woman you cannot work. Sometimes the husband says, 'I am the only one who works. You should not work; stay home. The woman's place is the home.'"

Other limiting stereotypes are that women cannot drive well or do not know much about cars. Women exert their independence by demonstrating their nontraditional skills, such as this twenty-eight-year-old dark-skinned African American woman who resides in Chicago who maintains her own car, a skill reserved for men:

> Yes. (laughs) Yes. So my dad um used to fix um cars so I picked up a lot of that from watching him. I don't ask for help. I do it myself because I know how to do it. So one thing that bugs me about people when they see me doing something to my car they're like, "Oh you need to have your boyfriend do it. You need to call a man and let them do it. I'll do it for you." And I'm like, "Dude I've changed the strut on the car already, I've done a tie rod already. I already did the sway bar link. I've already changed the water pump. What more do I need to tell you about me? I'm like, I've changed my own tire. I don't need you. I can do it myself."

In these examples, the women are stereotyped as not having skills outside of the home; they are expected to fulfill gendered roles by taking care of the household. Men, including spouses, expect them to stay home. These women acknowledge that they are being judged, and they resist this judgment by stepping out of these gendered roles and practicing skills reserved for men.

Stereotypes About the Capability of Young Mothers

Afro-descendant young mothers are stereotyped as not being capable of caring for children. They were also viewed as being inferior, and interview participants recalled that family members treated them poorly because of their gender. Some of this treatment includes physical and verbal abuse. A twenty-two-year-old dark-skinned mother who resides in Chicago felt judged because of her age:

> Yes. Like when I first got down here, everybody thought I was a little bitty girl because of how I look and how my age is. But when they found out my age, they're like, "You look like you 'bout 15, 16 [years old]. You got two kids? Like you kind of young." People judge me a lot sometimes.

And the parenting skills of an eighteen-year-old light-skinned Parda mother who resides in São Luis was questioned "for being a young mother. Even more because I wasn't with her dad. People say 'Ah, but you are not with her father. How are you going to raise her?' I can learn how to take care of her well just like I can learn to take care of a dog well."

In both cases, people doubted that these young women were capable because of their age. Furthermore, there is a societal expectation that women should raise their children with their father because they are not capable of properly taking care of them alone. In these examples, the women were discussing other people's criticism; however, some respondents also described unfair and abusive treatment. A twenty-four-year-old dark-skinned woman who resides in Chicago made this observation:

> Yeah. I haven't had many situations where it was like there's been sexism or nothing, but I do feel like guys treat women kind of low in this time of age. . . . Because if you carry yourself a certain way, you're just asking for a guy to treat you a certain way or whatever. . . . I feel like they think they can take advantage sometimes. Say, for instance, I'm not driving so I'm on the bus, so I try not to be all late because I don't want a guy to think, "Oh, she's [inaudible] or anything like that." That's like the first thing some guys think. I just feel like we have to defend ourselves more and kind of be ready more because they feel like they can walk on us sometimes.

A twenty-nine-year-old African American woman who resides in Chicago described verbal abuse from her own family members:

> It's from my own people. Black men. A couple of Black men that I know . . . I am not going to say people, my uncle and my step uncle because he is not my blood. But he says, "You ain't nothing but a woman." I hate when he says that.

And this nineteen-year-old dark-skinned woman self-identified as Black ("because she's not African") who resides in Chicago compared her boyfriend's treatment of her versus how he treats his male friends:

> Well, like, I was playing with my boyfriend. He likes to get physical with me when I don't listen to him, and he only does that

with me because I'm a woman. He don't do that with his guys, his homies, like, instantly want to jump at their throat. But since I'm a female, he just quicker to come at me and stuff like that. But that's with most men. They think that since you're a woman they can put their hands on you and stuff because you're a woman. And they know they can beat you up because you're a woman.

In these very concerning comments, Afro-descendant women social welfare beneficiaries faced poor treatment by society and by family members. The nineteen-year-old woman believes her boyfriend displays the behavior of "most men," thus normalizing his abusive behavior. In contrast, the twenty-nine-year-old woman expressed her dissatisfaction with the poor verbal treatment she receives from her male family members. Women respond to this poor treatment in a number of ways. One respondent tries to change her behavior to appeal to men, but at the same time she believes women have to defend themselves. In interviews with Brazilian women, at least one woman remarked that she divorced her husband. These strategies are difficult choices for women who occupy extremely vulnerable positions, both socially and economically, but women make these decisions despite the sexism and misogyny that exists within their communities.

SUMMARY

This chapter reveals national myths of racial democracy and American exceptionalism shape poor Afro-descendant women social welfare beneficiaries' perceptions of class discrimination and skin color discrimination. Poor Black women in the United States are less likely to perceive class discrimination than racial discrimination, whereas in Brazil, with the exception of São Paulo, women are more likely to perceive class discrimination than skin color discrimination. In Brazil, this is in line with the myth that discrimination is based on class rather than race. In the United States, women are less likely to recognize class discrimination and more likely to attribute discrimination to race, which confirms the myth that individual merit determines one's class status.

Generally, Afro-descendant women social welfare beneficiaries in Brazil and in the United States who experience gender discrimination are more likely than not to perceive skin color discrimination. Sexism and misogyny are present in the lives of these women in employment as well as in their everyday lives at home. This research confirms that marginalized Afro-descendant women are aware of sexism and that some actively push back against it. They resist by asserting their independence, learning skills, and gaining self-confidence that women are as capable as men. Although aware that sexism is normalized and that women are expected to fulfill specific roles, such as being a caretaker for the home, few who perceive gender discrimination fully accept these roles.

4

ARE POOR BLACK WOMEN TO BLAME FOR CONSERVATIVE POLITICIANS?

Social Welfare Beneficiaries' Political Knowledge, Voting Preferences, and Religion

Donald Trump (2016–2020) and Jair Bolsonaro (2018–2022) were conservative presidents elected by conservative political parties. Both leaders made racist and sexist public remarks such as these.

Look at my African American over here!

—U.S. presidential candidate Donald Trump, campaign rally, June 2016, Redding, California

I went to a quilombo. The lightest African descendant there weighed seven arrobas. They do nothing. I don't think they are even suitable to procreate. More than 1 billion reais a year is spent on them. . . . If I make it (to the presidency) there will be no money for NGOs. These bums will have to work . . . there will not be a centimeter demarcated for Indigenous and quilombola land.

—Brazilian presidential candidate Jair Bolsonaro, speech, April 2017, Rio de Janeiro

It seems unlikely that women marginalized because of their race, class, or gender would support these candidates. Mainstream media[1] and academic studies[2] often point to religion as a reason for Trump's and Bolsonaro's electoral success. Michele Margolis offers a more nuanced analysis: it is not simply whites who identify as evangelicals but whites who are devout evangelicals who were more supportive of Trump.[3] In their study on demographic polarization, Layton et al. found that cleavages among voters based on race, gender, and religion led to Bolsonaro's success in 2018.[4] Black and Brown Brazilians were less likely to vote for him than were whites, and evangelicals were more likely to vote for him. Given these findings, is the impact of religion on voting different for Afro-descendant evangelicals than for white evangelicals? Janelle Wong found that white evangelicals in the United States were more conservative than Black, Latinx, and Asian evangelicals.[5] In Brazil, Afro-descendant evangelical groups, such as Salvador's Aliança de Negras e Negros Evangélicos do Brasil (Black women and Black men evangelicals of the Brazil Alliance), were involved in "Evangelicals Against Bolsonaro" campaigns. This suggests that they are distinct from white evangelicals. How do religious Afro-descendant women social welfare beneficiaries fit into accounts of the role of religion in politics? What are their levels of political knowledge? What are their vote choices? What do they think about conservative presidents? Moreover, what role does religious affiliation play in their voting behavior?

In this chapter, I have used qualitative in-depth interviews of Afro-descendant women social welfare beneficiaries in Brazil and in the United States that were conducted in 2018 to examine political knowledge, voter choice, and evaluations of conservative presidents. The 2014 presidential election in Brazil and the 2016 U.S. presidential election were used as the basis for questions regarding voting. Critical evaluations of conservative presidents were based on respondents' perceptions of President Michel Temer and President Donald Trump, who were in office during the time of this study.

I tested three hypotheses. The first hypothesis is that Brazilian social welfare beneficiaries will have higher levels of political knowledge than American social welfare beneficiaries. I believe these differences are largely due to compulsory voting in Brazil and noncompulsory voting in the United States. I examined Afro-descendant women social welfare beneficiaries' political knowledge as measured by their ability to cite a political party. In general, Americans had lower levels of political knowledge than Brazilians.

The second hypothesis is that religiously affiliated Black women social welfare beneficiaries in Brazil and the United States are more likely to support leftist candidates than conservative political candidates. I do not expect respondents who identify as Christian, including evangelicals, to vote for conservative candidates. In both countries, Black women social welfare beneficiaries overwhelmingly supported leftist candidates. Moreover, those who are religiously affiliated, including evangelicals, also overwhelmingly supported the leftist candidate.

The third hypothesis is that Afro-descendant social welfare beneficiaries in both countries will be critical of their conservative presidents: Brazilian President Temer and U.S. President Trump. I tested this hypothesis by examining respondents' evaluations of these presidents. In both countries, I found that women were more likely to have negative evaluations of both presidents. An unexpected finding was that women in Brazil spoke about their discontent with President Temer in class terms, whereas those in the United States discussed discontent with President Trump in both class and racial terms.

POLITICAL KNOWLEDGE

My first hypothesis is that Brazilian social welfare beneficiaries will have higher levels of political knowledge than American social welfare beneficiaries largely due to Brazil's compulsory voting. Political knowledge was measured with the question, "Can you name any political parties?" The literature on political knowledge in the United States offers explanations about differences in political knowledge between Blacks and whites,[6] women and men,[7] and people with higher and lower levels of education,[8] but these scholars do not explain differences between similarly situated African-descended women in different countries. Dow found that Blacks and other groups may seek information when they are disadvantaged educationally.[9] Dow proposed that specific groups may have more knowledge when it is relevant for the group to which they belong, suggesting that general political knowledge may appear less relevant for their everyday lives. Cohen and Luttig challenged traditional measures of political knowledge, expanding this category to include knowledge of carceral violence.[10] They found that Black and Latinx youth have higher levels of knowledge of carceral violence than do white youth. Black and Latinx youth live in communities that suffer disproportionately from interactions with the carceral system, and youth are exposed to social media networks that discuss carceral violence. Brazilian police and secret squads kill four times more citizens than police in the United States do, and in Brazil, 75 percent of those killed by police are Afro-Brazilian. Brazil's population is 56 percent Afro-Brazilian, whereas the U.S. Black population is only 13 percent. Carceral violence is political knowledge that Afro-descendants would be more familiar with than their white counterparts in both countries. Expanding the definition of what counts as political knowledge is important, and I would expect similar findings for issues specific to marginalized groups because they are similarly situated. However, there are major differences in the political structure between these two countries (compulsory versus noncompulsory voting), so I expected to find differences in a traditional form of political knowledge. This is the only item in my interviews that measures some form of political knowledge.

Knowledge of Political Parties

In my interviews, political knowledge is measured by the ability of respondents to name a political party. In Brazil, 68 percent of respondents could name a political party, but only 40.4 percent of U.S. respondents could do so. In the United States, 16.2 percent of women named a politician instead of a political party, whereas in Brazil only 13 percent did so (table 4.1). In the United States, an overwhelming 59.6 percent could not name a political party. In Brazil, only 32 percent of women were unable to name a political party. Table 4.2 breaks down political knowledge by city. In Milwaukee, 69 percent of Afro-descendant women social

TABLE 4.1 POLITICAL KNOWLEDGE BY COUNTRY

	Named One or More Political Party (%)	Named a Politician (%)	Don't Know (%)	Total (%)
Brazil	68	13	19	100
United States	40.4	16.2	43.4	100

TABLE 4.2 POLITICAL KNOWLEDGE BY CITY

	Named One or More Political Party (%)	Named a Politician (%)	Don't Know (%)	Total (%)
Salvador	55	8	37	100
São Luis	77.5	7.5	15	100
São Paulo	65	11	24	100
Charlotte	61	6	33	100
Chicago	30	17	53	100
Milwaukee	31	22	47	100

welfare beneficiaries could not name a political party; in Chicago 70 percent could not do so. The southern city of Charlotte had the highest level of political knowledge, with 61 percent of women able to name a political party. This high percentage in the South may be explained by historical mobilization surrounding the civil rights movement as well as present-day mobilization around voting. In Brazil, São Luis has the highest percentage of respondents who named a political party (77.5 percent), followed by São Paulo (65 percent) and Salvador (55 percent).

Naming a person rather than a political party demonstrates personalism in U.S. politics. Voters rely less on a candidate's platform or the ideology of the political party and more on the personal characteristics of political candidates. In Brazil, Samuels found that voters affiliated with the Workers Party (PT) had higher levels of partisanship than voters supporting political party candidates that express more personal ties.[11] He suggested that the PT's efforts to mobilize voters aided in partisanship because voters could identify with the ideology and platform rather than support only charismatic politicians.

The ideologies of U.S. political parties continue to influence voting, but charismatic leaders also play a role in contemporary politics. Both Barack Obama and Donald Trump, although on different ends of the political spectrum, were charismatic leaders. Obama's platform of unification appealed to leftist and moderate voters; Trump's xenophobic, racist, homophobic, and ableism rhetoric appealed to his conservative and largely white base. Charismatic leaders are part of both Brazilian and U.S. politics. In the United States, 56 percent of respondents who named a politician rather than a political party named Donald Trump, making him the most cited politician. Although naming a politician shows some level of familiarity with politics, it is concerning that such a substantial percentage of low-income women do not have this basic level of political knowledge. A closer look at the role of personalism shows that some women in Brazil also named a politician, but these percentages were lower than in the United States. In Brazil, former president Lula was named by 60 percent of the women who named a politician. Lula remained popular and left office with an 87 percent approval rate. My hypothesis that Brazilian social welfare beneficiaries will have higher levels of political knowledge than their U.S. counterparts holds true. Compulsory voting requires interaction with the electoral system, which explains the higher levels of political knowledge in Brazil.

Afro-Descendant Women Social Welfare Beneficiary Voters

The Afro-descendant population in the United States generally supports the Democratic political candidate, and I expected Afro-descendant social welfare beneficiary voters to support the leftist candidate as well. In Brazil during Lula and Rousseff's years in office, studies found that Afro-descendants generally supported leftist candidates. However, Bolsonaro's candidacy created cleavages based on race, gender, and religion: men were more likely to vote for Bolsonaro, Blacks and Browns were less likely to vote for Bolsonaro, and Bolsa Família beneficiaries were more likely to vote for the PT candidate.[12] Considering the intersecting identities Afro-descendant social welfare beneficiaries occupy, I expected that these women would support the leftist presidential candidate.

In the United States, those with higher levels of education are more likely to vote[13] and to be politically engaged.[14] Afro-descendant women in the United States have high levels of voting and generally vote for Democratic candidates. In the 2020 presidential election, 66 percent of Black Americans voted.[15] In the 2016 election, Black women were more likely to vote than Black men: 64 percent and 54 percent, respectively. The tendency for women to outvote men is a trend among white, Black, and Latinx voters. Igielnik also reports that the gender gap in voting among less educated Black voters (less than a college degree) is even more substantial than the gap among voters with at least a college degree. In the 2016 presidential election, 74 percent of college-educated Black women voted compared to 71 percent of Black men; and 61 percent of less educated Black women voted but only 50 percent of less educated Black men voted.[16] In Brazil, voting is mandatory. However, "voting in white" (casting a blank vote) is one way to express dissatisfaction with candidates or to vote without actually voting. Brazilians can also intentionally annul their vote. These are two ways to avoid casting a vote in Brazil rather than not showing up at the polls.

TABLE 4.3 PRESIDENTIAL VOTING BY COUNTRY

	For Dilma Rousseff (%)	For Aecio Neves (%)	For Blank/ Annulled Vote/Did Not Vote (%)	For Hillary Clinton (%)	Write-In (%)	Did Not Vote (%)	Total (%)
Brazil	81	4	15				100
United States				67	1	32	100

In presidential voting, 68 percent of social welfare beneficiary women in the U.S. sample voted, and 32 percent did not vote (table 4.3). I did not count respondents who were too young to vote at the time of the 2016 presidential election. Of those who voted, 98 percent voted for Hillary Clinton in the 2016 election. This sample of Afro-descendant social welfare beneficiaries is similar to less educated Black women voters in the general population who also have fairly high levels of voting. In Brazil, 85 percent of Afro-descendant Bolsa Família beneficiaries voted in the 2014 presidential election; 81 percent voted for Dilma Rousseff and 15 percent voted in white, annulled their vote, or did not vote. U.S. women were more than twice as likely not to vote in the presidential election than their counterparts in Brazil. Thirty-two percent of the American sample did not vote. Despite these differences, in both cases women overwhelmingly supported women presidential candidates Dilma Rousseff and Hillary Clinton. In the next section, I examine voting patterns of Afro-descendant social welfare beneficiaries based on whether they are religious or nonreligious.

RELIGION AND AFRO-DESCENDANT COMMUNITIES IN BRAZIL AND THE UNITED STATES

In 1835, a group of African Muslims, the Malês, led a rebellion in Salvador, Bahia. This rebellion was not limited to Muslims and included a range of ethnic and nonreligious groups. In the United States, Harriet Tubman felt it was God's mission for her to lead enslaved people to freedom, and she led three hundred enslaved Blacks to freedom. Sojourner Truth, a pastor and an abolitionist, was inspired by God to sojourn and teach the word while fighting for freedom. In 1831, Nat Turner believed that God told him to organize and lead a rebellion against whites. African and Afro-descendant religious practitioners have been engaged in liberatory acts in Brazil and the United States for a long time. Religion has not always been liberatory in Black people's lives, but historically there has been a relationship between religion and freedom for those in the African Diaspora. Narrow understandings of the repressive role of Christianity fail to account for history and Black liberation theology, which argues that social justice and fighting racism is fundamental to the practice of Christianity.[17]

Religion and politics once again are at the forefront as scholars explore how Trump and Bolsonaro were elected to office. Scholars explain the 2018 presidential electoral win of the extreme right Brazilian candidate Jair Bolsonaro as a result of evangelical support.[18] In this unique study of Afro-descendant women social welfare beneficiaries, I examine the voting behavior of this segment of the Afro-descendant population in two of the world's largest democracies. In 2014 Dilma Rousseff, a Worker's Party candidate, ran for reelection in Brazil, and Hilary Clinton ran as a Democrat in the U.S.

presidential election of 2016. My hypothesis is that religion-affiliated social welfare beneficiaries in both countries are more likely to support leftist candidates than conservative political candidates.

Afro-Descendants and Religion

In the contemporary context, certain segments of Afro-descendant evangelicals and Christians in Brazil began to differentiate from their white counterparts with the rise of what John Burdick terms "Evangelical Black consciousness." In the United States, churches have traditionally been segregated, and some Black churches differ from their white counterparts as Black preachers include social justice and antiracism messages.[19] Burdick examined the rise in antiracism in evangelical churches in Brazil in the 1990s and states:

> The evangelical black consciousness/anti-racist movement—by which I mean projects, leaders, initiatives, networks, groups, and organisations that identify their agenda as combining a strong evangelical Protestant identity with a commitment to strengthen black identity and combat racism—is one of the newest, most rapidly proliferating, and potentially most consequential forces in Brazilian racial politics. What makes this movement so important is that, in contrast to non-Christian black movements, it speaks the language of one of the largest, broadest, best-organized segments of the Brazilian population. Indeed, by pushing evangelical rank-and-file to examine their consciences for evidence of racism, the movement may have the potential to help a whole new segment of the Brazilian population to bring the issue into the light of day.[20]

Burdick found that this movement was due to growing Black activism that increased with Brazil's political opening in 1985, the Durban conference, and more resources becoming available for Black activist groups. Black movement activists were historically skeptical of evangelicals; they believed activists should embrace African-derived religions and that evangelicals were simply out to convert people. However, Burdick found that some Black activists converted to Christianity and continued to practice antiracism within the church. Evangelicals were only granted the opportunity to discuss antiracism in church after the state embraced a more open discourse on racial issues.

Burdick argued that church leaders were more open to racial discussions when the state legitimized public racial discourse. Some activists opened or led their own churches, such as the Foursquare Gospel Church (Igreja Quadrangular) on the periphery of São Paulo, whose leader, Djalma, established it with the goal of discussing Black consciousness and antiracism.[21] Djalma felt excluded at his previous church and was passed over for a leadership role due to his skin color. In São Paulo, other groups were formed, including the Black Christian Women's Forum of São Paulo, which was made up of women from a variety of evangelical churches and was founded in 1991. Other groups formed in Rio de Janeiro and in other parts of Brazil.

In Brazil, the growing antiracism organizations in churches began in the 1990s. For this reason, it is possible to consider whether Afro-descendant evangelicals may not respond to political candidates in the same way as white evangelicals. Traditional studies on religion and politics in Brazil ignore how Christianity may interact with marginalized groups, especially Afro-descendant women.

In Brazil and the United States, there are divergences within Black Christians. Burdick's early work foreshadows the rise of progressive Black evangelicals. He described a meeting with three leaders of a group of Black progressive evangelicals in São Paulo. He asked who would have the greatest role in advocating an antiracist agenda in Brazil, and "they chimed in without hesitation: black evangelicals. 'Listen,' one of them said, 'the black movement that is out there is too divided. But we, evangelicals, we unite and become strong behind a single message—the message of Jesus Christ. And Jesus is asking us to fight racism. So nothing can stop us.'"[22] Black evangelicals are certainly not the most vocal Black movement today, but they are part of numerous voices fighting for Black rights. They also work with the umbrella Black movement group the Coalition for Black Rights, which was founded in 2018 after the election of Bolsonaro. An example of the role of progressive evangelicals is Pastor Eliad, an Afro-Brazilian Methodist pastor in São Paulo, who has been vocal about her discontent with Bolsonaro:

> I don't think Jair Bolsonaro took advantage of evangelicals. That rotten evangelical segment that's out there supported him from the beginning. They want power, they want money. It is a reactionary, fascist segment that wants the world to run according to what they believe. . . . Note that almost all of them, with very few exceptions, are white men and from wealthy churches. Bolsonaro has this support because, by joining this mob, these churches know they will have the power they dream of. . . . For us to understand this movement, it is necessary to go to the United States and see the project of the evangelical right there. By 2050 they want every leader in the Americas to be Christian, evangelicals (translation mine).[23]

Her statement is important because it exemplifies that Brazilian evangelicals are not monolithic, which is similar to the position of Black Christians in the United States. Some segments may be liberatory and committed to racial justice, and others may be conservative and supportive of restricting freedom and rights.

In the United States, scholars examining the influence of religion on African Americans have found that religion has had a positive impact on political activism,[24] political participation,[25] and the belief that the government plays a role in social and economic disparities.[26] Black churches with liberation messages are more likely to engage in politics. Black religious followers who embrace tenants of Black liberation theology are more likely to be accepting of gay people.[27] But not all Black churches are progressive. McDaniel, Dwidar, and Calderon found that Black Americans' solidarity with the poor and their political attitudes differ according to the type of Christianity they follow.[28] Those who follow Black liberation theology are more likely to demonstrate solidarity with the poor, are committed to racial solidarity, and embrace Black feminism. McDaniel, Dwidar, and Calderon stated that the social gospel is more aligned with the civil rights movement in terms of its commitment to social equality, and they found that its adherents are committed to social and racial equality. According to McDaniel, Dwidar, and Calderon, adherents of the social gospel believe that salvation is predicated on a relationship with God and a commitment to social equality. Prosperity gospel followers believe they will be rewarded on earth and in heaven by material gifts for their good deeds.[29] McDaniel, Dwidar, and Calderon found that those who follow the prosperity gospel are more likely to be conservative and do not show racial or class solidarity.[30] These differing worldviews among Black religious practitioners demonstrate significant divergences within Black churches, so it cannot be assumed that all Black congregants will make the same political choices.

I focused on Afro-descendants and did not compare Afro-descendants to whites. Many U.S. studies have analyzed white evangelicals and their politics. Scholarship on conservatism in

Brazilian politics has focused on evangelicals' political choices and ignored Afro-descendant Christians. This study brings Afro-descendant women into the scholarly conversation in both Brazil and the United States. More than a majority of the women in this sample identified as having a religious affiliation. Religious affiliation is an important area to consider when examining vote choice.

Religious Affiliation and Voting

I first discuss general findings of religious affiliation before analyzing results of vote choice and religious affiliation. In the Brazilian sample, 78 percent had a religious affiliation, and 22 percent did not. In the U.S. sample, 61 percent had a religious affiliation, and 39 percent did not. With the exception of Chicago, more than a majority of respondents in all cities in both countries had a religious affiliation (table 4.4). Although it may seem unsurprising for respondents in South America's largest city to have a religious affiliation, it is important to remember the intersectional identities of these women. Religion may

TABLE 4.4 CITY AND RELIGIOUS AFFILIATION

	Religious Affiliation (%)	No Religious Affiliation (%)	Total (%)
Salvador	79	21	100
São Luis	67.5	32.5	100
São Paulo	87	13	100
Charlotte	74	26	100
Chicago	43	57	100
Milwaukee	64	36	100

provide an opportunity for support and community. São Paulo had the most religious women (87 percent); the next highest were Salvador (79 percent) and Charlotte (74 percent). The lowest number of women with a religious affiliation was in Chicago (43 percent). It is perplexing that Chicago has such a low percentage. In general, Black Americans are more religious than any other racial group in the United States, with 59 percent of Blacks compared to 40 percent of the general population believing that religion is important to them.[31] However, Mohamed et al. also found that younger Black Americans are less connected to Black churches than are older Black Americans. The Chicago sample is relatively young, which may account for the Chicago sample being less religiously affiliated. Charlotte is located in the South, a region generally known for being more religious than other parts of the United States.

In Salvador, São Luis, and São Paulo, a significant majority of the women who voted in the 2018 Brazilian presidential election were affiliated with a religion (table 4.5). In Charlotte and Milwaukee, a significant majority of the women who voted in the 2016 U.S. presidential election were affiliated with a religion, whereas in Chicago only 37 percent of women voters were affiliated with a religion.

In Brazil, the most popular religious denominations of respondents were evangelical and Catholic. In the United States, the most popular denomination was Baptist: 37 percent identified as Baptist, and 29 percent identified as Christian, not specifying a denomination. Others identified as Jehovah's Witness (5 percent), Muslim (3 percent), and Hebrew Israelite (3 percent). In Brazil, 44 percent identified as evangelical, which included those who said evangelical, Assembly of God, Universal, Foursquare Church, and Congregational Christ of Brazil. Others identified as Catholic (32 percent), Candomblé or Umbanda (2 percent), and Baptist (10 percent).

TABLE 4.5 RELIGIOUS AFFILIATION OF BLACK WOMEN SOCIAL
WELFARE BENEFICIARY VOTERS IN PRESIDENTIAL ELECTIONS,
UNITED STATES (2016) AND BRAZIL (2018)

	Brazil		United States		
	Religious Affiliation (%)	No Religious Affiliation (%)	Religious Affiliation (%)	No Religious Affiliation (%)	Total (%)
Salvador	77	23			100
São Luis	70	30			100
São Paulo	87	13			100
Charlotte			71	29	100
Chicago			37	63	100
Milwaukee			70	30	100

Presidential Election Participation

In Brazil most participants voted for Dilma Rousseff, and in the United States most participants voted for Hillary Clinton. I did not expect variation in the U.S. sample because Afro-descendant women largely support Democratic candidates. In the United States, 68 percent of Afro-descendant social welfare beneficiaries voted in the 2016 presidential election, and 98 percent of them voted for former Secretary of State Hillary Clinton. Charlotte has the highest level of support for Hillary Clinton at 79 percent (table 4.6). These high levels of voter turnout mirror the high turnout rates of Black women generally in U.S. elections. Although nearly 60 percent of Afro-descendant women social welfare beneficiaries in the United States sample could not name a political party, they still showed up at the polls. Thus, for this population of women, there is an inverse relationship between political knowledge and voter turnout.

TABLE 4.6 VOTER PARTICIPATION BY CITY IN THE UNITED STATES

	For Hillary Clinton (%)	Write-In Candidate (Tupac Shakur) (%)	Did Not Vote (%)	Total (%)
Charlotte	79		21	100
Chicago	62		38	100
Milwaukee	61	3	36	100

Afro-Brazilians generally support PT candidates, but nearly half of them voted for Bolsonaro in the 2018 elections. Given the intersections of race, class, and gender, especially Bolsa Família status, I expected the Brazilian women in the sample to support Rousseff. São Luis had the highest number of voters (95 percent) supporting Rousseff (table 4.7). Only 58 percent of São Paulo's sample voted for Rousseff, and 34 percent annulled their vote, voted in white, or did not vote. The Brazil sample had both high voter turnout and a high level of political knowledge. In São Paulo, it appears that these women used their vote to show their dissatisfaction.

TABLE 4.7 VOTER PARTICIPATION BY CITY IN BRAZIL

	Dilma Rousseff (%)	Aecio Neves (%)	Voted in White/ Annulled Vote/ Did Not Vote (%)	Total (%)
Salvador	91	3	6	100
São Luis	95	0	5	100
São Paulo	58	8	34	100

Presidential Election Participation and Religious Affiliation

Among U.S. women with no religious affiliation, 31 percent did not vote, and 33 percent of Christians did not vote. These findings show that levels of abstaining by Afro-descendant social welfare beneficiaries are similar to those of religious and nonreligious women generally, although religious women are slightly more likely not to vote. The greatest difference in not voting was between nonreligious and religious Brazilian women. Among nonreligious women in Brazil, only 12 percent did not vote, annulled their vote, or voted in white, whereas 26 percent of Christians voted in white, annulled their vote, or did not vote. Among Brazilian social welfare beneficiaries, religious women were more than twice as likely as nonreligious women to avoid voting. In both countries, Christians had higher percentages than nonreligious people of not casting votes. However, this may be due to both samples having a high percentage of Christians.

My second hypothesis was that religion-affiliated Black women social welfare beneficiaries in Brazil and the United States are more likely to support leftist candidates than conservative candidates. There is support for this hypothesis. Afro-descendant social welfare beneficiaries in the United States tend to have a Christian religious affiliation, specifically Baptist, and 72 percent of these Christians voted for Clinton (table 4.8). Even though mainstream media and academic scholarship stated that conservative politician wins were in part due to evangelical support, 77 percent of evangelical Brazilian Afro-descendant social welfare beneficiaries voted for Rousseff. These findings contradict the mainstream media and academic discourse. Scholarship such as *The Politics of Survival* is important because it considers the intersection of race, class, gender, and religion. Afro-descendant

TABLE 4.8 EVANGELICALS AND CHRISTIANS WHO
SUPPORTED LEFTIST PRESIDENTIAL CANDIDATES

Evangelicals voted for Rousseff	77%
Evangelicals did not vote for Rousseff	23%
Christians voted for Clinton	72%
Christians did not vote for Clinton	28%

social welfare beneficiary religious women, including evangelicals, voted differently from evangelicals generally.

In Brazil, respondents who followed an African-derived religion, such as Candomblé or Umbanda, voted for Rousseff. However, in the United States, those who identified as Hebrew Israelite, a Black nationalist religion with sexist overtones, did not vote in the presidential election. These sample sizes are extremely small: four African-derived religious practitioners in Brazil and two Black nationalist practitioners in the United States. However, it demonstrates that a "Black" religious tradition in Brazil mobilizes voter participation, whereas in the United States low-income women voters are demobilized. I do not generalize these findings. In this study, Afro-descendant social welfare beneficiary voters in both countries were overwhelmingly supportive of leftist presidential candidates, and these findings go against the idea that evangelicals are more supportive of conservative leaders. I now turn to women social welfare beneficiaries' opinions of conservative presidents.

EVALUATIONS OF
CONSERVATIVE PRESIDENTS

In my study, Afro-descendant social welfare beneficiaries gave their strong support to leftist presidential candidates, so I am interested in how these women evaluate conservative presidents. But before discussing Michel Temer and Donald Trump, let me briefly explain the political environment that led to Temer's presidency and the aftermath of his presidency, in which another conservative president (Bolsonaro) was elected.

Oswaldo Amaral analyzed support for Jair Bolsonaro and Fernando Haddad in the 2018 presidential election and found that those who positively evaluated the Temer administration were more likely to vote for Bolsonaro.[32] Earlier scholars had claimed that Bolsa Família beneficiaries are more likely to support PT candidates.[33] Amaral also found that being a Bolsa Família beneficiary increased the likelihood of that person voting for Haddad in both rounds.[34] In previous studies on presidential voting, gender had not been a significant determinant of voting preferences. However, in the 2018 election, Amaral found that identifying as male increased the likelihood of voting for Bolsonaro. This was also supported by the work of Layton et al.[35] Amaral also stated that people who believed the economy was improving were more likely to support Bolsonaro.[36]

In the 2014 presidential election, PT President Dilma Rousseff won a second term, but she was removed from office in 2016. Rousseff received remarkable support from Afro-Brazilians through her affiliation with the Workers Party, but Brazil made a turn to the right after bogus corruption charges were laid against Rousseff. She was later found not guilty of being involved in Operation Car Wash, a corruption scheme involving both PT and non-PT politicians who received kickbacks in exchange for financial favors. Michel Temer, the center-right Vice President took over as president after Rousseff's impeachment. Activists and scholars who spoke out against Rousseff's removal from office—calling it a coup—were threatened, and academic freedom was tightened. The threat to free speech and to civil organizing threatened Brazilian democracy.[37] This deterioration in norms paved the way for a Bolsonaro win. The alliance between the Brazilian democratic movement (PMDB) and the Brazilian Social Democratic Party (PSDB) led the effort to impeach Rousseff, and they also criticized Temer's vice presidency and presidency. As Goldstein states, "Marcos Nobre's concept of Pemedebismo, the idea that the PMDB's accommodationism and conservatism have dominated Brazilian political culture since democratization, highlights the continuities in order between the Workers' Party administrations and those of Temer and Bolsonaro."[38] From this perspective, we can set aside the idea of an entirely new right-wing order, and we can also mark the continuities of this period with the relevant presence of the PMDB. This political culture and these continuities also explain how a Bolsonaro presidency was made possible.

The Brazilian Institute of Public Opinion and Statistics (IBOPE) reported that a remarkable 47 percent of Afro-Brazilians intended to vote for Bolsonaro, compared to 40 percent for Haddad.[39] The PT candidate was popular among the poor, those with less education, and those living in the northeast.[40] These categories—northeastern, women, and the poor—are sometimes analyzed as separate identities, but in reality they are intersectional. It is critical for researchers to examine subgroups to better understand how these intersections influence the political opinions of candidates.

Bolsonaro is sometimes referred to as the "Trump of the Tropics"; he has made racist, misogynist, and homophobic comments. During his campaign, Bolsonaro had a tough on crime stance and often posed for pictures pretending that his hand was a gun. He advocated for citizens to purchase guns, and he repeated the Brazilian aphorism that "a good thief is a dead thief." His tough on crime stance likely appealed to both low-income people who are concerned with crime in their

he's trying to deport people because my daughter's mixed. Some of her, her dad's side of the family, is from the island. Some of them aren't I guess legally, like citizens here. If he decided to do that, they could get deported. It's just messing up a lot of families. He just want to break up families. Like I said, he was trying to take away a lot of government assistance that people need. He's just trying to make us go lower than we are. I really can't respect nobody that does that, you know?

Although this woman believed that younger people voted for Trump as a joke, she quickly turned to a very serious issue: immigration. She admits that she is personally affected because members of her family are undocumented. She is also concerned that Trump would take away social welfare assistance.

A twenty-two-year-old dark-skinned Black woman with a high school diploma who resides in Milwaukee complained in class-related terms; she believes Trump is only motivated by money:

I think he is running America on a business . . . instead of . . . as a country. Instead of like a community, he's running it as a business. Instead of thinking about everyone, he's thinking about profiting and what he can get out of it or anyone.

These women believe Trump is disconnected from most Americans, who are not wealthy. They believe a president should care about everyone, including poor people.

For a twenty-nine-year-old dark-skinned woman self-identified as African American, Native who has a college degree and resides in Milwaukee she believes Trump is only concerned with his wealthy friends:

I feel like Donald Trump, he doesn't know how to relate to the major(ity) population. He doesn't understand different people, people's background and different lifestyles. He only thinks about his friends and about his lifestyle and about how people like him feel. He don't think about the other side of the population.

A thirty-year-old dark-skinned African American mother of four who is a high school graduate and resides in Milwaukee had a similar opinion and believes not caring for the poor makes someone nonhuman:

> Oh gosh, he's not human. I don't think he's a human. I don't think he has a soul. I don't think he has a heart. I don't think he cares. I feel like he is . . . more for the rich instead of the poor, so I don't like him at all. I don't wish anything bad on the man. I just don't think he takes the time out to actually see what's going on. He's just a famous person that all of a sudden became a president, and he just doing what he knows best; in front of the camera talking. He don't even know what's going on. He just like to talk, and be in front of [the] spotlight.

Trump's history of practicing racism and sexism was also of concern for these women. In fact, 16 percent of the U.S. respondents mentioned racism. A twenty-seven-year-old dark-skinned African American SNAP and WIC beneficiary who resides in Milwaukee offered these insightful comments:

> I can't stand him. I think he's just all full of himself. I think he acts like my five-year-old, and he pouts. . . . We got a big kid running the whole world! I be looking around like, who voted for him? He says stuff that doesn't even make sense. I'm like, dang, you didn't have anything to do with that. I'm not that deep into it, but when

I watch it I know he's saying something stupid. Yeah, I think he's racist, and I think he just uses people around him to get where he needs to get, and if they get knocked down, he doesn't care as long as he's covered. So, yeah. . . . All of them are lying for him, he's lying. It's just a whole bunch of mess. And we're in it because he's running everything. We're all in the mess. We're all messed up because he's running the mess. But I've got a God, so I'm not worried about what Trump is doing. So I pray.

A forty-seven-year-old dark-skinned self-identified Black woman who resides in Charlotte worried about the future of the country:

> (sighs) I guess the easiest way to say it is he's the biggest racist clown there is. I mean . . . yeah . . . he's a sexist. He has no respect for anybody. I mean he's . . . trying to turn this back to a slave country. I mean people can say "no he's not, he's trying to make it great again" (laughs). But how is he making it great when . . . we know . . . [he has] . . . connections to the Klan and people that keep saying all kind of hateful stuff that shows there's racism there? It makes me wonder as a Black person, where this country will be if this keeps happening, and what's going to happen to us, if all this stuff keeps going on?

A forty-three-year-old dark-skinned African American WIC beneficiary who resides in Charlotte was distressed by Trump's policy to separate children from their parents at the border:

> I just think he's a terrible person. I don't like how he speaks to women, especially African American women, and how he just doesn't have any respect for anybody. He says whatever he wants to say, whether you like it or you don't. And I don't like how he wants to build this wall, to keep the Mexican people out. Why?

They're human just like we are. They want a better life for their children, like anybody else would. And it bothered me when I saw how they was separating the parents from their children. And I'm like, "Oh, my God. My baby." I love him to death, I do need a break. But to not be able to see him, and have him worried about where his mom is, and thinking I left him. I just think he is the worst president that we have ever, ever had, and it's getting worse and worse. . . . It's just a scary time now. And then, with so much hatred. People that are not African Americans, for them to hate us so bad, because of the color of our skin. Back in the day you could go to the movies, you could go to the mall. You didn't have to worry about shootings. And now, those places you even nervous to go to. . . . But I'm just nervous now, because you don't know who going to flip out at any given moment because of the color of your skin and decide to shoot and kill you. And it bothers me when we have these shootings and stuff, and it's people that are not African American, first thing they'll say, "Oh, it's a mental illness. Oh, it's PTSD." But if it's an African American that has done something, "Oh, they [are] a thug. Oh, they are no good."

In Brazil, respondents believed that Temer also was concerned only with wealthy people and was self-interested. He was more concerned with corporations or businesspeople than with citizens. They didn't think he was concerned about the poor and Bolsa Família beneficiaries. A forty-year-old dark-skinned woman self-identified as Preta, Negona who resides in Salvador said that Temer does not have the interest of poor people at heart:

Out with Temer! Thief! Thief! Corrupt! . . . He wants the poor to stay poor and the rich to stay rich. . . . His mask will fall. It is already falling. Lula will return with everything. Lula's party will return . . . with everything.

A thirty-six-year-old dark-skinned self-identified Negra mother of four who completed high school and resides in São Luis also believed Temer is only interested in looking out for elite businesspeople. She said that he is "Irresponsible!" and that "He only thinks of the elite, those from the south; businesspeople." Another woman from São Luis believed he does not know what it feels like to be poor and therefore should not be the president. Former president Lula came from very humble beginnings and routinely discussed his experiences growing up poor and later as being in the working class. Some of the women echoed these differences including this thirty-two-year-old dark-skinned self-identified Negra mother of two with a high school education who resides in São Luis:

> Do I have to respond? Sincerely, he is in the wrong place because to be the president he has to be there for the nation. He does not do this. His family does not know how it is to be poor; to not [be able to] feed their family. He is in the wrong place.

A twenty-two-year-old Parda mother of two who has not completed high school and resides in São Luis echoed this sentiment:

> (Laughs). No, I don't like anything he does because he doesn't do anything. . . . In three months . . . what has he done? Nothing. He only takes. He didn't do anything. He didn't help anyone. . . . If he had done things like Dilma and Lula, I would not say anything about him. He didn't help us. He didn't help the poor.

Beyond not helping the poor, they are concerned with women not being able to receive Bolsa Família. An eighty-five-year-old Parda woman with an incomplete middle school education who resides in Salvador expressed this worry: "For me he should leave; he only wants to take away Bolsa Família. He only wants to take money from retired people; a lot of things are said on television."

Because of austerity measures, this thirty-five-year-old Negra mother of three with a high school education who resides in São Paulo was concerned with cuts to social security:

> Look, honestly I'm not liking him because he's messing with our Social Security. It is already difficult for you to receive what you have the right [to receive]. . . . It is difficult for you to retire. . . . He wants to make other rules for you to follow. I don't agree with his mandate to take away Social Security.

The Afro-descendant social welfare beneficiaries in both countries articulate their concerns in an intersectional way. They are concerned for immigrants, poor people, Black people, Black women, Black men, Mexican people, and children. Beneficiaries in the United States are concerned with racism and sexism, but they are also concerned with xenophobia and classism. Beneficiaries in Brazil are concerned with classicism and ageism as they discuss the rights that retired people should be granted. These respondents draw on an intersectional framework when evaluating their presidents.

The hypothesis that Afro-descendant social welfare beneficiaries will be critical of conservative presidents has been proven: women in Brazil and in the United States were extremely critical of their conservative leaders. They do not believe Temer and Trump are committed to most citizens, and they believe these presidents only uphold the interests of the wealthy. In fact, the women believe Trump and Temer are against the poor, pointing out that they want to cut benefits from social welfare beneficiaries.

More important, these women think radically and progressively as they consider life beyond their individual circumstances.

Resistance and empowerment come in myriad forms and are a part of Black feminism; the goal is to challenge and eliminate these interlocking forms of oppression. Poor Black women actively engage in challenging this domination by considering the needs of others even when these forms of domination do not involve them individually. In societies in which Black women find it difficult to sustain their lives and their families' lives, these women have in many ways won the battle of various intersecting oppressions through the simple act of living and sustaining their families.

SUMMARY

Afro-descendant women social welfare beneficiaries behaved in distinct ways when compared to other low-income people or religious people. A lack of political knowledge among beneficiaries in the United States does not depress voter turnout. Christianity, including evangelicalism, does not lead poor Afro-descendant women in Brazil or the United States to support conservative politicians. In fact, these women are critical of their conservative presidents for not meeting the needs of low-income people. In the United States, they are also critical of Trump's hostile attitude toward Black people and women. In Brazil, Afro-descendant women social welfare beneficiaries tend to be Christian and may be an important voting bloc for progressive Brazilian politicians because they are concerned with vulnerable populations and support leftist presidential candidates. Afro-descendant women in the United States and Brazil are often viewed as "saviors of democracy." The findings of my study point to low-income Afro-descendant women's political potential in progressive politics. They are aware that conservative leaders do not have their best interests or the interest of poor people at heart.

In the United States, the Democratic Party is a leftist political party when compared to the Republican Party, but it includes politicians and supporters who range from conservative to moderate to progressive. The Democratic Party welcomes members who have a broad spectrum of political leanings. Bernie Sanders and Alexandria Ocasio-Cortez support leftist politics such as free university education and free health care. However, moderate Democratic politicians do not share these left leaning policy ideas.

In addition, the way votes are counted in presidential elections in the United States and Brazil differ. In the U.S. electoral college system, each state is allotted a certain number of electoral votes, and all those votes are given to the winning candidate in that state. In Brazil, the winning candidate is the person who receives the most direct votes by individual citizens. Under the U.S. system, a candidate may "win" the popular vote but lose the election when electoral college votes are counted. Even though the election systems differ, media in both countries discuss the significant role Black women play. In the United States, Black women are overwhelmingly affiliated with the Democratic Party. In Brazil, Afro-Brazilian voters have a more diverse spread of affiliations, with some voting for conservative politicians, some for moderates, and others for leftist politicians. Nevertheless, the media and some politicians acknowledge that Afro-descendant women can determine which candidates will win in presidential elections in both countries.

How can poor Afro-descendant women survive and thrive in two of the world's largest democracies? And what should the role of poor Black women be in electoral politics beyond being saviors of democracy? I address this question in chapter 5, along with thinking beyond survival politics.

5

CONCLUSION

Are Poor Black Women the
Hope for Progressive Politics?

Sandra Lindsay, a Black nurse in New York, was the first person to take the Pfizer Covid-19 vaccine in the United States, and she became the public face of the vaccine. Another Black nurse, Mônica Calazans, was the first person in Brazil to receive the CaronaVac Covid-19 vaccine. In both cases, Black women's bodies became symbols of sacrifice. These Black women publicly demonstrated that the vaccine was safe and that others should take it. Symbolically, they were helping to save lives in these nations during the pandemic. This action connected them to the self-sacrifices Black women have made historically as caretakers. During slavery, Black women took care of their master's children and their own children. After emancipation from slavery, many Black women became domestic workers who cared for white households. Although labor markets are more open to Black women today, they still symbolically serve as saviors through their myriad sacrifices. In electoral politics, Black women are also viewed as potential saviors of the nation because they overwhelmingly vote for Democratic politicians in the United States. In Brazil, from the Worker's Party era (2002–2016) to Haddad's 2018 run for president, Afro-Brazilian women were a voting group that potentially could save Brazil's democracy.

In *The Politics of Survival*, I have shown that poor Afro-descendant women are saviors for their families and their communities. They sacrifice their time and energy to support others. They work at informal jobs to supplement insufficient social welfare benefits; lend money to daughters and sisters who are receiving social welfare benefits; and care for disabled and sick children, in some cases when they are disabled themselves.

Self-sacrifice can be dangerous, and self-sacrifice in all spheres of one's life—socially, economically, and politically—is even more dangerous. In *Birthing Black Mothers*, Jennifer Nash argued that the attention given to Black mothers is dangerous because they are seen as spectacles and as political currency for politicians and journalists:

> Black mothers in the United States have become spectacularly and dangerously visible through the frame of crisis, one that insists on their spatial and temporal location in a death-world that is described as reminiscent of the nation's imagined past, even as it is consistent with the conditions of the unfolding present. . . . It is precisely because Black motherhood is now cast as suffering rather than pathological, as tragic rather than self-destructive, as traumatized rather than deviant, that the crisis frame can be both deeply seductive and rhetorically effective. Yet the rhetoric of crisis is part of an enduring and troubling tradition of rendering Black women generally, and Black mothers specifically, into symbols, even if now Black mothers are symbols of tragic heroism rather than deviance.[1]

Nash focuses on how politicians and journalists use Black mothers as political currency. Her idea that Black mothers are tragic heroes and protectors but are also people who constantly suffer is relevant to this study of poor Afro-descendant social welfare beneficiaries. Poor Black women social welfare beneficiaries are viewed as deviant and undeserving, but at the same time Afro-descendant women generally are viewed as saviors.

Based on the framework of Black feminism, in *The Politics of Survival*, I propose a more nuanced way of exploring the juxtaposition between deviant and savior and demonstrate that these women are engaged in self-sacrifice and resistance. I challenge the way political scientists study social welfare beneficiaries, focusing on class in their examination of political preferences and vote choice. In this study, I consider racial, gender, and class discrimination to better understand how Afro-descendant women social welfare beneficiaries experience the world. I also focus on how intersectional identities explain why these women support leftist politicians and why their critique of conservative politicians is different from that of their white counterparts.

In Brazil, a segment of support for conservative politicians comes from evangelicals. Most of the Bolsa Família beneficiaries in this study are religious evangelicals and Catholics, but they support leftist politicians and are critical of conservative politicians. This is also true for Christian Afro-descendant social welfare beneficiaries in the United States. Brazilian social welfare beneficiaries have higher levels of political knowledge than their U.S. counterparts, but in both countries these women have high levels of voting. U.S. political science literature suggests a positive relationship between political knowledge and political participation, but the social welfare beneficiaries in the United States in this study exhibit an inverse relationship: low levels of political knowledge and high levels of voting. When considering African-based or Black American religions—Candomblé and Umbanda in Brazil and Black nationalist Hebrew Israelites in the United States—different political outcomes are found for social welfare beneficiaries. In Brazil, these religious followers vote, and in the United States they do not. Further research is needed to examine whether the general population of African-based religious practitioners in the United States and in Brazil share a similar trend.

Many studies on social welfare beneficiaries do not account for skin color even though scholars have found that skin color plays a role in economic, educational, and marriage outcomes for Black women. Using the Black feminist framework, skin color was included in the profile in both countries because it plays a significant role in the lives of Afro-descendant social welfare beneficiaries. The women in this study tended to have darker skin complexions. Darker skin color is a disadvantage. Considering skin color along with how other intersectional identities such as education, race, and gender intersect is important in understanding how identities shape experiences and life chances.

Single mother social welfare beneficiaries supplement their benefits and engage in the politics of survival, using whatever means are available to provide for their families. Afro-descendant women in Brazil and in the United States practice survival tactics such as relying on family, making extra money through odd jobs, and seeking emergency assistance from nonprofit organizations. These survival tactics challenge prevalent stereotypes that label these women as being unwilling to work. They resist society's attempts to humiliate them and to make survival of poor families impossible.

Some studies have demonstrated stigma against social welfare beneficiaries,[2] and others have shown that these women are empowered.[3] Mariano and Carloto have found that women are both stigmatized and empowered, which is similar to my findings in *The Politics of Blackness*.[4] Black women are more likely to perceive skin color discrimination than gender discrimination, and women also perceive discrimination against social welfare beneficiaries. However, the Afro-descendant women social welfare beneficiaries in Brazil and the United States in this study challenge these forms of discrimination. They are empowered by being able to provide food for their families, and the Brazilian beneficiaries live a dignified life because they can provide clothes and school materials for their children.

INCREASING THE NUMBER OF POOR BLACK WOMEN IN POLITICS

Black women must have roles as protagonists for change. Yes, they are voters, but they should also be in spaces of power. Black women politicians provide a unique perspective on the lives of those with little power. Cori Bush, a Black American politician who was a former social welfare beneficiary, offered this insight:

> I remember feeling like people don't understand, and how can I make them understand? It's not that we are bad people. It's not that we don't deserve to have a home or we don't deserve to have a better quality of life. . . . Because there's something that comes with standing in the line at a food pantry. Something happens to you, something happens when you have to explain how you're poor enough to be able to receive these resources, why you ended up in this position, you have to explain it, and I just remember feeling that and how it felt every time I pulled out my WIC vouchers in the grocery store. And whenever I paid for something with food stamps, all of that was just flooding back.[5]

Benny Briolly, a Black Brazilian transwoman politician experienced transphobia and racism before and after being elected to office:

> I remember that I wrote a bill for people to use the bathroom according to their identities, without segregation and I remember that I received messages from people on social media—from racist, transphobic, white men—that if they saw me in the same bathroom as their daughters and wives they would beat me up in these spaces.[6]

In 2021, Brazil's Congress was less than 3 percent Afro-Brazilian women although they are 27 percent of the population.[7] In 2021, Black American women made up 4.9 percent of the United States Congress, and they are less than 7 percent of the population.[8] Two solutions to meeting the needs of poor Afro-descendant women are that there should be an increase in the number of poor Black women in the electoral process and that society's views about who is deserving of rights and who is not must change.

Increasing the number of poor Black women who engage in politics and considering who is elected is important to expand progressive platforms. The politicians quoted here talked about their personal experiences belonging to vulnerable populations and how that shaped their progressive policies. At the same time, both exemplify the dangerous cultural elements of classism, racism, and transphobia in society that reduce empathy and tolerance for marginalized Black women. Bush's experience of stigma due to being a person living in poverty encapsulates American culture, which has a disdain for the poor, especially the Black poor, and blames poor people for their situation. Foreigners view Brazil as open-minded and friendly, but it is highly transphobic and has the highest number of deaths of trans people in the world. These Black women politicians, like many Black women, are expected to carry these burdens while continuing to provide for and serve their families and constituents.

The success of Afro-descendant women politicians has grown in Brazil and in the United States, but they remain underrepresented in both countries, especially in Brazil. Leading Black women political scientists such as Wendy Smooth, Christina Greer, Pearl Dowe, Nadia Brown, and Sharon Austin have done exemplary work on Black women's politics in the United States. They have shown the barriers Black women face as well as the successes of Black women politicians at the local and the national level. Kamala Harris's rise to the rank of U.S. Vice President was a watershed moment; she is the first woman and woman of color to hold that position. Harris is biracial: her mother is Indian and her father is Jamaican. President Biden has appointed more Black women as federal judges than any other president, and he recently chose Judge Ketanji Brown Jackson to join the U.S. Supreme Court.

These historic appointments are important in terms of descriptive representation, but descriptive representation does not ensure a progressive political agenda. Unfortunately, many politicians, including Black politicians, advocate most often for policies that help middle-class families and avoid poor people's issues. Politicians need to be willing to advocate for the needs of the poor. In 2021, Cori Bush was elected as a U.S. Representative from Missouri. A former WIC beneficiary and an activist in the Black Lives Matter movement, she also had experienced eviction. These experiences are very different from the experiences of more privileged politicians such as Vice President Harris. Bush knows what it feels like to experience hardship, and she advocates for economically vulnerable people. One example was her strong advocacy for an extension of the moratorium on evictions during the Covid-19 pandemic. It is important to support Black women who are visionaries and progressives. Poverty is not a dirty word, and Bush knows this.

Progressive politicians must respond to and implement legislation proposed by groups working on behalf and with poor people, which includes Black women. Reverend William Barber, leader of the Poor People's Campaign, a group that advocates for poor and working-class people, states, "I think we have to change the narrative when it comes to poor people. Too many people won't use the word poverty. Democrats have tended to run from poverty, while Republicans have tended to racialize poverty."[9] Institutions that promote or leave capitalism, classism, racism, and sexism unchecked produce poverty. The American myth that individual merit and hard work will ensure that one is protected from poverty is accepted even by lower-middle-class and working-class Blacks, who believe poor Blacks are poor because they are lazy and unwilling to work.[10] Wealthy people are not heavily taxed, which costs all Americans, yet they are viewed as people to admire whereas working-class people and poor people are viewed as wasteful spenders. As this study has shown, institutionalized racism and sexism contribute to low wages and unemployment. Poor women who seek employment often are not hired, and others cannot work because they are disabled or burdened with child care responsibilities.

Political support for poor Black women who advocate for their needs is one way to ensure that their needs are heard. Representative Barbara Lee, a Black woman from California, introduced H.Res. 438: "Third Reconstruction: Fully Addressing Poverty and Low Wages from the Bottom Up" in the House of Representatives on May 21, 2021. The resolution is meant to pressure the Biden administration to tackle poverty. Legislators supporting this resolution include Pramila Jayapal (Washington), Cori Bush (Missouri), Sara Jacobs (California), Gwen Moore (Wisconsin), Jamie Raskin (Maryland), Danny Davis and Jan Schakowsky (Illinois), and Rashida Tlaib (Michigan).[11] These legislators know the experience of needing social welfare. Lee grew up in a stable military family, however, when attending college she received public assistance to help her care for her two children. Lee has often championed progressive causes. Bush also benefited from social welfare, and Moore received food stamps before becoming a politician. Tlaib also benefited from receiving food stamps.[12] When Trump wanted to cut food stamps, these legislators were among nine Democrats calling on him not to cut the program because they had benefited from it when their families faced difficult times. Legislators who have experienced financial hardship and poverty know the benefits of these programs.

In Brazil, the word "poverty" is prevalent in political discourse, but some Brazilians also blame poor people for their condition. Increasing the number of progressive Afro-descendant women politicians is important but challenging as well. Many face political violence while running for office and after winning election. The best known example is Marielle Franco, who was assassinated on March 14, 2018. Franco was outspoken against the military takeover of favela communities in Rio de Janeiro and was a staunch advocate for the poor, especially Black women, the LGBTQ+ community, Black people, and young people. It is still not known who ordered her assassination and that of her driver Anderson Gomes.

Political violence is a serious threat, especially for those who advocate for human rights. Anielle Franco, Marielle Franco's sister and director of the Marielle Franco Institute, finds that those who have a similar agenda are even more vulnerable to political violence. The Marielle Franco Institute conducted a study of Black women politicians who work on human rights issues, including those who pressured the Bolsonaro administration to help people suffering from hunger due to Covid-19 and those who signed the Marielle Franco Agenda in 2020, which advocates for many of Franco's policies and causes. Eleven Black woman politicians were interviewed from eight states, and all were threatened with political violence as candidates and while in office. Benny Briolly, a Black transwoman, has been threatened while in office, and Talíria Petrone was also threatened while in office.

The Marielle Franco Institute advocates for more protection for Black women political candidates and those elected to office. Although decrees guaranteeing protection have been made, many of the security budgets have not been increased since 2018. The Protection of Defenders of Human Rights, Social Communicators and Environmentalists was instituted to protect and provide security for activists and politicians who are under threat because of their human rights work; however, only 44 percent of the budget of the Ministry of Women, Family, and Human Rights was allocated to this program in 2020.[13] There has been an increase in Black women running for elected positions, but the political environment remains especially dangerous for them.

Poor women also need resources to support their campaigns. Both universities and nongovernmental organizations have played a role in giving Black women and other progressive politicians a platform. The A Cor da Bahia program at the Federal University of Bahia organized several seminars that included roundtables with scholars, activists, and politicians during the 2020 elections in Brazil. Like Franco, many Black women politicians come from humble backgrounds and have experienced being vulnerable, which makes them more aware of policy solutions for poor people, including poor Black women. Hunger, unemployment, child care, and discrimination are all important issues to be addressed in Brazil.

> We have to stop this slave mentality. Three hundred fifty years of slavery still permeates in the heads (thinking) of people. They hate that the poor have ascended, they hate for poor people to go to downtown São Paulo; Ibiapuera. The poor can't go by plane? We have to stop with this imbecility! The poor are people!
>
> —Former president of Brazil, Luis "Lula" Inacio da Silva

> "Can the poor eat shrimp?" asked one of the hosts, Igao of PodPah. Lula responded, "Yes, and they should because they're the ones that caught them; that caught the shrimp, that built the car, made the clothes you are wearing. He has the right to the things he produced."
>
> —Podpah #295, December 2, 2021

CHALLENGING STEREOTYPES OF POOR BLACK WOMEN

It is important to challenge society's views about who is deserving and who is not. Social welfare beneficiaries are aware of negative stereotypes against beneficiaries. Ange-Marie Hancock's work shows the power the media has to negatively influence policy makers, which leads to a lack of support for social welfare policies.[14] Media expands far beyond traditional television and newspaper media today. Social media also contributes to stereotypes of social welfare beneficiaries. In Brazil and in the United States, respondents mentioned reading about stereotypes of social welfare beneficiaries on social media network platforms such as Facebook. In fact, the first time I saw the welfare queen stereotype made visible in the modern era in Brazil was when I saw memes of Bolsa Família beneficiaries.

Activists, scholars, and journalists can all play a role in challenging these stereotypes by changing the discourse. Progressive social media channels such as "Papo de Preta" in Brazil and "Jouelzy" and "For Harriet" in the United States challenge stereotypes based on racism, sexism, colorism, and classism. These channels discuss intersectionality with a focus on Black women. Along with mainstream media, social media "influencers" must use their platforms to challenge the stereotype that poor people are undeserving of the right to food. Former president Lula supported Bolsa Família because it allowed families to have dignity: mothers could buy food and clothing for their children. Lula acknowledged that many poor and working-class people are involved in making clothing and in producing food, yet they are not expected to want these things in life. He believes that poor and working-class people have the right to these items. Is it reasonable to expect poor and working-class people in capitalist countries like Brazil and the United States to have different wants than others have? Are they not worthy of having desires? When Lula was in office, some low-income and working-class people were able to travel, and they had access to some of the same spaces as people from other social classes. Lula noted that the problem is not poor people buying luxury items but that middle-class and wealthy Brazilians are uncomfortable with poor people sharing their spaces.

The Afro-descendant social welfare beneficiary women in this study were not privy to the luxuries they are stereotyped as having. The women appreciated receiving social welfare, but many had to supplement their income to provide for their families.

Academics who debate whether Bolsa Família is a form of clientelism should include intersectional analysis in their research. This approach considers the lived experiences of these women and how they are political subjects through their survival strategies. Voting is only one part of political participation. The study of the politics of social welfare beneficiaries must consider their identities and how these intersectional identities complicate our understanding of their political preferences. Furthermore, considering their strategies of resistance as a practice of politics will enable academics to go beyond viewing poor Afro-descendant women simplistically only as voters. Afro-descendant social welfare beneficiary women differ from other similarly situated poor voters because they also engage in other forms of politics—the *politics of survival*.

APPENDIX

BOLSA FAMÍLIA, PURCHASING EXPERIENCES, AND POLITICS IN BRAZIL

The Interview code is the number of the interview, type of hair and skin color. (Example: 01CA9) This should be recorded after you record consent to conduct the interview). Interviewer should not show this sheet (skin color and hair type) to the participant.

Hair Types

    Wavy
    Natural
    Relaxed, Wig, Weave Braids
    Cornrows
    Locs

Skin Tones (1 lightest – 10 darkest)

Skin tones of the following people were used to indicate skin tones of participants.

1. Camila Pitanga
2. Colin Kaepernick
3. Neymar da Silva Santos Júnior
4. Barack Obama
5. Eryka Badu
6. Kerry Washington
7. Michelle Obama
8. Lazaro Ramos
9. Joaquim Barbosa
10. Edson Santos

SURVEY QUESTIONS

1. In which year did you become a Bolsa Família recipient?
2. How long have you been a recipient?
3. How much do you receive each month?
4. How has the Bolsa Família program helped your family?
5. Has it ever been difficult to pay bills and make ends meet? If so, what did you do?
6. What do you think the government can do to make sure people have enough food and basic needs?
7. Do you think the policies of the national government threaten Bolsa Família?
8. Which items did you already have before receiving Bolsa Família? (refrigerator, cellphone, computer, television, car)
9. Have you made purchases you were not able to make before the Bolsa Família program?

10. If you bought some of these items after receiving Bolsa Família, which items were they? Also, how many of these items do you have? (refrigerator, cellphone, computer, television, car, washing machine)

SHOPPING EXPERIENCES: NOW WE WILL TALK ABOUT SHOPPING EXPERIENCES

11. Which neighborhood do you live in?
12. How would you describe your neighborhood?
13. Where do you shop for food?
14. Are these stores in your neighborhood? Can you describe your experience in the supermarket?
15. Where did you purchase your refrigerator? Was it brand new or secondhand? Was the store in your neighborhood? If no, which neighborhood? How would you describe the neighborhood?
16. Where did you purchase your cellphone? Was it brand new or secondhand? Was the store in your neighborhood? If no, which neighborhood?
17. Where did you purchase your computer? Was it brand new or secondhand? Was the store in your neighborhood? If no, which neighborhood?
18. Where did you purchase your television? Was it brand new or secondhand? Was the store in your neighborhood? If no, which neighborhood?
19. Where did you purchase your car? Was it brand new or secondhand? Was the store in your neighborhood? If no, which neighborhood?
20. Where did you purchase your washing machine? Was it brand new or secondhand? Was the store in your neighborhood? If no, which neighborhood?

COMMUNITY INVOLVEMENT: NOW WE WILL DISCUSS COMMUNITY INVOLVEMENT

21. Are you involved in any community groups (local groups, church groups)? If so, how are you involved and which groups?

22. Are you involved in any groups or organizations at the local school? If so, how are you involved and which groups?

POLITICS: NOW WE WILL DISCUSS POLITICS

23. Where do you get information about politics?

24. What do you think about Brazilian democracy?

25. Can you name some political parties? If so, please name some.

26. Which political party do you most relate to? Why?

27. On a scale of 1 to 10 with 1 being not a lot of support and 10 being a lot of support, how much do you support the [party respondent named]?

28. Do you remember the 2014 elections where Dilma Rousseff and Aécio Neves ran for president? Who did you vote for?

29. What do you think about Dilma Rousseff?

30. Do you feel there is a political party that is more supportive of people like you? If so, which one and why?

31. Do you feel like Bolsa Família is supported more by one political party or political parties? If so, how so?

32. What do you think of the current president (Michel Temer)?

33. Do you think Bolsa Família is more supported by Michel Temer, or was it more supported by Ex-President Dilma Rousseff?

34. Why do think Bolsa Família is more supported by (_____)?

DISCRIMINATION: NOW WE WILL DISCUSS DISCRIMINATION BRIEFLY

35. Have you ever been treated badly based on the color of your skin? If so, can you describe any experiences?
36. Do you feel like you have been judged because you are a woman? If so, can you describe these experiences?
37. Have you ever felt discriminated against because of where you live? If so, can you describe these experiences?
38. Do you think people have judged you or treated you differently because you receive Bolsa Família? If so, how? If no, why not?
39. Thinking back to when you were a kid, do you think the economic situation of Blacks has changed?

Demographic Information

40. Do you have a religious preference? If so, what is it?
41. If it is a church, what denomination is it?
42. If so, how many times a month do you attend church?
43. What is your color?
44. Considering the Brazilian Institute of Geography and Statistics, which do you consider yourself? (Choose one) White, Black, Asian, Brown, Indigenous, Other_____
45. How old are you? _____
46. What is your gender?
47. Which city do you live in?
48. What is your marital status? Married, Single, Widow, Not married but live with partner

49. How many years did you study? (For example, if you finished high school, you studied twelve years. If you went to high school up to your sophomore year, that would be ten years.)

    1–3 years

    4–7 years

    8–10 years

    11–14 years

    15 or more years

50. What is your level of schooling?

    did not finish high school, graduated from high school, currently enrolled in a program to obtain a GED, currently enrolled in a community college, graduated from a community college, currently at a four-year college, graduated from a four-year college, enrolled in a master's program, enrolled in a doctoral program, completed a graduate program

51. Are you currently working? a. Yes   No

    b. If yes, what is your occupation? _____

    c. If no, what is your occupation?

    Student   Retired   Housewife   Unemployed

52. How many children do you have? _____

53. How old are they? _____

54. How many people live in your family?

INCOME

55. Considering your principal work with other income you receive, how much do you receive each month (not including Bolsa Família)?

Up to 1 minimum salary

Between 1 and 2 minimum salaries

Between 2 and 4 minimum salaries

More than 4 minimum salaries

No income

56. Considering the income of everyone that lives in your household, what is the approximate family income of your household in the past month?

Up to 1 minimum salary

Between 2 and 5 minimum salaries

Between 5 and 10 minimum salaries

Between 10 and 20 minimum salaries

No income

BOLSA FAMÍLIA, EXPERIÊNCIAS DE COMPRAS E POLÍTICA NO BRASIL (BOLSA FAMÍLIA, PURCHASING EXPERIENCES, AND POLITICS IN BRAZIL)

Essa página não deverá ser visualizada pela entrevistada, sendo restrita apenas a entrevistadora. Código de entrevistado (Numero de entrevista, tipo de cabelo, cor de pele). Deve gravar esse código depois de voce gravar a permissão de fazer a entrevista.) Exemplo: (Entrevista 01, L, 9).

Tipo de Cabelo

Cacheado

Crespo

Relaxado, Peruca, Mega Hair, Tranças

Cornrows

Locs

Skin Tones (1 lightest – 10 darkest)
Skin tones of the following people were used to indicate skin tones of participants.

11. Camila Pitanga
12. Colin Kaepernick
13. Neymar da Silva Santos Júnior
14. Barack Obama
15. Eryka Badu
16. Kerry Washington
17. Michelle Obama
18. Lazaro Ramos
19. Joaquim Barbosa
20. Edson Santos

PERGUNTAS DA PESQUISA

1. Em que ano você se tornou uma beneficiária da Bolsa Família?
2. Há quantos anos você recebe a Bolsa Família?
3. Quanto você recebe do Bolsa Família por mês?
4. De que forma o programa Bolsa Família ajudou sua família?
5. Já foi difícil pagar suas contas, mesmo recebendo essa bolsa? Se sim, como você fez?
6. O que você acha que o governo pode fazer para garantir comidas suficientes e necessidades básicas supridas?
7. Você acha que as atuais políticas do governo federal ameaçam o programa de Bolsa Família? E porque?
8. Quais itens você já possuía antes de receber o benefício do programa Bolsa Família? (Geladeira, celular, computador, televisão, carro)

9. Você já fez compras que não era capaz de fazer antes do programa Bolsa Família?

10. Quais e quantos se você comprou algum desses ítens depois de receber o benefício do programa a Bolsa Família, especifique quais eram esses itens e quantas você têm? (Geladeira, celular, computador, televisão, carro, lavadora de roupa) Por exemplo 2 celulares.

EXPERIÊNCIAS DE COMPRAS: AGORA VAMOS FALAR SOBRE EXPERIÊNCIAS DE COMPRAS

11. Em que bairro você mora?

12. Como você descreveria o seu bairro?

13. Onde você faz compras de comida? Você pode descrever suas experiências onde faz compras de comida?

14. Os supermercados ou mercados estão em seu bairro?

15. Onde você comprou a sua geladeira? A loja está no seu bairro? Se não, em qual bairro? Como você descreveria esse bairro? Esses itens foram comprados totalmente novos ou foram comprados de segunda mão? (Não pergunte o entrevistado se ela não tem)

16. Onde você comprou seu celular? A loja está no seu bairro? Se não, em qual bairro você descreveria esse bairro? Esses itens foram comprados totalmente novos ou foram comprados de segunda mão? (Não pergunte o entrevistado se ela não tem)

17. Onde você comprou seu computador? A loja está no seu bairro? Se não, em qual bairro você descreveria esse bairro? Esses ítens foram comprados totalmente novos ou foram comprados de segunda mão? (Não pergunte o entrevistado se ela não tem)

18. Onde você comprou sua televisão? A loja está no seu bairro? Se não, em qual bairro você descreveria esse bairro? Esses ítens

foram comprados totalmente novos ou foram comprados de segunda mão? (Não pergunte o entrevistado se ela não tem)

19. Onde você comprou seu carro? A loja está no seu bairro? Se não, em qual bairro você descreveria esse bairro? Esses ítens foram comprados totalmente novos ou foram comprados de segunda mão? (Não pergunte o entrevistado se ela não tem)

20. Onde você comprou sua lavadora? A loja esta no seu bairro? Se não, em qual bairro como você descreveria esse bairro? Esses ítens foram comprados totalmente novos ou foram comprados de segunda mão? (Não pergunte o entrevistado se ela não tem)

ENVOLVIMENTO NA COMUNIDADE: AGORA VAMOS DISCUTIR O ENVOLVIMENTO NA COMUNIDADE

21. Você está envolvida em algum grupo comunitário (grupos locais, grupos religiosos)? Se sim, como você está envolvido e quais grupos?

22. Você está envolvido em algum grupo ou organização na escola local? Se sim, como você está envolvido e quais grupos?

POLÍTICA AGORA VAMOS DISCUTIR POLÍTICA

23. Onde você recebe informações sobre política?

24. O que você acha da democracia Brasileira?

25. Você pode citar alguns partidos políticos?

26. Se sim, qual partido político você mais se relaciona? Por quê?

27. Em uma escala de 1 a 10, com 1 sendo discordo muito e 10 sendo se apoio muito, quanto você apoia o [partido político número 21]?

28. Você se lembra das eleições de 2014, nas quais Dilma Rousseff e Aécio Neves concorreram à presidência? Em quem você votou? Qual era o partido deles?

29. O que você acha da Dilma Rousseff?

30. Você acha que existe um partido político que apoia mais pessoas como você? Se sim, qual e por quê?

31. Você acha que o Programa Bolsa Família é mais apoiado por um partido político ou por partidos políticos? Se sim, como assim?

32. O que você acha do atual presidente (Michel Temer)?

33. Você acha que o Programa Bolsa Família é mais apoiado pelo Presidente Michel Temer ou que foi mais apoiado pela Ex-Presidenta Dilma Rousseff?

34. Porque você acha que o Bolsa Família é mais apoiado pelo/a (_____)

DISCRIMINAÇÃO: AGORA VAMOS DISCUTIR BREVEMENTE A DISCRIMINAÇÃO

35. Você já se sentiu discriminado por conta da cor da sua pele? Se sim, você pode descrever alguma experiência?

36. Você já se sentiu discriminado por conta de ser mulher? Se sim, você pode descrever essas experiências?

37. Você já se sentiu discriminado por conta de onde mora? Se sim, você pode descrever essas experiências?

38. Você acha que as pessoas que recebem o Bolsa Família são discriminadas? Se sim, como? Se não, porque não?

39. Você acha que a situação econômica dos negros mudou?

INFORMAÇÃO DEMOGRÁFICA

40. Você frequenta algum culto ou religião? Se sim, qual?
    Se sim, quantas vezes você frequenta a igreja por mês?

41. Se é uma igreja, que tipo (por exemplo, pentecostal, batista)?

42. Qual é a sua cor? _____

43. Dentro das categorias utilizadas pelo IBGE, como você se considera? (Escolha um) Branco Preto Amarelo Pardo Índio Outro_____

44. Qual é a sua idade? _____

45. Qual é o seu sexo. _____

46. Você mora em qual cidade? _____

47. Qual é o seu estado conjugal? Casada Solteira Viúva Não casado/a mas moro com namorada/o

48. Quantos anos você estudou?

    1 a 3 anos de estudo

    4 a 7 anos de estudo

    8 a 10 anos de estudo

    11 a 14 anos de estudo

    15 anos ou mais de estudo

49. Qual é seu nível de ensino?

    fundamental incompleto

    fundamental completo

    médio incompleto

    médio completo

    pré-vestibular

    superior incompleto

    superior completo

    mestrado

    doutorado

50. Você está trabalhando atualmente? a. Sim   Não

    b. Se sim, qual é a sua profissão? _____

    c. Se não, qual é a sua ocupação?

      Estudante   Aposentado   Dona de casa   Desempregado

51. Quantos filhos você tem? _____

52. Quais são as idades dos seus filhos? _____

53. Quantas pessoas moram na sua casa? _____

RENDA

54. Adicionando a renda do seu trabalho principal com outros tipos de renda, quanto você ganhou ao todo no mês passado? (não incluindo o beneficiário a Bolsa Família)

    Até 1 salário mínimo

    Entre 1 e 2 salários mínimos

    Entre 2 e 4 salários mínimos

    Mais de 4 salários mínimos

    Não teve renda

55. Adicionando a sua renda com as rendas de todas as pessoas que moram com você, quanto foi aproximadamente a renda familiar em sua casa no mês passado? (não incluindo o beneficiário a Bolsa Família)

    Até 2 salários mínimos

    Entre 2 e 5 salários mínimos

    Entre 5 e 10 salários mínimos

    Entre 10 e 20 salários mínimos

    Não teve renda

AFRICAN AMERICAN WOMEN SUPPLEMENTAL NUTRITION ASSISTANCE PROGRAM (SNAP), WOMEN, INFANTS, AND CHILDREN (WIC) FOOD AND NUTRITION SERVICE RECIPIENTS' PROGRAM OPINIONS, AND POLITICAL OPINIONS IN THE UNITED STATES

The Interview code is the number of the interview, type of hair and skin color (Example: 01CA9). This should be recorded after you record consent to conduct the interview. Interviewer should not show this sheet (skin color and hair type) to participant.

Hair Types

Wavy
Natural
Relaxed, Wig, Weave Braids
Cornrows
Locs

Skin Tones (1 lightest –10 darkest)

Skin tones of the following people were used to indicate skin tones of participants.

21. Camila Pitanga
22. Colin Kaepernick
23. Neymar da Silva Santos Júnior
24. Barack Obama
25. Eryka Badu
26. Kerry Washington
27. Michelle Obama
28. Lazaro Ramos
29. Joaquim Barbosa
30. Edson Santos

SURVEY QUESTIONS

The survey questions are broken into five different sections. First, we'll discuss the SNAP or WIC program,; second we'll discuss where you shop; third we'll discuss involvement in organizations; fourth we'll briefly discuss politics,; and last we'll discuss racial experiences. If you are uncomfortable answering any questions, we can skip that question. You can discontinue the interview at any time.

1. Do you receive SNAP or WIC benefits?
2. When did you start receiving SNAP or WIC benefits?
3. How long have you received them?
4. How much do you receive each month?
5. What do you think about SNAP or WIC?
6. Has it helped your family?
7. What do you think the government can do to make sure people have enough food and basic needs?
8. Has it ever been difficult to pay bills and make ends meet? If so, what did you do?
9. Do you think the policies of the national government threaten SNAP/WIC? (Research assistant: Refer to whichever program respondent mentions.)

SHOPPING EXPERIENCES: NOW WE WILL TALK ABOUT SHOPPING EXPERIENCES.

7. Which neighborhood do you live in?
8. How would you describe your neighborhood?
9. Where do you shop for food?
10. Are these stores in your neighborhood?

11. Which items do you own in the household and how many? (Add all items in the household not just yours. For example, if you, your husband, and your child each has a cellphone, there are three cellphones in the household.)

    Refrigerator _____, cellphone _____, computer _____, television _____, car _____
    washing machine_____

12. Where did you purchase your refrigerator? Was it brand new or secondhand? Was the store in your neighborhood? If no, which neighborhood? How was your experience in the store or shopping mall where you purchased your refrigerator? Did you feel welcome, and were sales associates friendly?

13. Where did you purchase your cellphone? Was it brand new or secondhand? Was the store in your neighborhood? If no, which neighborhood? How was your experience in the store or shopping mall where you purchased your cellphone? Did you feel welcome, and were sales associates friendly?

14. Where did you purchase your computer? Was it brand new or secondhand? How was your experience in the store or shopping mall where you purchased your computer? Did you feel welcome, and were sales associates friendly?

15. Where did you purchase your television? Was it brand new or secondhand? Was the store in your neighborhood? If no, which neighborhood? How was your experience in the store or shopping mall where you purchased your television? Did you feel welcome, and were sales associates friendly?

16. Where did you purchase your car? Was it brand new or secondhand? How was your experience in the store or shopping mall where you purchased your car? Did you feel welcome, and were sales associates friendly?

17. Where did you purchase your washing machine? Was it brand new or secondhand? Was the store in your neighborhood? If no, which neighborhood? Did you feel welcome, and were sales associates friendly?

COMMUNITY INVOLVEMENT: NOW WE WILL DISCUSS COMMUNITY INVOLVEMENT

18. Are you involved in any community groups (local groups, church groups)? If so, how are you involved and which groups?
19. Are you involved in any groups or organizations at the local school? If so, how are you involved and which groups?

POLITICS: NOW WE WILL DISCUSS POLITICS

20. Where do you get information about politics?
21. What do you think about American democracy?
22. Can you name some political parties? If so, please name some.
23. Which political party do you most relate to? Why?
24. On a scale of 1 to 10 with 1 being not a lot of support and 10 being a lot of support, how much do you support the [party respondent named]?
25. Do you remember the 2016 elections where Hillary Clinton and Donald Trump ran for president? Who did you vote for?
26. What do you think about Donald Trump?
27. Do you feel there is a political party that is more supportive of people like you? If so, which one and why?

28. Do you feel like SNAP/WIC is supported more by one political party or political parties? If so, how so?

29. Do you know what it means to be liberal or conservative? If so, please explain this.

30. On a 7-point scale where 1 is extremely liberal and 7 is extremely conservative, where would you place yourself?

   1. Extremely liberal
   2. Liberal
   3. Slightly liberal
   4. Moderate, middle
   5. Slightly conservative
   6. Conservative
   7. Extremely conservative

DISCRIMINATION: NOW WE WILL DISCUSS DISCRIMINATION BRIEFLY

31. Have you ever been treated badly based on the color of your skin? If so, can you describe any experiences?

32. Do you feel like you have been judged because you are a woman? If so, can you describe these experiences?

33. Have you ever felt discriminated against because of where you live? If so, can you describe these experiences?

34. Do you think people have judged you or treated you differently because you receive SNAP/WIC ? If so, how? If no, why not?

35. Thinking back to when you were a kid, do you think the economic situation of Blacks has changed?

Demographic Information

36. Do you have a religious preference? If so, what is it?

37. If it is a church, what denomination is it?

38. If so, how many times a month do you attend church?

39. What is your race or ethnicity?

40. How old are you?

41. What is your gender?

42. Which city do you live in?

43. What is your marital status?

- ◯ Married
- ◯ Single
- ◯ Widow
- ◯ Not married but live with partner

44. How many years did you study? (For example, if you finished high school, you studied twelve years. If you went to high school up to your sophomore year, that would be ten years.)

- ◯ 1–3 years
- ◯ 4–7 years
- ◯ 8–10 years
- ◯ 11–14 years
- ◯ 15 or more years

45. What is your level of schooling?

- ◯ did not finish high school
- ◯ graduated from high school
- ◯ currently enrolled in a program to obtain a GED
- ◯ currently enrolled in a community college
- ◯ graduated from a community college
- ◯ currently at a four-year college

○ graduated from a four-year college

○ enrolled in a master's program

○ enrolled in a doctoral program

○ completed a graduate program

46. Are you currently working? a. ○ Yes   ○ No

    b. If yes, what is your occupation? _____

    c. If no, what is your occupation?

    ○ Student   ○ Retired   ○ Housewife   ○ Unemployed

47. How many children do you have? _____

48. How old are they? _____

INCOME

49. Considering your principal work with other income you receive, how much is your monthly income (before taxes) (excluding SNAP/WIC)?

50. Considering the income of everyone that lives in your household, what is the approximate family income of your household in the past month?

51. What is the total number of people that live in the household?

NOTES

INTRODUCTION

1. Kia Caldwell, "'Look at Her Hair': The Body Politics of Black Womanhood in Brazil," *Transforming Anthropology* 11, no. 2 (2004): 18–29; Elizabeth Hordge-Freeman, *Color of Love: Racial Features, Stigmas, and Socialization in Brazilian Black Families* (Austin: University of Texas Press, 2015); Sheryl Felecia Means, "Bikuda: Hair, Aesthetic, and Bodily Perspectives from Women in Salvador, Bahia, Brazil," *African and Black Diaspora: An International Journal* 13, no. 3 (2020): 269–82.

2. USDA Food and Nutrition Service, "WIC-Racial Ethnic Group Enrollment Data 2016," 2016, https://www.fns.usda.gov/wic/wic-racial -ethnic-group-enrollment-data-2016.

3. Gangopadhyay, as cited in Mansfield and Rudra 2020, 212.

4. Center on Budget and Policy Priorities, "A Quick Guide to SNAP Eligibility and Benefits," October 4, 2020, https://www.cbpp.org/research /food-assistance/a-quick-guide-to-snap-eligibility-and-benefits.

5. USDA Food and Nutrition Service, "Characteristics of SNAP Households: FY 2018," August 31, 2020, https://www.fns.usda.gov/snap /characteristics-households-fy-2018.

6. USDA Food and Nutrition Service, "WIC Participant and Program Characteristics 2018 Food Packages and Costs Report," January 11, 2021, https://www.fns.usda.gov/wic/participant-program-characteristics -2018-food-packages-costs-report.

7. Kimberle Crenshaw, "Mapping the Margins: Intersectionality, Identity Politics, and Violence Against Women of Color," *Stanford Law Review* 43, no. 6 (1991): 1241–99; Ange-Marie Hancock, "Trayvon Martin, Intersectionality, and the Politics of Disgust," *Theory & Event* 15, no. 3 (2012). Project MUSE muse.jhu.edu/article/484428.

8. Joe Soss, Richard C. Fording, and Sanford F. Schram, *Disciplining the Poor: Neoliberal Paternalism and the Persistent Power of Race* (Chicago: University of Chicago Press, 2011), 5.

9. Eileen Patten, "Racial, Gender Wage Gaps Persist in U.S. Despite Some Progress," Pew Research Center, July 1, 2016, https://www.pewresearch.org/fact-tank/2016/07/01/racial-gender-wage-gaps-persist-in-u-s-despite-some-progress/.

10. Heloisa Mendonca, "Mulheres Negras Recebem Menos da Metade do Salário dos Homens Brancos no Brasil," *El Pais Brasil*, November 13, 2019, https://brasil.elpais.com/brasil/2019/11/12/politica/1573581512_623918.html.

11. Anna Carolina Papp, Bianca Lima, and Luiz Guilherme Gerbelli, "Na mesma Profissão, Homem Branco chega a Ganhar mais que o dobro que Mulher Negra, diz estudo," global.com G1, September 15, 2020, https://g1.globo.com/economia/concursos-e-emprego/noticia/2020/09/15/na-mesma-profissao-homem-branco-chega-a-ganhar-mais-que-o-dobro-da-mulher-negra-diz-estudo.ghtml.

12. Patricia Hill Collins, *Black Feminist Theory: Knowledge, Consciousness, and the Politics of Empowerment* (Abingdon, UK: Routledge, 1990).

13. Carl Degler, *Neither Black nor White: Slavery and Race Relations in Brazil and the United States* (New York: MacMillan, 1971); Thomas Skidmore, *Black Into White: Race and Nationality in Brazilian Thought* (New York: New York University Press, 1974); David Hellwig, *African American Reflections on Brazil's Racial Paradise* (Philadelphia: Temple University Press, 1992); Anthony Marx, *Making Race and Nation: A Comparison of South Africa, the United States, and Brazil* (Cambridge: Cambridge University Press, 1998); Reginald G. Daniel, *Race and Multiraciality in Brazil and the United States: Converging Paths?* (University Park: Pennsylvania State University Press, 2006); Michele Lamont, Graziella Moraes Silva, Jessica Welburn, Joshua Guetzkow, Nissim Mizrachi, Hanna Herzog, and Elis Reis, *Getting Respect: Responding to Stigma and Discrimination in the United States, Brazil, and Israel*

(Princeton, NJ: Princeton University Press, 2016); Joao Vargas, *The Denial of Anti-Blackness: Multiracial Redemption and Black Suffering* (Minneapolis: University of Minnesota Press, 2018); Chinyere Osuji, *Boundaries of Love: Interracial Marriage and the Meaning of Race* (New York: New York University Press, 2019); Jasmine Mitchell, *Imagining the Mulatta: Blackness in U.S. and Brazilian Media* (Urbana: University of Illinois Press, 2020).

14. Pedro Lima Coelho and Andrea Sales Soares de Azevedo Melo, "Impacto do Programa 'Bolsa Família' sobre a qualidade da dieta das famílias de Pernambuco no Brasil," *Ciência e Saúde Coletiva* 22, no. 2 (2017): 393–402, https://doi.org/10.1590/1413-81232017222.13622015; Mariana Cristina Silva Santos, Lucas Rocha Delatorre, Maria das Graças Braga Ceccato, and Palmira de Fátima Bonolo, "Programa Bolsa Família e indicadores educacionais em crianças, adolescentes e escolas no Brasil: Revisão sistemática," *Ciência e Saúde Coletiva* 24, no. 6 (2019): 2233–47, https://doi.org/10.1590/1413-81232018246.19582017; Elizabeth Racine, Ashley S. Vaughn, and Sarah Laditka, "Farmers' Market Use Among African-American Women Participating in the Special Supplemental Nutrition Program for Women, Infants, and Children," *Journal of the American Dietetic Association* 110, no. 3 (2010): 441–46.

15. Anne C. Beal, Karen Kuhlthau, and James Perrin, "Breastfeeding Advice Given to African American and White Women by Physicians and WIC Counselors," *Public Health Reports* 118, no. 4 (2003): 368–76, https://doi.org/10.1093/ohr/118.4.368; Holloway Sparks, "Queens, Teens, and Model Mothers," in *Race and the Politics of Welfare Reform*, ed. Sanford Schram, Joe Soss, and Richard Fording (Ann Arbor: University of Michigan Press, 2003), 171–95; Matthew Layton, "Welfare Stereotypes and Conditional Cash Transfer Programmes: Evidence from Brazil's Bolsa Família," *Journal of Politics in Latin America* 12, no. 1 (2020): 53–76, https://doi.org/10.1177/1866802X20914429; Stephanie M. Baran, "An Intersectional Analysis of the Role Race and Gender Play in Welfare Recipients' and Case Manager Experiences" (PhD diss., University of Wisconsin–Milwaukee, 2019).

16. Soss, Fording, and Schram, *Disciplining the Poor.*

17. Jamila Michener, *Fragmented Democracy: Medicaid, Federalism, and Unequal Politics* (Cambridge: Cambridge University Press, 2018).

18. Silvana Aparecida Mariano and Cassia Maria Carloto, "Aspectos Diferenciais da Inserção das Mulheres Negras no Programa Bolsa Família," *Sociedade e Estado* 28, no. 2 (August 2013): 393–417, http://www.scielo.br /scielo.php?script=sci_arttext&pid=S0102-69922013000200011&lng =en&nrm=iso.

19. Natasha Sugiyama and Wendy Hunter, *Transforming Subjects Into Citizens: Insights from Brazil's Bolsa Família* (Cambridge: Cambridge University Press, 2014).

20. Wendy Hunter and Natasha Sugiyama, "Transforming Subjects Into Citizens: Insights from Brazil's Bolsa Família," *Perspectives on Politics* 12, no. 4 (2014): 829–45.

21. Nathalia Carvalho Moreira, Marco Aurélio Marques Ferreira, Afonso Augusto Teixeira de Freitas Carvalho Lima, and Ivan Beck Ckagnazaroff, "Bolsa Família na percepção dos agentes dos Centros de Referência de Assistência Social," *Revista de Administração Pública* 46, no. 2 (2012): 403–23.

22. Hareli Cecchin and Temis Parente, "Relações de gênero no Acampamento Ilha Verde: Discutindo o (des) empoderamento das mulheres beneficiárias do Bolsa Família," *Interações* 20, no. 3 (2019): 907–21.

23. Mariano and Carloto, "Aspectos Diferenciais da Inserção das Mulheres Negras no Programa Bolsa Família."

24. David De Micheli, "The Racialized Effects of Social Programs in Brazil," *Latin American Politics and Society* 6, no. 1 (2018): 52–75, https:// doi.org/10.1017/lap.2017.6.

25. Tanya Hernandez, *Racial Subordination in Latin America: The Role of the State, Customary Law, and the New Civil Rights Response* (Cambridge: Cambridge University Press, 2012).

26. Gianna Melillo, "Racial Disparities Persist in Maternal Morbidity, Mortality and Infant Health," *American Journal of Managed Care*, June 13, 2020, https://www.ajmc.com/view/racial-disparities-persist-in -maternal-morbidity-mortality-and-infant-health.

27. Layton, "Welfare Stereotypes and Conditional Cash Transfer Programmes"; Baran, "An Intersectional Analysis of the Role Race and Gender Play in Welfare Recipients' and Case Manager Experiences"; Bridgette Baldwin, "Stratification of the Welfare Poor: Intersections of Gender, Race, and 'Worthiness' in Poverty Discourse and Policy," *Modern American* 6, no. 1 (Spring 2010): 4–14; Karen Seccombe, *So You*

Think I Drive a Cadillac?: Welfare Recipients' Perspectives on the System and Its Reform (Boston: Allyn and Bacon, 1999); Ange-Marie Hancock, *The Politics of Disgust: The Public Identity of the Welfare Queen* (New York: New York University Press, 2004); Martin Gilens, *Why Americans Hate Welfare: Race, Media, and the Politics of Antipoverty Policy* (Chicago: University of Chicago Press, 1999); Martin Gilens, "How the Poor Became Black: The Racialization of American Poverty in the Mass Media," in *Race and the Politics of Welfare Reform*, ed. Sanford Schram, Joe Soss, and Richard Fording (Ann Arbor: University of Michigan Press, 2003), 101–30; Sparks, "Queens, Teens, and Model Mothers"; Lucy Williams, "Race, Rat Bites and Unfit Mothers: How Media Disclosure Informs Welfare Legislation Debate," *Fordham Urban Law Journal* 22, no. 4 (1995): 1159–96.

28. Layton, "Welfare Stereotypes and Conditional Cash Transfer Programmes."

29. Beal, Kuhlthau, and Perrin, "Breastfeeding Advice Given to African American and White Women by Physicians and WIC Counselors."

30. Baran, "An Intersectional Analysis of the Role Race and Gender Play in Welfare Recipients' and Case Manager Experiences."

31. Hancock, *The Politics of Disgust.*

32. Williams, "Race, Rat Bites and Unfit Mothers"; Gilens, *Why Americans Hate Welfare*; Gilens, "How the Poor Became Black"; Rosalee Clawson and Rakuya Trice, "Poverty as We Know It: Media Portrayals of the Poor," *Public Opinion Quarterly* 64, no. 1 (2000): 53–64.

33. Gilens, "How the Poor Became Black," 102.

34. Sparks, "Queens, Teens, and Model Mothers."

35. Katherine Tate, *Black Faces in the Mirror: African Americans and Their Representatives in the U.S. Congress* (Princeton, NJ: Princeton University Press, 2003); Michael Dawson, *Behind the Mule: Race and Class in African American Politics* (Princeton, NJ: Princeton University Press, 1994).

36. Chryl Laird and Ismail White, *Steadfast Democrats: How Social Forces Shape Black Political Behavior* (Princeton, NJ: Princeton University Press, 2020).

37. Ana Lucia E. F. Valente, *Politica e Relacoes Raciais: Os Negros e As Eleicoes Paulistas de 1982* (São Paulo: FFLCH-US, 1986); Amaury de Souza, "Raça e Política no Brasil Urbano," *Revista de Administração de Empresas* 11, no. 4 (1971): 61–70.

38. Glaucio Ary Dillon Soares and Nelson do Valle Silva, "Urbanization, Race, and Class in Brazilian Politics," *Latin American Research Review* 22, no. 2 (1987): 155–76.

39. Gladys Mitchell-Walthour, *The Politics of Blackness: Racial Identity and Political Behavior in Contemporary Brazil* (Cambridge: Cambridge University Press, 2018).

40. Gabriela Caesar, "Haddad Ganha no Nordeste: e Bolsonaro, nas Demais regiões do País Maiores Diferenças Entre os Votos dos Candidatos Foram Registradas no Nordeste e no Sul," Globo.com G1, October 29, 2018, https://g1.globo.com/politica/eleicoes/2018/eleicao-em-numeros/noticia/2018/10/29/haddad-ganha-no-nordeste-e-bolsonaro-nas-demais-regioes-do-pais.ghtml.

41. Simone Bohn, "The Electoral Behavior of the Poor in Brazil: A Research Agenda," *Latin American Research Review* 48, no. 2 (2013): 25–31.

42. Natasha Sugiyama and Wendy Hunter, "Whither Clientelism? Good Governance and Brazil's Bolsa Familia Program," *Comparative Politics* 46, no. 1 (2013): 43–62; Brian Fried, "Distributive Politics and Conditional Cash Transfers: The Case of Brazil's Bolsa Familia," *World Development* 40, no. 5 (2012): 1042–53.

43. Cesar Zucco and Timothy Power, "Bolsa Família and the Shift in Lula's Electoral Base, 2002–2006," *Latin American Research Review* 48, no. 2 (2013): 3–24.

44. Diego Sanches Corrêa, "Conditional Cash Transfer Programs, the Economy, and Presidential Elections in Latin America," *Latin American Research Review* 50, no. 2 (2015): 63–85.

45. Gladys Mitchell-Walthour, "Intersectionality, Discrimination, and Presidential Approval: An Intersectional Analysis of Bolsa Família Recipients' Presidential Satisfaction of Dilma Rousseff and Political Trust," *National Political Science Review* 20, no. 1 (2019): 73–90.

46. Claudia Pons Cardoso, "Feminisms from the Perspective of Afro-Brazilian Women," trans. Miriam Adelman, *Meridians* 14, no. 1 (2016): 1–29; Lelia Gonzalez, "For an Afro-Latin American Feminism," in *Confronting the Crisis in Latin America: Women Organizing for Change*, Isis International: Development Alternatives with Women for a New Era (Santiago, Chile: Isis International, 1988), 95–101.

47. Nikol Alexander-Floyd, "Disappearing Acts: Reclaiming Intersectionality in the Social Sciences in a Post–Black Feminist Era," *Feminist Formations* 24, no. 1 (Spring 2012): 1–25; Collins, *Black Feminist Theory*.

48. Christen Smith, Archie Davies, and Bethania Gomes, "In Front of the World: Translating Beatriz Nascimento," *Antipode* 53, no. 1 (2021): 279–316; Djamila Ribeiro, *Quem Tem Medo do Feminismo Negro?* (São Paulo, Brazil: Companhia das Letras, 2018); Collins, *Black Feminist Theory*; Gonzalez, "For an Afro-Latin American Feminism"; Evelyn Simien, "Doing Intersectionality Research: From Conceptual Issues to Practical Examples," *Politics and Gender* 3, no. 2 (2007): 36–43; Julia Jordan-Zachery, "I Ain't Your Darn Help: Black Women as the Help in Intersectionality Research in Political Science," *National Political Science Review* 16 (2014): 19–30; Jaira Harrington, "A Place of Their Own: Black Feminist Leadership and Economic and Educational Justice in São Paulo and Rio de Janeiro, Brazil," *Latin American Caribbean and Ethnic Studies* 10, no. 3 (2015): 271–87.

49. Collins, *Black Feminist Theory*; Brittney Cooper, *Beyond Respectability: The Intellectual Thought of Race Women* (Chicago: University of Illinois Press, 2017); Mikki Kendall, *Hood Feminism: Notes from the Women That a Movement Forgot* (New York: Penguin Random House, 2020).

50. Cardoso, "Feminisms from the Perspective of Afro-Brazilian Women."

51. Cardoso, "Feminisms from the Perspective of Afro-Brazilian Women," 4.

52. Gonzalez, "For an Afro-Latin American Feminism."

53. Alexander-Floyd, "Disappearing Acts"; Jordan-Zachery, "I Ain't Your Darn Help"; Simien, "Doing Intersectionality Research."

54. Luiza Bairros and Sonia E. Alvarez, "Feminisms and Anti-Racism: Intersections and Challenges. An Interview with Luiza Bairros, Minister, Brazilian Secretariat of Public Policies for the Promotion of Racial Equality (SEPPIR), 2011–2014," trans. Miriam Adelman, *Meridians* 14, no. 1 (2016): 50–69.

55. Antonio José Bacelar da Silva, *Between Brown and Black: Anti-Racist Activism in Brazil* (New Brunswick, NJ: Rutgers University Press, 2022).

56. Kendall, *Hood Feminism*, 42–43.

57. Jaime Alves, *The Anti-Black City: Police Terror and Urban Life in Brazil* (Minneapolis: University of Minnesota Press, 2018).

58. Margaret Hunter finds evidence that lighter-skinned African American women fare better on sociodemographic factors such as marriage, employment, and education than their darker-skinned counterparts. See Margaret Hunter, "Colorstruck: Skin Color Stratification in the Lives of African American Women," *Sociological Inquiry* 68, no. 4 (1998): 517–35. Hamilton, Goldsmith, and Darity also find that lighter-skinned Black women are more preferred for marriage than darker-skinned Black women. See Darrick Hamilton, Arthur H. Goldsmith, and William Darity Jr., "Shedding 'Light' on Marriage: The Influence of Skin Shade on Marriage for Black Females," *Journal of Economic Behavior and Organization* 72, no. 1 (2009): 30–50. Diette, Goldsmith, Hamilton, and Darity also find that rates of depression due to unemployment are greater for dark-skinned Black women than lighter-skinned Black women. See Timothy M. Diette, Arthur H. Goldsmith, Darrick Hamilton, and William Darity Jr., "Skin Shade Stratification and the Psychological Cost of Unemployment: Is There a Gradient for Black Females?," *Review of Black Political Economy* 42, no. 1–2 (2009): 155–77.

59. Flávia Rios, "O que o colorismo diz sobre as relações raciais brasileiras? 28/ Outubro," Portal Geledes, https://www.geledes.org.br/o-que-o-colorismo-diz-sobre-as-relacoes-raciais-brasileiras/?amp=1, 2019.

60. Mitchell, "Imagining the Mulatta."

61. Lamont et al., *Getting Respect*; Angela Figueiredo, "Out of Place: The Experience of the Black Middle Class," in *Brazil's New Racial Politics*, ed. B. Reiter and Gladys Mitchell (Boulder, CO: Lynn Reiner, 2010), 51–63; Karyn Lacy, *Blue-Chip Black: Race, Class, and Status in the New Black Middle Class* (Berkeley: University of California Press, 2007); Adia Wingfield, *No More Invisible Man: Race and Gender in Men's Work* (Philadelphia: Temple University Press, 2013).

62. Jazmin L. Brown-Iannuzzi, Ron Dotsch, Erin Cooley, and B. Keith Payne, "The Relationship Between Mental Representations of Welfare Recipients and Attitudes Toward Welfare," *Psychological Science* 28, no. 1 (2017): 92–103, and Ryan F. Lei and Galen V. Bodenhausen, "Racial Assumptions Color the Mental Representation of Social Class," *Frontiers in Psychology* 8 (2017): 519. doi: 10.3389/fpsyg.2017.00519, PMID: 28424651.

63. Mark Paul, Sarah Gaither, and William Darity, "About Face: Seeing Class and Race," *Journal of Economic Issues* 56, no. 1 (2022): 1–17.

64. Alana Semuels, "Chicago's Awful Divide," *Atlantic*, March 28, 2018, https://www.theatlantic.com/business/archive/2018/03/chicago -segregation-poverty/556649/.

65. Tim Henderson, "Where Black Homeownership Is the Norm," Pew Trust, August 15, 2018, https://www.pewtrusts.org/en/research-and-analysis /blogs/stateline/2018/08/15/where-black-homeownership-is-the-norm.

66. Michael Rosen, "The Rise and Fall of Black Milwaukee's Blue Collar Middle Class with Sheila Cochran and Dr. Michael Rosen," University of Wisconsin–Milwaukee African and African Diaspora Studies Department Series, 2021, https://m.facebook.com/UWMAADS /videos/the-rise-and-fall-of-black-milwaukees-blue-collar-middle -class-with-sheila-cochr/485887322402824/?locale=pa_IN&_rdr.

67. Marc V. Levine, "The State of Black Milwaukee in National Perspective: Racial Inequality in the Nation's 50 Largest Metropolitan Areas. In 65 Charts and Tables," Center for Economic Development, July 20, 2020, https://dc.uwm.edu/ced_pubs/56.

68. Levine, "The State of Black Milwaukee in National Perspective."

69. Noah Smith, "Why Charlotte and Raleigh Work for Black Residents," *Pocono Record*, April 1, 2018, https://www.poconorecord.com/story /opinion/2018/04/02/why-charlotte-raleigh-work-for/12847906007/.

70. Derek Pardue, *Brazilian Hip-Hoppers Speak from the Margin: We's on Tape* (London: Palgrave Macmillan, 2011).

71. Means, "Bikuda: Hair, Aesthetic, and Bodily Perspectives from Women in Salvador, Bahia, Brazil."

72. Keisha-Khan Perry, *Black Women Against the Land Grab: The Fight for Racial Justice in Brazil* (Minneapolis: University of Minnesota Press, 2013).

73. Gladys Mitchell-Walthour, *The Politics of Blackness: Racial Identity and Political Behavior in Contemporary Brazil* (Cambridge: Cambridge University Press, 2018); Lauren Davenport, *Politics Beyond Black and White: Biracial Identity and Attitudes in America* (Cambridge: Cambridge University Press, 2018).

74. Lee Sigelman, Steven Tuch, and Jack Martin, "What's in a Name? Preference for 'Black' versus 'African-American' Among Americans of African Descent," *Public Opinion Quarterly* 69, no. 3 (2005): 429–38.

75. Candis Watts Smith, *Black Mosaic: The Politics of Black Pan-Ethnic Diversity* (New York: New York University Press, 2014).

76. Davenport, *Politics Beyond Black and White*.

77. Jill Viglione, Lance Hannon, and Robert DeFina, "The Impact of Light Skin on Prison Time for Black Female Offenders," *Social Science Journal* 48, no. 1 (2011): 250–58.

78. Jamila Blake, Bettie Butler, Chance Lewis, and Alicia Darensbourg, "Unmasking the Inequitable Discipline Experiences of Urban Black Girls: Implications for Urban Educational Stakeholders," *Urban Review* 43, no. 1 (2011): 90–106.

79. Zucco and Power, "Bolsa Família and the Shift in Lula's Electoral Base, 2002–2006."

80. Corrêa, "Conditional Cash Transfer Programs, the Economy, and Presidential Elections in Latin America."

81. Layton, "Welfare Stereotypes and Conditional Cash Transfer Programmes."

82. Hancock, *The Politics of Disgust*.

1. THE POLITICS OF SURVIVAL

1. Patricia Hill Collins, *Black Feminist Theory: Knowledge, Consciousness, and the Politics of Empowerment* (Abingdon, UK: Routledge, 1990), 140.

2. Nikol Alexander-Floyd, "Disappearing Acts: Reclaiming Intersectionality in the Social Sciences in a Post–Black Feminist Era," *Feminist Formations* 24, no. 1 (Spring 2012): 1–25.

3. Cláudia Pons Cardoso, "'Amefricanizing' the Feminism: The Thought of Lélia Gonzalez," Debate Colonialidade do Gênero e Feminismos Descoloniais, *Revista Estudos Feministas* 22, no. 3 (November 28, 2014), https://doi.org/10.1590/S0104-026X2014000300015.

4. Carolina Maria Jesus, *Quarto de Despejo: Diário de Uma Favelada* (São Paulo, Brazil: Ática, 1960); Conceição Evaristo, *Becos Da Memoria* (Rio de Janeiro, Brazil: Pallas, 2017); Toni Morrison, *The Bluest Eye* (New York: Vintage International, 1970); Alice Walker, *The Color Purple: A Walker* (New York: Penguin, 2019).

5. Cristiane Sobral, "Não vou Mais Lavar os Pratos," *Cadernos Negros: Poemas Afro-Brasileiros* (vol. 23), São Paulo, Brazil: Quilombhoje, 2000.

6. Djamila Ribeiro, *Quem Tem Medo do Feminismo Negro?* (São Paulo, Brazil: Companhia das Letras, 2018).

7. Christen Smith, Archie Davies, and Bethania Gomes, "In Front of the World: Translating Beatriz Nascimento," *Antipode* 53, no. 1 (2021): 279–316; Keisha-Khan Perry, *Black Women Against the Land Grab: The Fight for Racial Justice in Brazil* (Minneapolis: University of Minnesota Press, 2013); Kia Caldwell, *Negras in Brazil: Re-envisioning Black Women, Citizenship, and the Politics of Identity* (New Brunswick, NJ: Rutgers University Press, 2006).

8. Tafnes Martins, Tiago Jessé Souza de Lima, and Walberto Silva Santos, "O efeito das Microagressões Raciais de Gênero na Saúde Mental De Mulheres Negras," *Ciência & Saúde Coletiva* 25, no. 7 (2020): 2793–2802, https://doi.org/10.1590/1413-81232020257.29182018.

9. Cheryl Woods-Giscombe, "Superwoman Schema: African American Women's Views on Stress, Strength, and Health," *Qualitative Health Research* 20, no. 5 (May 2010): 668–83, https://doi.org/10.1177/104973 2310361892.

10. Karen Seccombe, *So You Think I Drive a Cadillac?: Welfare Recipients' Perspectives on the System and Its Reform* (Boston: Allyn and Bacon, 1999).

11. Nikol Alexander-Floyd, *Re-Imagining Black Women: A Critique of Post-Feminist and Post-Racial Melodrama in Culture and Politics* (New York: New York University Press, 2021).

12. Jaime Alves, *The Anti-Black City: Police Terror and Urban Life in Brazil* (Minneapolis: University of Minnesota Press, 2018).

13. Darrick Hamilton, Arthur H. Goldsmith, and William Darity Jr., "Shedding 'Light' on Marriage: The Influence of Skin Shade on Marriage for Black Females," *Journal of Economic Behavior and Organization* 72, no. 1 (2009): 30–50.

2. SUPPORT OF SOCIAL WELFARE PROGRAMS, STIGMA, AND RESISTANCE

1. Matthew Layton, "Welfare Stereotypes and Conditional Cash Transfer Programmes: Evidence from Brazil's Bolsa Família," *Journal of Politics in Latin America* 12, no. 1 (2020): 53–76, https://doi.org/10.1177 /1866802X20914429; Ange-Marie Hancock, *The Politics of Disgust: The Public Identity of the Welfare Queen* (New York: New York University Press, 2004).

2. Wendy Hunter and Natasha Sugiyama, "Transforming Subjects Into Citizens: Insights from Brazil's Bolsa Família," *Perspectives on Politics* 12, no. 4 (2014): 829–45.

3. Suzanne Mettler and Jeffrey Stonecash, "Government Program Usage and Political Voice," *Social Science Quarterly* 89, no. 2 (2008): 273–93.

4. Joe Soss, Richard C. Fording, and Sanford F. Schram, *Disciplining the Poor: Neoliberal Paternalism and the Persistent Power of Race* (Chicago: University of Chicago Press, 2011); Wendy Hunter, Leila Patel, and Natasha Borges Sugiyama, "How Family and Child Cash Transfers Can Empower Women: Comparative Lessons from Brazil and South Africa," *Global Social Policy* 21, no. 2 (2021): 258–77.

5. Hunter and Sugiyama, "Transforming Subjects Into Citizens."

6. Cesar Zucco and Timothy Power, "Bolsa Família and the Shift in Lula's Electoral Base, 2002–2006," *Latin American Research Review* 48, no. 2 (2013): 3–24.

7. Diego Sanches Corrêa, "Conditional Cash Transfer Programs, the Economy, and Presidential Elections in Latin America," *Latin American Research Review* 50, no. 2 (2015): 63–85.

8. Hancock, *The Politics of Disgust*.

9. Harold R. Kerbo, "Stigma of Welfare and a Passive Poor," *Sociology and Social Research* 60, no. 2 (1972): 175–87.

10. Ann Nichols-Casebolt, "The Psychological Effects of Income Testing Income-Support Benefits," *Social Service Review* 60, no. 2 (1986): 287–302.

11. Karen Seccombe, *So You Think I Drive a Cadillac?: Welfare Recipients' Perspectives on the System and Its Reform* (Boston: Allyn and Bacon, 1999).

12. Robin L. Jarrett, "Welfare Stigma Among Low-Income African American Single Mothers," *Family Relations* 45, no. 4 (1996): 368–74.

13. Tracy Loveless, "Supplemental Nutrition Assistance Program (SNAP) Receipt for Households: 2018," American Community Survey Briefs, 2020, https://www.census.gov/content/dam/Census/library/publications/2020/demo/acsbr20-01.pdf.

14. Patricia Hill Collins, *Black Feminist Theory: Knowledge, Consciousness, and the Politics of Empowerment* (Abington, UK: Routledge, 1990), 133.

15. Juanita Chinn, Iman K. Martin, and Nicole Redmond, "Health Equity Among Black Women in the United States," *Journal of Women's Health* 30, no. 2 (February 2021): 212–19.

16. USDA Food and Nutrition Service, "Farmers' Markets Accepting SNAP Benefits," May 2021, https://www.fns.usda.gov/snap/farmers-markets-accepting-snap-benefits.

17. William Darity Jr., Darrick Hamilton, Mark Paul, Alan Aja, Anne Price, Antonio Moore, and Caterina Chiopris, "What We Get Wrong About Closing the Racial Wealth Gap," Samuel DuBois Cook Center on Social Equity, April 2018, https://socialequity.duke.edu/wp-content/uploads/2019/10/what-we-get-wrong.pdf.

18. Darrick Hamilton and Ngina Chiteji, "Wealth," in *International Encyclopedia of Race and Racism*, 2nd ed., ed. Patrick Mason (New York: Macmillan Reference, 2013); Maury Gittleman and Edward N. Wolff, "Racial Differences in Patterns of Wealth Accumulation," *Journal of Human Resources* 39, no. 1 (Winter 2004): 193–227.

19. Daniel Silvera, "63,7% dos Desempregados no Brasil são Pretos ou Pardos, Aponta IBGE," November 17, 2017, https://g1.globo.com/economia/noticia/637-dos-desempregados-no-brasil-sao-pretos-ou-pardos-aponta-ibge.ghtml.

20. Hunter and Sugiyama, "Transforming Subjects Into Citizens."

21. Collins, *Black Feminist Theory*.

22. Martin Luther King Jr., "The Other America," Grosse Pointe Historical Society, March 14, 1968, http://www.gphistorical.org/mlk/index.htm.

23. Marc V. Levine, "The State of Black Milwaukee in National Perspective: Racial Inequality in the Nation's 50 Largest Metropolitan Areas. In 65 Charts and Tables." Center for Economic Development, July 20, 2020, https://dc.uwm.edu/ced_pubs/56.

24. Levine, "The State of Black Milwaukee in National Perspective," 29.

25. Levine, "The State of Black Milwaukee in National Perspective," 29.

26. Hunter, Patel, and Sugiyama, "How Family and Child Cash Transfers Can Empower Women"; Silvana Aparecida Mariano and Cassia Maria Carloto, "Aspectos Diferenciais da Inserção das Mulheres Negras no Programa Bolsa Família," *Sociedade e Estado* 28, no. 2 (August 2013): 393–417, https://doi.org/10.1590/S0102-69922013000200011.

27. Darity et al., "What We Get Wrong About Closing the Racial Wealth Gap."

28. Marcelo Paixão and Luiz M. Carvano, *Relatório Anual das Desigual-dades Raciais no Brasil: 2007–2008* (Rio de Janeiro, Brazil: Garamond, 2008).
29. Seccombe, "So You Think I Drive a Cadillac?," 61.
30. Levine, "The State of Black Milwaukee in National Perspective"; Mary Patillo-McCoy, *Black Picket Fences* (Chicago: University of Chicago Press, 1999).
31. Chris M. Herbst and Joanna Lucio, "Happy in the Hood? The Impact of Residential Segregation on Self-Reported Happiness," *Journal of Regional Science* 56, no. 3 (2016): 494–52.
32. Claudia Pons Cardoso, "Feminisms from the Perspective of Afro-Brazilian Women," trans. Miriam Adelman, *Meridians* 14, no. 1 (2016): 1–29.

3. PERCEPTIONS OF CLASS, SKIN COLOR, AND GENDER DISCRIMINATION

1. Karen Seccombe, *So You Think I Drive a Cadillac?: Welfare Recipients' Perspectives on the System and Its Reform* (Boston: Allyn and Bacon, 1999).
2. Matthew O. Hunt, Lauren A. Wise, Marie-Claude Jipguep, Yvette C. Cozier, and Lynn Rosenberg, "Neighborhood Racial Composition and Perceptions of Racial Discrimination: Evidence from the Black Women's Health Study," *Social Psychology Quarterly* 70, no. 3 (2007): 272–89.
3. Kimberle Crenshaw, "Mapping the Margins: Intersectionality, Identity Politics, and Violence Against Women of Color," *Stanford Law Review* 43, no. 6 (July 1991):1241–99.
4. Catherine E. Harnois, "Are Perceptions of Discrimination Unidimensional, Oppositional, or Intersectional? Examining the Relationship Among Perceived Racial–Ethnic-, Gender-, and Age-Based Discrimination," *Sociological Perspectives* 57, no. 4 (2014): 470–87.
5. Matthew Layton and Amy Smith, "Is It Race, Class, or Gender? The Sources of Perceived Discrimination in Brazil," *Latin American Politics and Society* 59, no. 1 (2017): 52–73.
6. Kira Banks, Laura P. Kohn-Wood, and Michael Spencer, "An Examination of the African American Experience of Everyday Discrimination

and Symptoms of Psychological Distress," *Community Mental Health Journal* 42, no. 6 (2006): 555–70.

7. Cathy Cohen, *The Boundaries of Blackness: AIDS and the Breakdown of Black Politics* (Chicago: University of Chicago Press, 1999).

8. William Darity Jr., Darrick Hamilton, Mark Paul, Alan Aja, Anne Price, Antonio Moore, and Caterina Chiopris, "What We Get Wrong About Closing the Racial Wealth Gap," Samuel DuBois Cook Center on Social Equity, April 2018, https://socialequity.duke.edu/wp-content/uploads/2019/10/what-we-get-wrong.pdf.

9. Layton and Smith, "Is It Race, Class, or Gender?"; Timothy M. Diette, Arthur H. Goldsmith, Darrick Hamilton, and William Darity Jr., "Skin Shade Stratification and the Psychological Cost of Unemployment: Is There a Gradient for Black Females?," *Review of Black Political Economy* 42, no. 1–2 (2009): 155–77.

10. Edward Telles, *Pigmentocracies: Ethnicity, Race, and Color in Latin America* (Chapel Hill: University of North Carolina Press, 2014).

11. Adia Wingfield, *No More Invisible Man: Race and Gender in Men's Work* (Philadelphia: Temple University Press, 2013).

12. Devah Pager, Bruce Western, and Bart Bonikowski, "Discrimination in a Low Wage Labor Market: A Field Experiment," *American Sociological Review* 74, no. 5 (2009): 777–99; Devah Pager, "Identifying Discrimination at Work: The Use of Field Experiments," *Journal of Social Issues* 68, no. 2 (2012): 221–27; William Darity Jr., "Employment Discrimination, Segregation, and Health," *American Journal of Public Health* 93, no. 2 (2003): 226–31; Elizabeth Higgenbotham and Lynn Weber, "Perceptions of Workplace Discrimination Among Black and White Professional-Managerial Women," in *Latinas and African American Women at Work: Race, Gender, and Economic Inequality*, ed. Irene Browne (New York: Russell Sage Foundation, 1999), 327–53.

13. Chinyere Osuji, *Boundaries of Love: Interracial Marriage and the Meaning of Race* (New York: New York University Press, 2019); Elizabeth Hordge-Freeman, *Color of Love: Racial Features, Stigmas, and Socialization in Brazilian Black Families* (Austin: University of Texas Press, 2015); Marcos Rangel, "Is Parental Love Colorblind? Human Capital Accumulation Within Mixed Families," *Review of Black Political Economy* 42, no. 1–2 (2015): 57–86; Robin Sheriff, *Dreaming Equality: Color, Race, and Racism in Urban Brazil* (New Brunswick, NJ: Rutgers University Press, 2001).

14. Darity, "Employment Discrimination, Segregation, and Health"; Fernando Mendes Massignam, João Luiz Dornelles Bastos, and Fúlvio Borges Nedel, "Discriminação e saúde: Um problema de Acesso," *Epidemiologia e Serviços de Saúde* 24, no. 3 (2015): 541–44.

15. Michele Lamont, Graziella Moraes Silva, Jessica Welburn, Joshua Guetzkow, Nissim Mizrachi, Hanna Herzog, and Elis Reis, *Getting Respect: Responding to Stigma and Discrimination in the United States, Brazil, and Israel* (Princeton, NJ: Princeton University Press, 2016).

16. Angela Figureido, "Out of Place: The Experience of the Black Middle Class," in *Brazil's New Racial Politics*, ed. B. Reiter and Gladys Mitchell (Boulder, CO: Lynne Reiner, 2010), 51–63.

17. Nolan Kopkin and Gladys Mitchell-Walthour, "Color Discrimination, Occupational Prestige, and Skin Color in Brazil," *Latin American & Caribbean Ethnic Studies* 15, no. 1 (2020): 44–69.

18. Wingfield, *No More Invisible Man.*

19. Figureido, "Out of Place"; Graziella Silva and Elisa Reis, "Perceptions of Racial Discrimination Among Black Professionals in Rio de Janeiro," *Latin American Research Review* 46, no. 2 (2011): 55–78.

20. Lamont et al., *Getting Respect.*

21. Jennifer Roth-Gordon, *Race and the Brazilian Body: Blackness, Whiteness, and Everyday Language in Rio de Janeiro* (Oakland: University of California Press, 2016); Sheriff, *Dreaming Equality.*

22. Ellis Monk, "The Consequences of 'Race and Color' in Brazil," *Social Problems* 43, no. 3 (2016): 413–30.

23. Graziella Silva and Marcelo Paixão, "Mixed and Unequal: New Perspectives on Brazilian Ethnoracial Relations," in *Pigmentocracies: Ethnicity, Race, and Color in Latin America*, ed. Edward Telles (Chapel Hill: University of North Carolina Press, 2014), 172–217.

24. Jaira Harrington, "A Place of Their Own: Black Feminist Leadership and Economic and Educational Justice in São Paulo and Rio de Janeiro, Brazil," *Latin American Caribbean and Ethnic Studies* 10, no. 3 (2015): 271–87; Cecilia McCallum, "Racialized Bodies, Naturalized Classes: Moving Through the City of Salvador da Bahia," *American Ethnologist* 32, no. 1 (2005): 100–17; Sheriff, *Dreaming Equality.*

25. Arthur H. Goldsmith, Darrick Hamilton, and William Darity, "Shades of Discrimination: Skin Tone and Wages," *American Economic Review* 96, no. 2 (2006): 242–45.

26. Dawn Szymanski and Destin Stewart, "Racism and Sexism as Correlates of African American Women's Psychological Distress," *Sex Roles* 63, no. 3–4 (2010): 226–38.

27. Layton and Smith, "Is It Race, Class, or Gender?"

28. Wisconsin Department of Health Services, "African Americans in Wisconsin: An Overview," 2018, https://www.dhs.wisconsin.gov /minority-health/population/afriamer-pop.htm.

29. Amanda Y. Agan and Sonja B. Starr, "Employer Neighborhoods and Racial Discrimination," NBER Working Paper 28153, November 2020, https://www.nber.org/system/files/working_papers/w28153/w28153.pdf.

30. Layton and Smith, "Is It Race, Class, or Gender?"

31. Harnois, "Are Perceptions of Discrimination Unidimensional, Oppositional, or Intersectional?"

4. ARE POOR BLACK WOMEN TO BLAME FOR CONSERVATIVE POLITICIANS? SOCIAL WELFARE BENEFICIARIES' POLITICAL KNOWLEDGE, VOTING PREFERENCES, AND RELIGION

1. Elizabeth Dias, "How Evangelicals Helped Donald Trump Win," *Time*, November 9, 2016, https://www.google.com/amp/s/time.com/4565010 /donald-trump-evangelicals-win/%3famp=true; Trip Gabriel, "Donald Trump, Despite Impieties, Wins Hearts of Evangelical Voters," *New York Times*, February 26, 2016, https://www.google.com/amp/s/www .nytimes.com/2016/02/28/us/politics/donald-trump-despite-impieties -wins-hearts-of-evangelical-voters.amp.html; Philip Bump, "A Third of Trump's Support in 2016 Came from Evangelicals—And He Hasn't Lost Them Yet," *Washington Post*, June 5, 2020, https://www .washingtonpost.com/politics/2020/06/05/third-trumps-support -2016-came-evangelicals-and-he-hasnt-lost-them-yet/.

2. Ronaldo de Almeida, "The Broken Wave: Evangelicals and Conservatism in the Brazilian Crisis," *Journal of Ethnographic Theory* 10, no. 1 (2020): 32–40; Oswaldo Amaral, "The Victory of Jair Bolsonaro According to the Brazilian Electoral Study of 2018," *Brazilian Political Science Review* 14, no. 1 (2020):1–13, https://doi.org/10.1590/1981 -3821202000010004; Matthew Layton, "Welfare Stereotypes and

Conditional Cash Transfer Programmes: Evidence from Brazil's Bolsa Família," *Journal of Politics in Latin America* 12, no. 1 (2020): 53–76, https://doi.org/10.1177/1866802X20914429; Dante Scala, "Polls and Elections: The Skeptical Faithful: How Trump Gained Momentum Among Evangelicals," *Presidential Studies Quarterly* 50, no. 4 (2020): 927–47.

3. Michele Margolis, "Who Wants to Make America Great Again? Understanding Evangelical Support for Donald Trump," *Politics and Religion* 13, no. 1 (2020): 89–118.

4. Matthew Layton, Amy Erica Smith, Mason W. Moseley, and Mollie J. Cohen, "Demographic Polarization and the Rise of the Far Right: Brazil's 2018 Presidential Election," *Research and Politics* 8, no. 1 (January 2021): 1–7.

5. Janelle Wong, "The Evangelical Vote and Race in the 2016 Presidential Election," *Journal of Race, Ethnicity, and Politics* 3, no. 1 (2018): 81–106.

6. Sidney Verba, Kay Lehman Schlozman, and Henry E. Brady, *Voice and Equality: Civic Voluntarism in American Politics* (Cambridge, MA: Harvard University Press, 1995).

7. Kathleen Dolan, "Do Women and Men Know Different Things? Measuring Gender Differences in Political Knowledge," *Journal of Politics* 73, no. 1 (2011): 97–107; Jay Dow, "Gender Differences in Political Knowledge: Distinguishing Characteristics-Based and Returns-Based Differences," *Political Behavior* 31, no. 1 (2009): 117–36.

8. Michael X. Delli Carpini and Scott Keeter, "Measuring Political Knowledge: Putting the Cart Before the Horse," *American Journal of Political Science* 37, no. 4 (1993): 1179–1206.

9. Dow, "Gender Differences in Political Knowledge."

10. Cathy Cohen and Matthew Luttig, "Reconceptualizing Political Knowledge: Race, Ethnicity, and Carceral Violence," *Perspectives on Politics* 18, no. 3 (2020): 805–18, https://doi.org/10.1017/S1537592718003857.

11. David Samuels, "Sources of Mass Partisanship in Brazil," *Latin American Politics and Society* 48, no. 2 (2006): 1–27, https://doi.org/10.1111/j.1548-2456.2006.tb00345.x.

12. Matthew Layton, Amy Erica Smith, and Mollie J. Cohen, "Demographic Polarization and the Rise of the Far Right: Brazil's 2018 Presidential Election," *Research and Politics* 8, no. 1 (2021).

13. Verba, Scholzman, and Brady, *Voice and Equality*.

14. William Galston, "Political Knowledge, Political Engagement, and Civic Education," *Annual Review of Political Science* 4 (June 2001): 217–34, https://doi.org/10.1146/annurev.polisci.4.1.217; Norman H. Nie, Jane Junn, and Kenneth Stehlik-Barry, *Education and Democratic Citizenship in America* (Chicago: University of Chicago Press, 1996).

15. Scott Clement and Daniela Santamariña, "What We Know About the High, Broad Turnout in the 2020 Election," *Washington Post*, May 13, 2021, https://www.washingtonpost.com/politics/2021/05/13/what-we-know-about-high-broad-turnout-2020-election/.

16. Ruth Igielnik, "Men and Women in the U.S. Continue to Differ in Voter Turnout Rate, Party Identification," Pew Research Center, August 18, 2020, https://www.pewresearch.org/fact-tank/2020/08/18/men-and-women-in-the-u-s-continue-to-differ-in-voter-turnout-rate-party-identification/.

17. James Cone, *Black Theology and Black Power* (Louisville, KY: Westminster John Knox Press, 1969); J. Deotis Roberts, *Liberation and Reconciliation: A Black Theology* (Louisville, KY: Westminster John Knox Press, 1971); Jeremiah A. Wright Jr., *Africans Who Shaped Our Faith* (Nashville, TN: Urban Ministries, 1995); Katie Cannon, *Katie's Canon: Womanism and the Soul of the Black Community* (London: Continuum, 1998); Ronilso Pacheco, *Teologia Negra: O Sopro Antiracista do Espirito* (Brasilia: Novos Diálogos; São Paulo: Editora Recriar, 2019); Leontino Faria dos Santos, "Por uma Teologia Negra no Brasil," *Cross Currents* 67, no. 1 (2017): 35–54.

18. Ronaldo Almeida, "Bolsonaro President: Evangelicals, Conservatism, and Political Crisis," Novos Estudos. *CEBRAP* 38, no. 1 (2019): 185–213, https://doi.org/10.25091/S01013300201900010010; Amaral, "The Victory of Jair Bolsonaro According to the Brazilian Electoral Study of 2018."

19. St. Clair Drake and Horace R. Cayton, *Black Metropolis: A Study of Negro Life in a Northern City* (Chicago: University of Chicago Press, 1970); Peter J. Paris, *The Social Teaching of the Black Churches* (Philadelphia: Fortress, 1985); C. Eric Lincoln and Lawrence H. Mamiya, *The Black Church in the African American Experience* (Durham, NC: Duke University Press, 1990).

20. John Burdick, "Why Is the Black Evangelical Movement Growing in Brazil?," *Journal of Latin American Studies* 37, no. 2 (2005): 311–32, at 313.

21. Burdick, "Why Is the Black Evangelical Movement Growing in Brazil?"
22. Burdick, "Why Is the Black Evangelical Movement Growing in Brazil?," 332.
23. Henrique Rodrigues, "Não Acredito Nesse Deus Homem, Branco e Macho, Que Escolhe Quem Vai Matar," *Revista Forum*, May 18, 2021, https://revistaforum.com.br/brasil/nao-acredito-nesse-deus-homem -branco-e-macho-que-escolhe-quem-vai-matar/#.
24. Frederick Harris, *Something Within: Religion in African American Political Activism* (Oxford: Oxford University Press, 2001).
25. Alison Calhoun-Brown, "Will the Circle Be Unbroken? The Political Involvement of Black Churches Since the 1960s," in *Black Political Organizations in the Post-Civil Rights Era*, ed. Ollie. A. Johnson III and Karin L. Stanford (New Brunswick, NJ: Rutgers University Press, 2002), 14–27.
26. Laura A. Reese and Ronald E. Brown, "The Effects of Religious Messages on Racial Identity and System Blame Among African Americans," *Journal of Politics* 57, no. 1 (1995): 24–43.
27. Todd Shaw and Eric McDaniel, "'Whosoever Will': Black Theology, Homosexuality, and the Black Political Church," *National Political Science Review* 11 (2007): 137–55.
28. Eric L. McDaniel, Maraam A. Dwidar, and Hadill Calderon, "The Faith of Black Politics: The Relationship Between Black Religious and Political Beliefs," *Journal of Black Studies* 49, no. 3 (2018): 256–83.
29. Tamelyn Tucker-Worgs, *The Black Megachurch: Theology, Gender, and the Politics of Public Engagement* (Waco, TX: Baylor University Press, 2011).
30. McDaniel, Dwidar, and Calderon, "The Faith of Black Politics."
31. Besheer Mohamed, Kiana Cox, Jeff Diamant, and Claire Gecewicz, "Faith Among Black Americans," Pew Forum, February 16, 2021, https:// www.pewforum.org/2021/02/16/faith-among-black-americans/.
32. Amaral, "The Victory of Jair Bolsonaro According to the Brazilian Electoral Study of 2018."
33. Cesar Zucco and Timothy Power, "Bolsa Família and the Shift in Lula's Electoral Base, 2002–2006," *Latin American Research Review* 48, no. 2 (2013): 3–24.
34. Amaral, "The Victory of Jair Bolsonaro According to the Brazilian Electoral Study of 2018."

35. Layton, Smith, Moseley, and Cohen, "Demographic Polarization and the Rise of the Far Right."

36. Amaral, "The Victory of Jair Bolsonaro According to the Brazilian Electoral Study of 2018."

37. Benjamin Junge, Sean T. Mitchell, Alvaro Jarrin, and Lucia Cantero, eds., *Precarious Democracy: Ethnographies of Hope, Despair, and Resistance in Brazil* (New Brunswick, NJ: Rutgers University Press, 2021).

38. Ariel Alejandro Goldstein, "The New Far-Right in Brazil and the Construction of a Right-Wing Order," *Latin American Perspectives* 46, no. 1 (April 2019): 245–62. Marcos Nobre, *Imobilismo em Movimento: da Abertura Democrática ao Governo Dilma* (São Paulo, Brazil: Companhia das Letras, 2013).

39. Gilberto Costa, "Ibope: Bolsonaro Lidera Entre Mulheres, Negros e Em Quatro Regiões mais Pobres, Menos Escolarizados e Nordestinos Preferem Haddad," Agência Brasil, October 17, 2018, https://agenciabrasil .ebc.com.br/politica/noticia/2018-10/ibope-bolsonaro-lidera-entre -Mulheres-negros-e-em-quatro-regioes.

40. Costa, "Ibope: Bolsonaro Lidera Entre Mulheres, Negros e Em Quatro Regiões mais Pobres, Menos Escolarizados e Nordestinos Preferem Haddad."

41. Jaime Alves, *The Anti-Black City: Police Terror and Urban Life in Brazil* (Minneapolis: University of Minnesota Press, 2018).

42. Michael Tesler, "The Spillover of Racialization Into Health Care: How President Obama Polarized Public Opinion by Racial Attitudes and Race," *American Journal of Political Science* 56, no. 3 (2012): 690–704, https://doi.org/10.1111/j.1540-5907.2011.00577.x; Nicholas A. Valentino, Vincent L. Hutchings, and Ismail K. White, "Cues That Matter: How Political Ads Prime Racial Attitudes During Campaigns," *American Political Science Review* 96, no. 1 (2002): 75–90.

5. CONCLUSION: ARE POOR BLACK WOMEN THE HOPE FOR PROGRESSIVE POLITICS?

1. Jennifer Nash, *Birthing Black Mothers* (Durham, NC: Duke University Press, 2021), 4.

2. Karen Seccombe, *So You Think I Drive a Cadillac?: Welfare Recipients' Perspectives on the System and Its Reform* (Boston: Allyn and Bacon,

1999); Ange-Marie Hancock, *The Politics of Disgust: The Public Identity of the Welfare Queen* (New York: New York University Press, 2004); Matthew Layton, Amy Erica Smith, Mason W. Moseley, and Mollie J. Cohen, "Demographic Polarization and the Rise of the Far Right: Brazil's 2018 Presidential Election," *Research and Politics* 8, no. 1 (2021): 1–7; Silvana Aparecida Mariano and Cassia Maria Carloto, "Aspectos Diferenciais da Inserção das Mulheres Negras no Programa Bolsa Família," *Sociedade e Estado* 28, no. 2 (August 2013): 393–417, https://doi.org/10.1590/S0102-69922013000200011.

3. Natasha Sugiyama and Wendy Hunter. *Transforming Subjects Into Citizens: Insights from Brazil's Bolsa Família* (Cambridge: Cambridge University Press, 2014).

4. Marian and Carloto, "Aspectos Diferenciais da Inserção das Mulheres Negras no Programa Bolsa Família"; Gladys Mitchell-Walthour, *The Politics of Blackness: Racial Identity and Political Behavior in Contemporary Brazil* (Cambridge: Cambridge University Press, 2018).

5. Cori Bush and Ryan Grim, "Cori Bush on the Shame and Power of Poverty," The Intercept, August 6, 2021, https://theintercept.com/2021/08/06/deconstructed-cori-bush-eviction-poverty/.

6. Fabiana Pinto, Marcelle Decothé, and Brisa Lima, *Violência Política de Gênero e Raça no Brasil 2021* (Rio de Janeiro, Brazil: Marielle Franco Institute, 2021), 28.

7. Jefferson Nascimento, *Democracia Inacabada: Um Retrato das Desigualdades Brasileiras* (São Paulo, Brazil: Oxfam Brasil, 2021).

8. April O. Turner and Daniel De Simone, "By the Numbers: Black Women in the 117th Congress," Higher Heights (press release), January 3, 2021, https://cawp.rutgers.edu/sites/default/files/resources/press-release-black-women-117th-congress_0.pdf.

9. Sean Liing, "'Racism May Target Black People, but It Damns a Democracy and It Damns Humanity.' Why Rev. William Barber Thinks We Need a Moral Revolution," Vox, August 18, 2020, https://www.vox.com/policy-and-politics/2020/8/18/21327358/william-barber-poor-peoples-campaign-moral-mondays.

10. Karyn Lacy, *Blue-Chip Black: Race, Class, and Status in the New Black Middle Class* (Berkeley: University of California Press, 2007).

11. Jack Jenkins, "Poor People's Campaign, Lawmakers Unveil Sweeping Resolution to Tackle Poverty," *Episcopal News Service*, May 21, 2021,

https://www.episcopalnewsservice.org/2021/05/21/poor-peoples
-campaign-lawmakers-unveil-sweeping-resolution-to-tackle-poverty/.

12. Susan Cornwell, "Nine U.S. Lawmakers Who Were Once on Food
Stamps Ask Trump Not to Shrink Program," *Reuters*, February 13,
2020, https://www.reuters.com/article/us-usa-trump-budget-foodstamps
/nine-u-s-lawmakers-who-were-once-on-food-stamps-ask-trump
-not-to-shrink-program-idUSKBN2071BM.

13. Pinto, Decothé, and Lima, *Violência Política de Gênero e Raça no Brasil
2021.*

14. Hancock, *The Politics of Disgust.*

REFERENCES

Adams, Elizabeth, Beth E. Krutz-Costes, and Adam J. Hoffman. "Skin Tone Bias Among African Americans: Antecedents and Consequences Across the Life Span." *Developmental Review* 40 (June 2016): 93–116.

Agan, Amanda Y., and Sonja B. Starr. "Employer Neighborhoods and Racial Discrimination." NBER Working Paper 28153. November 2020. https://www.nber.org/system/files/working_papers/w28153/w28153.pdf.

Alexander-Floyd, Nikol. "Disappearing Acts: Reclaiming Intersectionality in the Social Sciences in a Post–Black Feminist Era." *Feminist Formations* 24, no.1 (Spring 2012): 1–25.

——. *Re-Imagining Black Women: A Critique of Post-Feminist and Post-Racial Melodrama in Culture and Politics*. New York: New York University Press, 2021.

Almeida, Ronaldo de. "Bolsonaro President: Evangelicals, Conservatism, and Political Crisis." *Novos Estudos CEBRAP* 38, no. 1 (2019): 185–213. https://doi.org/10.25091/S01013300201900010010.

——. "The Broken Wave: Evangelicals and Conservatism in the Brazilian Crisis." *Journal of Ethnographic Theory* 10, no. 1 (2020): 32–40.

Alves, Jaime. *The Anti-Black City: Police Terror and Urban Life in Brazil*. Minneapolis: University of Minnesota Press, 2018.

Amaral, Oswaldo. "The Victory of Jair Bolsonaro According to the Brazilian Electoral Study of 2018." *Brazilian Political Science Review* 14, no. 1 (2020): 1–13. https://doi.org/10.1590/1981-3821202000010004.

Bairros, Luiza, and Sonia E. Alvarez. "Feminisms and Anti-Racism: Intersections and Challenges: An interview with Luiza Bairros, Minister, Brazilian Secretariat of Public Policies for the Promotion of Racial Equality (SEPPIR), 2011–2014." Trans. Miriam Adelman. *Meridians* 14, no. 1 (2016): 50–69.

Baldwin, Bridgette. "Stratification of the Welfare Poor: Intersections of Gender, Race, and 'Worthiness' in Poverty Discourse and Policy." *Modern American* 6, no. 1 (Spring 2010): 4–14.

Banks, Kira, Laura P. Kohn-Wood, and Michael Spencer. "An Examination of the African American Experience of Everyday Discrimination and Symptoms of Psychological Distress." *Community Mental Health Journal* 42, no. 6 (2006): 555–70.

Baran, Stephanie M. "An Intersectional Analysis of the Role Race and Gender Play in Welfare Recipients' and Case Manager Experiences." PhD diss., University of Wisconsin–Milwaukee, 2019.

Beal, Anne C., Karen Kuhlthau, and James Perrin. "Breastfeeding Advice Given to African American and White Women by Physicians and WIC Counselors." *Public Health Reports* 118, no. 4 (2003): 368–76. https://doi.org/10.1093/ohr/118.4.368.

Blake, Jamila, Bettie Butler, Chance Lewis, and Alicia Darensbourg. "Unmasking the Inequitable Discipline Experiences of Urban Black Girls: Implications for Urban Educational Stakeholders." *Urban Review* 43, no. 1 (2011): 90–106.

Bohn, Simone. "The Electoral Behavior of the Poor in Brazil: A Research Agenda." *Latin American Research Review* 48, no. 2 (2013): 25–31.

"Bolsonaro: 'Quilombola Não Serve Nem Para Procriar.'" *Congresso em Foco.* May 4, 2017.

Brown-Iannuzzi, Jazmin L., Ron Dotsch, Erin Cooley, and B. Keith Payne. "The Relationship Between Mental Representations of Welfare Recipients and Attitudes Toward Welfare." *Psychological Science* 28, no. 1 (2017): 92–103.

Bump, Philip. "A Third of Trump's Support in 2016 Came from Evangelicals—And He Hasn't Lost Them Yet." *Washington Post*, June 5, 2020. https://www.washingtonpost.com/politics/2020/06/05/third-trumps-support-2016-came-evangelicals-and-he-hasnt-lost-them-yet/.

Burdick. John. "Why Is the Black Evangelical Movement Growing in Brazil?" *Journal of Latin American Studies* 37, no. 2 (2005): 311–32.

Bush, Cori, and Ryan Grim. "Cori Bush on the Shame and Power of Poverty." The Intercept. August 6, 2021. https://theintercept.com/2021/08/06/deconstructed-cori-bush-eviction-poverty/.

Caesar, Gabriela. "Haddad Ganha no Nordeste: e Bolsonaro, nas Demais regiões do País Maiores Diferenças Entre os Votos dos Candidatos Foram Registradas no Nordeste e no Sul." Globo.com G1. October 29, 2018. https://g1.globo.com/politica/eleicoes/2018/eleicao-em-numeros/noticia/2018/10/29/haddad-ganha-no-nordeste-e-bolsonaro-nas-demais-regioes-do-pais.ghtml.

Caldwell, Kia. "'Look at Her Hair': The Body Politics of Black Womanhood in Brazil." *Transforming Anthropology* 11, no. 2 (2004): 18–29.

——. *Negras in Brazil: Re-envisioning Black Women, Citizenship, and the Politics of Identity*. New Brunswick, NJ: Rutgers University Press, 2006.

Calhoun-Brown, Alison. "Will the Circle Be Unbroken? The Political Involvement of Black Churches Since the 1960s." In *Black Political Organizations in the Post–Civil Rights Era*, ed. Ollie. A. Johnson III and Karin. L. Stanford, 14–27. New Brunswick, NJ: Rutgers University Press, 2002.

Cannon, Katie. *Katie's Canon: Womanism and the Soul of the Black Community*. London: Continuum, 1998.

Cardoso, Cláudia Pons. "'Amefricanizing' the Feminism: The Thought of Lélia Gonzalez." Debate Colonialidade do Gênero e Feminismos Descoloniais. *Revista Estudos Feministas* 22, no. 3 (November 28, 2014). https://doi.org/10.1590/S0104-026X2014000300015.

Cardoso, Claudia Pons. "Feminisms from the Perspective of Afro-Brazilian Women." Trans. Miriam Adelman. *Meridians* 14, no. 1 (2016): 1–29.

Cecchin, Hareli, and Temis Parente. "Relações de gênero no Acampamento Ilha Verde: Discutindo o (des) empoderamento das mulheres beneficiárias do Bolsa Família." *Interações* 20, no. 3 (2019): 907–21.

Chinn, Juanita, Iman K. Martin, and Nicole Redmond. "Health Equity Among Black Women in the United States." *Journal of Women's Health* 30, no. 2 (February 2021): 212–19.

Clawson, Rosalee, and Rakuya Trice. "Poverty as We Know It: Media Portrayals of the Poor." *Public Opinion Quarterly* 64, no. 1 (2000): 53–64.

Clement, Scott, and Daniela Santamariña. "What We Know About the High, Broad Turnout in the 2020 Election." *Washington Post*, May 13, 2021. https://www.washingtonpost.com/politics/2021/05/13/what-we-know-about-high-broad-turnout-2020-election/.

Coelho, Pedro Lima, and Andrea Sales Soares de Azevedo Melo. "Impacto do Programa 'Bolsa Família' sobre a qualidade da dieta das famílias de Pernambuco no Brasil." *Ciência e Saúde Coletiva* 22, no. 2 (2017): 393–402. https://doi.org/10.1590/1413-81232017222.13622015.

Cohen, Cathy. *The Boundaries of Blackness: AIDS and the Breakdown of Black Politics*. Chicago: University of Chicago Press, 1999.

Cohen, Cathy, and Matthew Luttig. "Reconceptualizing Political Knowledge: Race, Ethnicity, and Carceral Violence." *Perspectives on Politics* 18, no. 3 (2020): 805–18. https://doi.org/10.1017/S1537592718003857.

Collins, Patricia Hill. *Black Feminist Theory: Knowledge, Consciousness, and the Politics of Empowerment*. Abingdon, UK: Routledge, 1990.

Cone, James. *Black Theology and Black Power*. Louisville, KY: Westminster John Knox Press, 1969.

Cooper, Brittney. *Beyond Respectability: The Intellectual Thought of Race Women*. Chicago: University of Illinois Press, 2017.

Cornwell, Susan. "Nine U.S. Lawmakers Who Were Once on Food Stamps Ask Trump Not to Shrink Program." *Reuters*, February 13, 2020. https://www.reuters.com/article/us-usa-trump-budget-foodstamps/nine-u-s-lawmakers-who-were-once-on-food-stamps-ask-trump-not-to-shrink-program-idUSKBN2071BM.

Corrêa, Diego Sanches. "Conditional Cash Transfer Programs, the Economy, and Presidential Elections in Latin America." *Latin American Research Review* 50, no. 2 (2015): 63–85.

Costa, Gilberto. "Ibope: Bolsonaro Lidera Entre Mulheres, Negros e Em Quatro Regiões mais Pobres, Menos Escolarizados e Nordestinos Preferem Haddad." Agência Brasil. October 17, 2018. https://agenciabrasil.ebc.com.br/politica/noticia/2018-10/ibope-bolsonaro-lidera-entre-Mulheres-negros-e-em-quatro-regioes.

Crenshaw, Kimberle. "Mapping the Margins: Intersectionality, Identity Politics, and Violence Against Women of Color." *Stanford Law Review* 43, no. 6 (July 1991): 1241–99.

Daniel, Reginald G. *Race and Multiraciality in Brazil and the United States: Converging Paths?* University Park: The Pennsylvania State University Press, 2006.

Darity, William, Jr. "Employment Discrimination, Segregation, and Health." *American Journal of Public Health* 93, no. 2 (2003): 226–31.

Darity, William, Jr., Darrick Hamilton, Mark Paul, Alan Aja, Anne Price, Antonio Moore, and Caterina Chiopris. "What We Get Wrong About Closing the Racial Wealth Gap." Samuel DuBois Cook Center on Social Equity. April 2018. https://socialequity.duke.edu/wp-content/uploads/2019/10/what-we-get-wrong.pdf.

Davenport, Lauren. *Politics Beyond Black and White: Biracial Identity and Attitudes in America*. Cambridge: Cambridge University Press, 2018.

Dawson, Michael. *Behind the Mule: Race and Class in African American Politics*. Princeton, NJ: Princeton University Press, 1994.

Degler, Carl. *Neither Black nor White: Slavery and Race Relations in Brazil and the United States*. New York: MacMillan, 1971.

Delli Carpini, Michael X., and Scott Keeter. "Measuring Political Knowledge: Putting the Cart Before the Horse." *American Journal of Political Science* 37, no. 4 (1993): 1179–1206.

Dias, Elizabeth. "How Evangelicals Helped Donald Trump Win." *Time*, November 9, 2016. https://www.google.com/amp/s/time.com/4565010/donald-trump-evangelicals-win/%3famp=true.

Diette, Timothy M., Arthur H. Goldsmith, Darrick Hamilton, and William Darity Jr. "Skin Shade Stratification and the Psychological Cost of Unemployment: Is There a Gradient for Black Females?" *Review of Black Political Economy* 42, no. 1–2 (2009): 155–77.

Dolan, Kathleen. "Do Women and Men Know Different Things? Measuring Gender Differences in Political Knowledge." *Journal of Politics* 73, no. 1 (2011): 97–107.

Dow, Jay. "Gender Differences in Political Knowledge: Distinguishing Characteristics-Based and Returns-Based Differences." *Political Behavior* 31, no. 1 (2009): 117–36.

Drake, St. Clair, and Horace. R. Cayton. *Black Metropolis: A Study of Negro Life in a Northern City*. Chicago: University of Chicago Press, 1970.

Evaristo, Conceição. *Becos Da Memoria*. Rio de Janeiro, Brazil: Pallas, 2017.

Figureido, Angela. "Out of Place: The Experience of the Black Middle Class." In *Brazil's New Racial Politics*, ed. Bernd Reiter and Gladys Mitchell, 51–63. Boulder, CO: Lynn Reiner, 2010.

Fried, Brian. "Distributive Politics and Conditional Cash Transfers: The Case of Brazil's Bolsa Familia." *World Development* 40, no. 5 (2012): 1042–53.

Gabriel, Trip. "Donald Trump, Despite Impieties, Wins Hearts of Evangelical Voters." *New York Times*, February 26, 2016. https://www.google.com/amp/s/www.nytimes.com/2016/02/28/us/politics/donald-trump-despite-impieties-wins-hearts-of-evangelical-voters.amp.html.

Galston, William. "Political Knowledge, Political Engagement, and Civic Education." *Annual Review of Political Science* 4 (June 2001): 217–34. https://doi.org/10.1146/annurev.polisci.4.1.217.

Gilens, Martin. "How the Poor Became Black: The Racialization of American Poverty in the Mass Media." In *Race and the Politics of Welfare Reform*, ed. Sanford Schram, Joe Soss, and Richard Fording, 101–30. Ann Arbor: University of Michigan Press, 2003.

——. *Why Americans Hate Welfare: Race, Media, and the Politics of Antipoverty Policy*. Chicago: University of Chicago Press, 1999.

Gittleman, Maury, and Edward N. Wolff. "Racial Differences in Patterns of Wealth Accumulation." *Journal of Human Resources* 39, no. 1 (Winter 2004): 193–227.

Goldstein, Ariel Alejandro. "The New Far-Right in Brazil and the Construction of a Right-Wing Order." *Latin American Perspectives* 46, no. 1 (April 2019): 245–62.

Gonzalez, Lelia. "For an Afro-Latin American Feminism." In *Confronting the Crisis in Latin America: Women Organizing for Change*, Isis International: Development Alternatives with Women for a New Era, 95–101. Santiago, Chile: Isis International, 1988.

Hamilton, Darrick, and Ngina Chiteji. "Wealth." In *International Encyclopedia of Race and Racism*, 2nd ed., ed. Patrick Mason. New York: Macmillan Reference, (2013): 259–65.

Hamilton, Darrick, Arthur H. Goldsmith, and William Darity Jr. "Shedding 'Light' on Marriage: The Influence of Skin Shade on Marriage for Black Females." *Journal of Economic Behavior and Organization* 72, no. 1 (2009): 30–50.

Hancock, Ange-Marie. *The Politics of Disgust: The Public Identity of the Welfare Queen*. New York: New York University Press, 2004.

Hancock, Ange-Marie. "Trayvon Martin, Intersectionality, and the Politics of Disgust." *Theory & Event* 15, no. 3 (2012). Project MUSE muse.jhu.edu/article/484428.

Harnois, Catherine E. "Are Perceptions of Discrimination Unidimensional, Oppositional, or Intersectional? Examining the Relationship Among

Perceived Racial–Ethnic-, Gender-, and Age-Based Discrimination." *Sociological Perspectives* 57, no. 4 (2014): 470–87.

Harrington, Jaira. "A Place of Their Own: Black Feminist Leadership and Economic and Educational Justice in São Paulo and Rio de Janeiro, Brazil." *Latin American Caribbean and Ethnic Studies* 10, no. 3 (2015): 271–87.

Harris, Frederick. *Something Within: Religion in African American Political Activism.* Oxford: Oxford University Press, 2001.

Hellwig, David. *African American Reflections on Brazil's Racial Paradise.* Philadelphia: Temple University Press, 1992.

Henderson, Tim. "Where Black Homeownership Is the Norm." Pew Trusts. August 15, 2018. https://www.pewtrusts.org/en/research-and-analysis/blogs /stateline/2018/08/15/where-black-homeownership-is-the-norm.

Herbst, Chris M., and Joanna Lucio. "Happy in the Hood? The Impact of Residential Segregation on Self-Reported Happiness." *Journal of Regional Science* 56, no. 3 (2016): 494–52.

Hernandez, Tanya. *Racial Subordination in Latin America: The Role of the State, Customary Law, and the New Civil Rights Response.* Cambridge: Cambridge University Press, 2012.

Higgenbotham, Elizabeth, and Lynn Weber. "Perceptions of Workplace Discrimination Among Black and White Professional-Managerial Women." In *Latinas and African American Women at Work: Race, Gender, and Economic Inequality*, ed. Irene Browne, 327–53. New York: Russell Sage Foundation, 1999.

Hordge-Freeman, Elizabeth. *Color of Love: Racial Features, Stigmas, and Socialization in Brazilian Black Families.* Austin: University of Texas Press, 2015.

Hunt, Matthew O., Lauren A. Wise, Marie-Claude Jipguep, Yvette C. Cozier, and Lynn Rosenberg. "Neighborhood Racial Composition and Perceptions of Racial Discrimination: Evidence from the Black Women's Health Study." *Social Psychology Quarterly* 70, no. 3 (2007): 272–89.

Hunter, Margaret. "Colorstruck: Skin Color Stratification in the Lives of African American Women." *Sociological Inquiry* 68, no. 4 (1998): 517–35.

Hunter, Wendy, Leila Patel, and Natasha Borges Sugiyama. "How Family and Child Cash Transfers Can Empower Women: Comparative Lessons from Brazil and South Africa." *Global Social Policy* 21, no. 2 (2021): 258–77.

Hunter, Wendy, and Natasha Sugiyama. "Transforming Subjects Into Citizens: Insights from Brazil's Bolsa Família." *Perspectives on Politics* 12, no. 4 (2014): 829–45.

Igielnik, Ruth. "Men and Women in the U.S. Continue to Differ in Voter Turnout Rate, Party Identification." Pew Research Center. August 18, 2020. https://www.pewresearch.org/fact-tank/2020/08/18/men-and-women -in-the-u-s-continue-to-differ-in-voter-turnout-rate-party-identification/.

Jarrett, Robin L. "Welfare Stigma Among Low-Income African American Single Mothers." *Family Relations* 45, no. 4 (1996): 368–74.

Jenkins, Jack. "Poor People's Campaign, Lawmakers Unveil Sweeping Resolution to Tackle Poverty." *Episcopal News Service*, May 21, 2021. https:// www.episcopalnewsservice.org/2021/05/21/poor-peoples-campaign -lawmakers-unveil-sweeping-resolution-to-tackle-poverty/.

Jesus, Carolina Maria. *Quarto de Despejo: Diário de Uma Favelada.* São Paulo, Brazil: Ática, 1960.

Jordan-Zachery, Julia. "I Ain't Your Darn Help: Black Women as the Help in Intersectionality Research in Political Science." *National Political Science Review* 16 (2014): 19–30.

Junge, Benjamin, Sean T. Mitchell, Alvaro Jarrin, and Lucia Cantero, eds. *Precarious Democracy: Ethnographies of Hope, Despair, and Resistance in Brazil.* New Brunswick, NJ: Rutgers University Press, 2021.

Kendall, Mikki. *Hood Feminism: Notes From the Women That a Movement Forgot.* New York: Penguin Random House, 2020.

Kerbo, Harold. R. "Stigma of Welfare and a Passive Poor." *Sociology and Social Research* 60, no. 2 (1972): 175–87.

King, Martin Luther, Jr. "The Other America." Gross Pointe Historical Society. March 14, 1968. http://www.gphistorical.org/mlk/index.htm.

Kopkin, Nolan, and Gladys Mitchell-Walthour. "Color Discrimination, Occupational Prestige, and Skin Color in Brazil." *Latin American & Caribbean Ethnic Studies* 15, no. 1 (2020): 44–69.

Lacy, Karyn. *Blue-Chip Black: Race, Class, and Status in the New Black Middle Class.* Berkeley: University of California Press, 2007.

Laird, Chryl, and Ismail White. *Steadfast Democrats: How Social Forces Shape Black Political Behavior.* Princeton, NJ: Princeton University Press, 2020.

Lamont, Michele, Graziella Moraes Silva, Jessica Welburn, Joshua Guetzkow, Nissim Mizrachi, Hanna Herzog, and Elis Reis. *Getting Respect:*

Responding to Stigma and Discrimination in the United States, Brazil, and Israel. Princeton, NJ: Princeton University Press, 2016.

Layton, Matthew. "Welfare Stereotypes and Conditional Cash Transfer Programmes: Evidence from Brazil's Bolsa Família." *Journal of Politics in Latin America* 12, no. 1 (2020): 53–76. https://doi.org/10.1177/1866802X20914429.

Layton, Matthew, and Amy Smith. "Is It Race, Class, or Gender? The Sources of Perceived Discrimination in Brazil." *Latin American Politics and Society* 59, no. 1 (2017): 52–73.

Layton, Matthew, Amy Erica Smith, Mason W. Moseley, and Mollie J. Cohen. "Demographic Polarization and the Rise of the Far Right: Brazil's 2018 Presidential Election." *Research and Politics* 8, no. 1 (2021): 1–7.

Lei, Ryan F., and Galen V. Bodenhausen. "Racial Assumptions Color the Mental Representation of Social Class. *Frontiers in Psychology* 5, no. 8 (2017): 519. doi: 10.3389/fpsyg.2017.00519. PMID: 28424651; PMCID: PMC5380730.

Lemos, Leila Ribeiro, and Caroline Ramos do Carmo de Souza. "Interseccionalidade e Feminismo Negro: A Violência Contra a Mulher Não é Apenas Uma Questão de Gênero." *ANAIS—21a SEMOC* (October 22–26, 2018): 194.

Levine, Marc V. "The State of Black Milwaukee in National Perspective: Racial Inequality in the Nation's 50 Largest Metropolitan Areas. In 65 Charts and Tables." Center for Economic Development. July 20, 2020. https://dc.uwm.edu/ced_pubs/56.

Liing, Sean. "'Racism May Target Black People, but It Damns a Democracy and It Damns Humanity.' Why Rev. William Barber Thinks We Need a Moral Revolution." Vox. August 18, 2020. https://www.vox.com/policy-and-politics/2020/8/18/21327358/william-barber-poor-peoples-campaign-moral-mondays.

Lincoln, C. Eric, and Lawrence H. Mamiya. *The Black Church in the African American Experience.* Durham: NC: Duke University Press, 1990.

Loveless, Tracy. "Supplemental Nutrition Assistance Program (SNAP) Receipt for Households: 2018." American Community Survey Briefs. 2020. https://www.census.gov/content/dam/Census/library/publications/2020/demo/acsbr20-01.pdf.

Margolis, Michele. "Who Wants to Make America Great Again? Understanding Evangelical Support for Donald Trump." *Politics and Religion* 13, no. 1 (2020): 89–118.

Mariano, Silvana Aparecida, and Cassia Maria Carloto. "Aspectos Diferenciais da Inserção das Mulheres Negras no Programa Bolsa Família." *Sociedade e Estado* 28, no. 2 (August 2013): 393–417. https://doi.org/10.1590/S0102-69922013000200011.

Martins, Tafnes, Tiago Jessé Souza de Lima, and Walberto Silva Santos. "O efeito das Microagressões Raciais de Gênero na Saúde Mental De Mulheres Negras." Ciência & Saúde Coletiva 25, no. 7 (2020): 2793–2802. https://doi.org/10.1590/1413-81232020257.29182018.

Marx, Anthony. *Making Race and Nation: A Comparison of South Africa, the United States, and Brazil.* Cambridge: Cambridge University Press, 1998.

Massignam, Fernando Mendes, João Luiz Dornelles Bastos, and Fúlvio Borges Nedel. "Discriminação e saúde: Um problema de Acesso." *Epidemiologia e Serviços de Saúde* 24, no. 3 (2015): 541–44.

McDaniel, Eric L., Maraam A. Dwidar, and Hadill Calderon. "The Faith of Black Politics: The Relationship Between Black Religious and Political Beliefs." *Journal of Black Studies* 49, no. 3 (2018): 256–83.

Means, Sheryl Felecia. "Bikuda: Hair, Aesthetic, and Bodily Perspectives from Women in Salvador, Bahia, Brazil." *African and Black Diaspora: An International Journal* 13, no. 3 (2020): 269–82.

Melillo, Gianna. "Racial Disparities Persist in Maternal Morbidity, Mortality and Infant Health." *American Journal of Managed Care.* June 13, 2020. https://www.ajmc.com/view/racial-disparities-persist-in-maternal-morbidity-mortality-and-infant-health.

Mendonca, Heloisa. "Mulheres Negras Recebem Menos da Metade do Salário dos Homens Brancos no Brasil." *El Pais Brasil.* November 13, 2019. https://brasil.elpais.com/brasil/2019/11/12/politica/1573581512_623918.html.

Mettler, Suzanne, and Jeffrey Stonecash. "Government Program Usage and Political Voice." *Social Science Quarterly* 89, no. 2 (2008): 273–93.

Micheli, David De. "The Racialized Effects of Social Programs in Brazil." *Latin American Politics and Society* 6, no 1 (2018): 52–75. https://doi.org/10.1017/lap.2017.6.

Michener, Jamila. *Fragmented Democracy: Medicaid, Federalism, and Unequal Politics.* Cambridge: Cambridge University Press, 2018.

Mitchell, Jasmine. *Imagining the Mulatta: Blackness in U.S. and Brazilian Media.* Urbana: University of Illinois Press, 2020.

Mitchell-Walthour, Gladys. "Intersectionality, Discrimination, and Presidential Approval: An Intersectional Analysis of Bolsa Família Recipients'

Presidential Satisfaction of Dilma Rousseff and Political Trust." *National Political Science Review* 20, no. 1 (2019): 73–90.

——. *The Politics of Blackness: Racial Identity and Political Behavior in Contemporary Brazil*. Cambridge: Cambridge University Press, 2018.

Mohamed, Besheer, Kiana Cox, Jeff Diamant, and Claire Gecewicz. "Faith Among Black Americans." Pew Forum. February 16, 2021. https://www.pewforum.org/2021/02/16/faith-among-black-americans/.

Monk, Ellis. "The Consequences of 'Race and Color' in Brazil." *Social Problems* 43, no. 3 (2016): 413–30.

Moreira, Nathalia Carvalho, Marco Aurélio Marques Ferreira, Afonso Augusto Teixeira de Freitas Carvalho Lima, and Ivan Beck Ckagnazaroff. "Bolsa Família na percepção dos agentes dos Centros de Referência de Assistência Social." *Revista de Administração Pública* 46, no. 2 (2012): 403–23.

Morrison, Toni. *The Bluest Eye*. New York: Vintage International, 1970.

Nascimento, Jefferson. *Democracia Inacabada: Um Retrato das Desigualdades Brasileiras*. São Paulo, Brazil: Oxfam Brasil, 2021.

Nash, Jennifer. *Birthing Black Mothers*. Durham, NC: Duke University Press, 2021.

Nichols-Casebolt, Ann. "The Psychological Effects of Income Testing Income-Support Benefits." *Social Service Review* 60, no. 2 (1986): 287–302.

Nie, Norman H., Jane Junn, and Kenneth Stehlik-Barry. *Education and Democratic Citizenship in America*. Chicago: University of Chicago Press, 1996.

Nobre, Marcos. *Imobilismo em Movimento: da Abertura Democrática ao Governo Dilma*. São Paulo, Brazil: Companhia das Letras, 2013.

Osuji, Chinyere. *Boundaries of Love: Interracial Marriage and the Meaning of Race*. New York: New York University Press, 2019.

Pacheco, Ronilso. *Teologia Negra: O Sopro Antiracista do Espírito*. Brasília: Novos Diálogos, São Paulo: Editora Recriar, 2019.

Pager, Devah. "Identifying Discrimination at Work: The Use of Field Experiments." *Journal of Social Issues* 68, no. 2 (2012): 221–27.

Pager, Devah, Bruce Western, and Bart Bonikowski. "Discrimination in a Low Wage Labor Market: A Field Experiment." *American Sociological Review* 74, no. 5 (2009): 777–99.

Paixão, Marcelo, and Luiz M. Carvano. *Relatório Anual das Desigualdades Raciais no Brasil: 2007–2008*. Rio de Janeiro, Brazil: Garamond, 2008.

Papp, Anna Carolina, Bianca Lima, and Luiz Guilherme Gerbelli. "Na mesma Profissão, Homem Branco chega a Ganhar mais que o dobro que Mulher Negra, diz estudo." global.com G1. September 15, 2020. https:// g1.globo.com/economia/concursos-e-emprego/noticia/2020/09/15/na -mesma-profissao-homem-branco-chega-a-ganhar-mais-que-o-dobro -da-mulher-negra-diz-estudo.ghtml.

Pardue, Derek. *Brazilian Hip-Hoppers Speak from the Margin: We's on Tape.* London: Palgrave Macmillan, 2011.

Paris, Peter J. *The Social Teaching of the Black Churches.* Philadelphia: Fortress Press, 1985.

Patillo-McCoy, Mary. *Black Picket Fences.* Chicago: University of Chicago Press, 1999.

Paul, Mark, Sarah Gaither, and William Darity. "About Face: Seeing Class and Race." *Journal of Economic Issues* 56, no. 1 (2022): 1–17.

Perry, Keisha-Khan. *Black Women Against the Land Grab: The Fight for Racial Justice in Brazil.* Minneapolis: University of Minnesota Press, 2013.

Pinto, Fabiana, Marcelle Decothé, and Brisa Lima. *Violência Política de Gênero e Raça no Brasil 2021.* Rio de Janeiro, Brazil: Marielle Franco Institute, 2021.

Racine, Elizabeth, Ashley. S. Vaughn, and Sarah Laditka. "Farmers' Market Use Among African–American Women Participating in the Special Supplemental Nutrition Program for Women, Infants, and Children." *Journal of the American Dietetic Association* 110, no. 3 (2010): 441–46.

Rangel, Marcos. "Is Parental Love Colorblind? Human Capital Accumulation Within Mixed Families. *Review of Black Political Economy* 42, no. 1–2 (2015): 57–86.

Reese, Laura A., and Ronald E. Brown. "The Effects of Religious Messages on Racial Identity and System Blame Among African-Americans," *Journal of Politics* 57, no. 1 (1995): 24–43.

Ribeiro, Djamila. *Quem Tem Medo do Feminismo Negro?* São Paulo, Brazil: Companhia das Letras, 2018.

Rios, Flávia. "O que o colorismo diz sobre as relações raciais brasileiras? 28/ Outubro." Portal Geledes. 2019. https://www.geledes.org.br/o-que-o -colorismo-diz-sobre-as-relacoes-raciais-brasileiras/?amp=1.

Roberts, J. Deotis. *Liberation and Reconciliation: A Black Theology.* Louisville, KY: Westminster John Knox Press, 1971.

Rodrigues, Henrique. "Não Acredito Nesse Deus Homem, Branco e Macho, Que Escolhe Quem Vai Matar." *Revista Forum.* May 18, 2021. https://revistaforum.com.br/brasil/nao-acredito-nesse-deus-homem-branco-e-macho-que-escolhe-quem-vai-matar/#.

Rosen, Michael. "The Rise and Fall of Black Milwaukee's Blue Collar Middle Class with Sheila Cochran and Dr. Michael Rosen." University of Wisconsin-Milwaukee African and African Diaspora Studies Department Series. 2021. https://m.facebook.com/UWMAADS/videos/the-rise-and-fall-of-black-milwaukees-blue-collar-middle-class-with-sheila-cochr/485887322402824/?locale=pa_IN&_rdr.

Roth-Gordon, Jennifer. *Race and the Brazilian Body: Blackness, Whiteness, and Everyday Language in Rio de Janeiro.* Oakland: University of California Press, 2016.

Samuels, David. "Sources of Mass Partisanship in Brazil." *Latin American Politics and Society* 48, no. 2 (2006): 1–27. https://doi.org/10.1111/j.1548-2456.2006.tb00345.x.

Santos, Leontino Faria dos. "Por uma Teologia Negra no Brasil." *Cross Currents* 67, no. 1 (2017): 35–54.

Santos, Mariana Cristina Silva, Lucas Rocha Delatorre, Maria das Graças Braga Ceccato, and Palmira de Fátima Bonolo. "Programa Bolsa Família e indicadores educacionais em crianças, adolescentes e escolas no Brasil: revisão sistemática." *Ciência e Saúde Coletiva* 24, no. 6 (2019): 2233–47. https://doi.org/10.1590/1413-81232018246.19582017.

Scala, Dante. "Polls and Elections: The Skeptical Faithful: How Trump Gained Momentum Among Evangelicals." *Presidential Studies Quarterly* 50, no. 4 (2020): 927–47.

Seccombe, Karen. *So You Think I Drive a Cadillac?: Welfare Recipients' Perspectives on the System and Its Reform.* Boston: Allyn and Bacon, 1999.

Semuels, Alana. "Chicago's Awful Divide." *Atlantic.* March 28, 2018. https://www.theatlantic.com/business/archive/2018/03/chicago-segregation-poverty/556649/

Shaw, Todd, and Eric McDaniel. "'Whosoever Will': Black Theology, Homosexuality, and the Black Political Church." *National Political Science Review* 11 (2007): 137–55.

Sheriff, Robin. *Dreaming Equality: Color, Race, and Racism in Urban Brazil.* New Brunswick, NJ: Rutgers University Press, 2001.

Sigelman, Lee, Steven Tuch, and Jack Martin. "What's in a Name? Preference for 'Black' versus 'African-American' Among Americans of African Descent." *Public Opinion Quarterly* 69, no. 3 (2005): 429–38.

Silva, Antonio José Bacelar da. *Between Brown and Black: Anti-Racist Activism in Brazil*. New Brunswick, NJ: Rutgers University Press, 2022.

Silva, Graziella, and Marcelo Paixão. "Mixed and Unequal: New Perspectives on Brazilian Ethnoracial Relations." In *Pigmentocracies: Ethnicity, Race, and Color in Latin America*, ed. Edward Telles, 172–217. Chapel Hill: University of North Carolina Press, 2014.

Silva, Graziella, and Elisa Reis. "Perceptions of Racial Discrimination Among Black Professionals in Rio de Janeiro." *Latin American Research Review*, 46. no. 2 (2011): 55–78.

Simien, Evelyn. "Doing Intersectionality Research: From Conceptual Issues to Practical Examples." *Politics and Gender* 3, no. 2 (2007): 36–43.

Skidmore, Thomas. *Black Into White: Race and Nationality in Brazilian Thought*. New York: New York University Press, 1974.

Smith, Candis Watts. *Black Mosaic: The Politics of Black Pan-Ethnic Diversity*. New York: New York University Press, 2014.

Smith, Christen, Archie Davies, and Bethania Gomes. "In Front of the World: Translating Beatriz Nascimento." *Antipode* 53, no. 1 (2021): 279–316.

Smith, Noah. "Why Charlotte and Raleigh Work for Black Residents." *Pocono Record*. April 1, 2018. https://www.poconorecord.com/story/opinion/2018/04/02/why-charlotte-raleigh-work-for/12847906007/.

Soares, Glaucio Ary Dillon, and Nelson do Valle Silva. "Urbanization, Race, and Class in Brazilian Politics." *Latin American Research Review* 22, no. 2 (1987): 155–76.

Sobral, Cristiane. "Não vou Mais Lavar os Pratos." In *Cadernos Negros: Poemas Afro-Brasileiros* Vol. 23. São Paulo, Brazil: Quilombhoje, 2000.

Soss, Joe, Richard C. Fording, and Sanford F. Schram. *Disciplining the Poor: Neoliberal Paternalism and the Persistent Power of Race*. Chicago: University of Chicago Press, 2011.

Souza, Amaury de. "Raça e Política no Brasil Urbano." *Revista de Administração de Empresas* 11, no. 4 (1971): 61–70.

Sparks, Holloway. "Queens, Teens, and Model Mothers." In *ag and the Politics of Welfare Reform*, ed. Sanford Schram, Joe Soss, and Richard Fording, 171–95. Ann Arbor: University of Michigan Press, 2003.

Sugiyama, Natasha, and Wendy Hunter. *Transforming Subjects Into Citizens: Insights from Brazil's Bolsa Família.* Cambridge: Cambridge University Press, 2014.

——. "Whither Clientelism? Good Governance and Brazil's Bolsa Familia Program." *Comparative Politics* 46, no. 1 (2013): 43–62.

Szymanski, Dawn, and Destin Stewart. "Racism and Sexism as Correlates of African American Women's Psychological Distress." *Sex Roles* 63, no. 3–4 (2010): 226–38.

Tate, Katherine. *Black Faces in the Mirror: African Americans and Their Representatives in the U.S. Congress.* Princeton, NJ: Princeton University Press, 2003.

Telles, Edward. *Pigmentocracies: Ethnicity, Race, and Color in Latin America.* Chapel Hill: University of North Carolina Press, 2014.

Tesler, Michael. "The Spillover of Racialization Into Health Care: How President Obama Polarized Public Opinion by Racial Attitudes and Race." *American Journal of Political Science* 56, no. 3 (2012): 690–704. https://doi.org/10.1111/j.1540-5907.2011.00577.x.

Tucker-Worgs, Tamelyn. *The Black Megachurch: Theology, Gender, and the Politics of Public Engagement.* Waco, TX: Baylor University Press, 2011.

Turner, April O., and Daniel De Simone. "By the Numbers: Black Women in the 117th Congress." Higher Heights (press release). January 3, 2021. https://cawp.rutgers.edu/sites/default/files/resources/press-release -black-women-117th-congress_0.pdf.

USDA Food and Nutrition Service. "Farmers' Markets Accepting SNAP Benefits." May 2021. https://www.fns.usda.gov/snap/farmers-markets -accepting-snap-benefits.

——. "WIC-Racial Ethnic Group Enrollment Data 2016." 2016. https:// www.fns.usda.gov/wic/wic-racial-ethnic-group-enrollment-data-2016.

Valente, Ana Lucia E. F. *Politica e Relacoes Raciais: Os Negros e As Eleicoes Paulistas de 1982.* São Paulo, Brazil: FFLCH-US, 1986.

Valentino, Nicholas A., Vincent L. Hutchings, and Ismail K. White. "Cues That Matter: How Political Ads Prime Racial Attitudes During Campaigns." *American Political Science Review* 96, no. 1 (2002): 75–90.

Vargas, Joao. *The Denial of Anti-Blackness: Multiracial Redemption and Black Suffering.* Minneapolis: University of Minnesota Press, 2018.

Verba, Sidney, Kay Lehman Schlozman, and Henry E. Brady. *Voice and Equality: Civic Voluntarism in American Politics.* Cambridge, MA: Harvard University Press, 1995.

Viglione, Jill, Lance Hannon, and Robert DeFina. "The Impact of Light Skin on Prison Time for Black Female Offenders." *Social Science Journal* 48, no. 1 (2011): 250–58.

Walker, Alice. *The Color Purple: A Walker.* New York: Penguin Books, 2019.

Williams, Lucy. "Race, Rat Bites and Unfit Mothers: How Media Disclosure Informs Welfare Legislation Debate." *Fordham Urban Law Journal* 22, no. 4 (1995): 1159–96.

Wingfield, Adia. *No More Invisible Man: Race and Gender in Men's Work.* Philadelphia: Temple University Press, 2013.

Wisconsin Department of Health Services. "African Americans in Wisconsin: Overview." 2018. https://www.dhs.wisconsin.gov/minority-health/population/afriamer-pop.htm.

Wong, Janelle. "The Evangelical Vote and Race in the 2016 Presidential Election." *Journal of Race, Ethnicity, and Politics* 3, no. 1 (2018): 81–106.

Woods-Giscombe, Cheryl. "Superwoman Schema: African American Women's Views on Stress, Strength, and Health." *Qualitative Health Research* 20, no. 5 (May 2010): 668–83. https://doi.org/10.1177/1049732310361892.

Wright, Jeremiah A., Jr. *Africans Who Shaped Our Faith.* Nashville, TN: Urban Ministries, 1995.

Zucco, Cesar, and Timothy Power. "Bolsa Família and the Shift in Lula's Electoral Base, 2002–2006." *Latin American Research Review* 48, no. 2 (2013): 3–24.

INDEX